MY RUSSIAN BRIDE

HOW I SCAMMED THE SCAMMER

CHRISTOPHER NADEAU

SUNBRIGHT PUBLISHING/NEW YORK

Published by Sunbright Publishing Inc.
PO Box 173
Harriman NY 10926
Email: sunbrightpub@gmail.com

ISBN-13: 978-0615567440
ISBN-10: 0615567444

PRINTED IN THE UNITED STATES OF AMERICA

First Printing – December 2011

Cover, artwork, and interior design by the author

For anyone who's ever been scammed.

Contents

My Russian Bride

Introduction

It came from out of the blue one fall day. A simple email. Tiny bits of information floating along the information superhighway. It was so ambiguous. Did I know this person? Was it someone I once knew a long time ago? I wasn't really sure. So I wrote back. It became immediately clear from the response what I was dealing with. An email scammer. It's no secret that online dating is a big business. All those web dating sites you see advertised all over the TV generate big money. Why is this? Because there are a lot of lonely people out there looking for love. The scammer community knows this and exploits peoples need for love to its fullest extent.

Russia and the former blocks of the Soviet Union have become somewhat of a mythical nirvana of what is perceived as a land of desperate beautiful women dying to be saved from a lonely loveless life. The reasons behind the myths are numerous and of course with most myths, there is some truths behind them.

According to Elena Petrova from Russian Brides Cyber Guide (www.womenrussia.com), most Russian women dating western men are affected by "the grass is always greener on the other side" syndrome and they are looking for a knight in shining armor. They believe that foreign men are more courteous, attentive and loving than their Russian counterparts. "For the most women the country of their future partner is of no importance; they care more for the quality of the man", says Elena.

"They feel once they have found the right man, their life is going to change like in a fairy-tale: first the wedding, and then they will live happily ever after."

Russia has one of the lowest men to women ratio in the world. According to the latest Russian census, there are 10 million more women than men, or only 88 men for 100 women. At the same time Russian culture requires a woman to be married in order to acquire a respectable social status. Because of the demographics and the cultural notion, Russian women are driven to seek partners elsewhere if they have failed to find them in a "normal" way. As the internet becomes more affordable in Russia it can happen that the numbers of Russian women seeking partners abroad will soar. "Until Russia develops a new culture that will not require women to be married, in order to gain a respectable social status, or Russian demographics change, the situation with Russian women marrying western men can continue its dynamics," says Elena.

While it is true that there are plenty of lonely Russia women, there are plenty, if not more so, crafty scammers out there that are using this information (and misinformation) about Russian women to their benefit. The transition from the prior scams of "you've won the lottery" or "this is the Bank of Nigeria's president looking to send you a million dollars" to, "I'm lonely and desperate in Russia" and "I want to marry you my American prince", is becoming more prevalent every day.

What you are about to read is a transcript between myself and a few of these new age scammers. I was naïve enough to answer their first email, but it was them who were dumb enough to keep replying. It seemed to me early on, that they didn't seem to understand or more likely, didn't even read what I wrote back. With each response, I kept pushing the boundaries further and further to see just how far I can go without them noticing.

It became very clear in a short period of time that I could push them as far out as I wanted them to go. And that is just what you are about to experience.

If you could think of the most twisted, wacky, most nonsensical story in your life, what kind of story would you tell? Would it include dragons? Or pirates? The hell with it. Why not pirates that fly on dragons? Heck, why not have Captain Kirk commanding the USS Flying Dragon and fighting pirates. These are the kinds of tales you will find within these pages. What can I say? I was bored at work and these scammers gave me a reason to slack off. You can only play so many games of solitaire and read so many newspapers in a day.

As my story became more and more elaborate, I had to start pulling in friends to create characters. One such friend who you will meet here is Stacy "Aces" Bell, who you will come to know as "Curly". Now I love Aces (in a brofriend way), but I also love to bust his chops. Anything I can dish out at him, he takes like a man. Early on when I got the thoughts of making this a book of an epic tale, I needed to put a face to the character I was creating. So why not use it as an opportunity to have some fun with my buddies. I showed him the email exchanges and he gave me the blessing to go ahead and turn him into Curly. However he wanted me to give him a bit of a disguise. So of course, a "mouthstash" fit the bill. And so my main character was created and sent off to parts unknown. Other friends appear within the pages including Thomas England who I am certain, may never talk to me again after his portrayal of "Tornado Tommy". To which I take this space to formally apologize to him. I'm sorry I turned you into a lonely sheep and goat lover Tommy. Please forgive me.

Also featured are John Lipori, Terry Sargent, Anthony Nadeau, Christopher Howard, Mike Downs, Gordon DeVoss , Jim Stokkeland, Jenn Wilson, Wayne Jorgensen, James F DiFilippo Jr., and Caro England. Without them, many characters wouldn't have been able to be brought to life. I thank them all deeply from the bottom of my heart. Also a special thanks to Kristin Hill, Bert Else, David Henry Sterry, and Arielle Eckstut for all of their help in bringing this book to fruition.

All communications back and forth that you will read are real and laid out in the order in which they were received and sent. I have no idea if anything I communicated or any pictures I sent to my scammers were understood. I suspect that they were using an online translator as there is heavy butchering of the English language and grammar. I of course fed into this by butchering the English language myself. The transcripts here are completely unedited. If you are a spelling, grammar, and punctuation fanatic, you will be certainly horrified by the mutilation of the English language. You have been warned. My advice for you is to read it all with a Russian accent. The photos that appear within were sent (or received from the scammer) along with the emails. I created all the photos with Photoshop. The photos are of the actual photos sent and received.

If it's one bit of advice I can give to you the reader, is if you encounter a scammer and have the time, go ahead and have fun with them. Give them a taste of their own medicine. They have created a fake life and world in which they live in. Why not create your own too? But don't, for the love of God, DON'T ever give your scammer any personal information or money. No matter how real they might seem, they aren't. The odds that some beautiful 25 year old girl from some distant land is somehow going to fall madly in love with you after 5 emails are astronomical. It just doesn't happen in the real world. Don't be stupid. Don't be taken.

I invite you now to sit back, relax, and experience the most elaborate fuck you ever written to an email scammer. Enjoy!

"Listen, I will now tell you the truth
and there is no other."

-Isaac Stern

CHAPTER 1:
LITTLE RED ROCKET

Little Red Rocket

INSERT
MOUNT
HERE
Little Red Rocket

From: Larisa <gilkakisska@xxxxx.com>
Sent: Wednesday, November 10 8:50 AM
To: Chris <coldbastrd@xxxxx.com>
Subject: [No Subject]

Hello Chris,
I found you on websearch. I am looking for someone like you. Tell me please if you like to write to me. We shall have great fun! Your friend, Larisa.

From: Chris <coldbastrd@xxxxx.com>
Sent: Wednesday, November 10 1:33 PM
To: Larisa <gilkakisska@xxxxx.com>
Subject: [RE: No Subject]

Hi Larisa,
Do I know you? Did we go to school together or something? I honestly don't remember you.
Chris

From: Larisa <gilkakisska@xxxxx.com>
Sent: Thursday, November 11 9:07 AM
To: Chris <coldbastrd@xxxxx.com>
Subject: [No Subject]

Hello Chris!
How are you, my friend? I'm glad that you respond to my message. I think when we learn each other better, we meet soon. Tell me what you do in your life. How do you spend your free time? I am curious to learn everything. Send me your pictures please. In my letter I would like to say a few words about me. My name is Larisa. I am 25 years old. I live Tomsk. is one city east of West Siberia. Have you heard of my town? I think this is not a problem the distance between us? What do you think? We are two want to find someone serious in. Am I correct? We can start to learn each other but if you do not want it's your choice. In my letter I send my photos. I finish here. I await your e-mail. At the next time I shall write the greatest message. I beg you to accept, Excellency, the assurances of my respectful feelings.
Your friend, Larisa.

From: Chris <coldbastrd@xxxxx.com>
Sent: Thursday, November 11 2:26 PM
To: Larisa <gilkakisska@xxxxx.com>
Subject: [RE: No Subject]

Hi Larisa (if that is your name),
Let me get this straight, you live in Russia??!!?? Or is it Nigeria? I'm not really looking for anything. I thought that you knew me. But I am fairly certain that this is a scam. Thanks for the try though. It made me laugh.
Later

From: Larisa <gilkakisska@xxxxx.com>
Sent: Friday, November 12 9:12 AM
To: Chris <coldbastrd@xxxxx.com>
Subject: [No Subject]

Hello Chris! I was surprised to receive your reply frankly speaking. Thanks that you paid affection to me. I was pleased to read your letter. I didn't expect to see your message in my e-mail-box. But still I'm happy!

I think if's high time to tell you some words about myself. My full name is Larisa. But my friends call me in different ways Larisa. You may also call me like this. It will be pleasant for me. And how do your friends call you? If you want I will address to you in the same way. I'm 25 years old, a young European lady. My growth is about 168 cm, my weight is 52 kg I live in Russia. My native town is called Tomsk. It's the capital of Tomsk Area. My city is big and very beautiful. I adore it. Sometimes I go for a walk alone. There is a "my place" where I can think a lot alone and have a rest. I think each person has his special in his city. Do you agree? Do you have such a place? I live alone in small flat. My parents are on pension now. I love and admire my parents. I'm grateful because they did their best to bring me up in a good way. I think when I have children in the future I will use the same methods of upbringing. Do you like children? As for me I love them very much. They are so innocent and need our care. I spend a lot of time with my friends son. He is 3 years old. I can't explain it by words but I get a great pleasure when I go for a walk with him or stay at home with him. It's wonderful to answer his childish questions. Sometimes I feel a desire to have my own child. But for it I must have a husband in whom I will be sure and to whom I can rely in this life. And it's rather difficult to find such a man nowadays. But still I hope that my dream will come true soon and I will be happy having a real family. I'm working as a shop-assistant in the department store. I sell home appliances. I can't say that I'm happy with my job.

I had a lot of hopes before graduating from the University but when I tried to find a well-paid job it turned to be that they need specialists with 3-5 year of experience. I don't want to live like my parents who had been working honestly for all their life and it wasn't estimated in a worthy manner. I don't say that they are poor.

They can afford buying necessary things but even to afford such thing they worked so hard. It's no fair. I can't understand the politics of Russian government. To my mind in your country the situation is different, isn't it? It was one of the reasons why I decided to find a man from abroad. It's rather interesting for me to learn about your character, your habits. I also would like to learn about the customs and traditions of your country.

I really hope that our correspondence will continue. I think in the next letter I will tell you more about myself: my character, Hobby and so on. But now I'm finishing. I repeat again that I was glad to receive your letter. And I'm looking for another one. Very soon. Have a good day. Best regards, Larisa.

P.S. I would like to see your photos and the photos of the place where you live!!! I will send you the of photos. I think, that to you to like!!!

From: Chris <coldbastrd@xxxxx.com>
Sent: Friday, November 12 3:16 PM
To: Larisa <gilkakisska@xxxxx.com>
Subject: [RE: No Subject]

Hi Asiral,
See I called you name in different way. What do my friends call me? Some people call me Larry and some call me Larry in different ways. You can call me Curly but when you say it in a different way, it sounds like Moe. Yes every person should have a special place. My special place is under my bed where I keep my action figure collection. I often go under my bed and play with myself. Do I like children? Yes generally served with BBQ sauce with garnish on the side. The only photo I have is of my trouser snake. Do you want that? Your bestest friend in the whole world,
Curly Larry Moe

From: Larisa <gilkakisska@xxxxx.com>
Sent: Monday, November 15 8:53 AM
To: Chris <coldbastrd@xxxxx.com>
Subject: [No Subject]

Hi Chris!!!
How are today ? I am pleased to get your e-mail again. It cheered me up even . I have recently Done for a walk . I was in the park. I noticed the coupe there . They were so happy with each other. They looked at each other with warmth & tenderness . This is a real love. I rankly speaking . I envied them a bit I want to love & be loved. I'm dreaming of sincere love when people understand each other & even without words. They trust each other & prepare plans about their future life together . That's great. Love is the best feeling in the world. I have not met a worthy person who really loved me. I dated with some Russian men but none them I could trust & be sure in . You probably were surprised that I' m single. I have never been married & don't have children. During my lifetime I had serious relationship with the person , we were going to marry but he betrayed me. He committed adultery with my friend . It was a double betrayals for me . Two closest people let me down . I can't describe by words my state at that lime. I can't wish it even for an enemy . But the time is the great healer. I managed to survive & my vounds were tightened . Now I'm open for relationship but even a year before I was sure that I won't trust anybody any more. But my family & true friends encouraged me. Now I'm optimist I believe that about you? Do you want to have serious relationship? I hope you didn't have such a bad experience in love as me. What women do you like ? What features don't you bare in women? Please tell me . As for me I want to be with a man with a strong character , clever, ambitions , communicative , cheerful , careful & gentle . He should be a man of a word. I hate conceited men. They say only words but in reality they do nothing. I don't have a lot of friends. And you? I have one best friend.

Her name is Lena. She advised me to fry to get acquainted with a person on the Internet. Frankly speaking first I could meet you on the Internet. Unfortunately I don't have my on computer. I write to you from internet-cafe . First I didn't know now to use computers . Bat my friend showed me & gave instructions .

So now I understand that computer is quite an essential thing in our society . I'm Christian . What religion do you have ? Do you trust the God ? As for me trust the God. God is one for all people do you agree with me ? He gives forces for living. When I go to the church it makes me feel easier & forged abut problems . Do you go to the church ? I also wanted to tell you one thing. I like cooking. I can say that I'm good at it. I cook different dishes : soups, ragout, salads, pies & many other things . But my Borsch is the best one. Did you hear about this dish ? I like ice - cream & chocolate very much . I also like Chinese Cuisine . What cuisine do you prefer ? Chris, pls tell me your birthday . What is your sign of the zodiac? As for me I was born 13. Mart I'm a Fishes . Well, its to finish .... I'm really glad to real your letters. Good luck at work Sincerely yours, Larisa!!!

GLAMOUR SHOTS
BY BORIS

EXCUSE ME WHILE I
PROP UP MY
FAKE LEG

SASSY AND

SOPHISTICATED

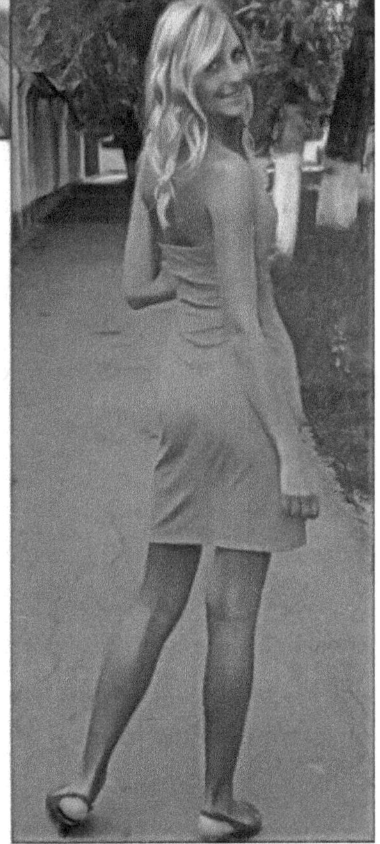

SORRY YOU HAVE

CHOSEN TO WALK

BEHIND ME. I THINK I

JUST FARTED.

From: Chris <coldbastrd@xxxxx.com>
Sent: Monday, November 15 12:46 PM
To: Larisa <gilkakisska@xxxxx.com>
Subject: [RE: No Subject]

Dearest Larisa,
I am exceptional today. Thank you kindly for asking. I would LOVE to try your pie...but not your ragout...or your pie if it's on the ragout. What cuisine do I like? I like pies...cream pies, peach pies, cherry pies. I also like beaver, bearded oysters, beef curtains, pink tacos, and furburgers. That is very sad about you not having lots of friends. That makes me cry...I weep for you now. Weeppppp weeppp weeppp weeppp. Maybe you and Lena can get together and hug...maybe she can kiss you. Come to think of it, that is the kind of woman I like. What guy wouldn't right? Church? Sure. I worship Beelzebub. Heard of him? My birth? Mart me as the 6. The sign of the beast. Welp it finish now. What wonderful time it is! Forever sincerely, Curly

From: Chris <coldbastrd@xxxxx.com>
Sent: Monday, November 15 12:55 PM
To: Larisa <gilkakisska@xxxxx.com>
Subject: [RE: No Subject]

My dearest sweat Larisa,
I almost forgot to send you picture of me. Here you will find it attached. As you see I have the mouthstache. How do you say in your country? It is a macho? I am like the great American cowboy Cliff Eastwood ready to ride the pony into the sunrise. It is good for the sexy time yes? Now you send me sexy time pictures of you? I wait in great anticipation for them.
Curly

IT IS I, THE CURLY, YOU LIKE?

From: Larisa <gilkakisska@xxxxx.com>
Sent: Tuesday, November 16 9:03 AM
To: Chris <coldbastrd@xxxxx.com>
Subject: [No Subject]

Hello my dear Chris! Can I call you like this?
I hope your mood is ok. As for me I'm fired a bit. I had a difficult day at work But when T san your letter my mood became higher! I have a question for you. I thought about it last did you expert that you would be able to find a person for serious relationship? Pls answer to me honestly. I hope that you are serious about me. I'm fired of different games in my life. I have recently watched the program. It said about the traditions of your country. It was so interesting & I can't but say these traditions are different from ours. Do you agree? As I've told you before I'm satisfied with my work. My salary is abut 250 euro. It certainly doesn't satisfy all my needs but in general it's ok. I earn good money so I can't complain.
And how much do you earn? Do you like your job?

Today I want to tell about my city. Nowadays Tomsk is a administrative, economic, cultural, scientific, centre of Tomsk Oblast. This city is very green is summer & write in winter. There are a lot of places of interest. . It lakes my breath away when I look at it. Did you hear smth about Tomsk? It's about 3755 km from Moscow. And pls describe your town too. I want to learn more & about you. T wanted to confess. I'm interested in you. I like your manner of writing to me. I hope that you like me too. Well, the future will show us what happens. Do you support me in this idea? I hope so.

Some words about my family. I'm the only chi in my family. My family is not big. My dad is 52. He' s name is Andrey. He is retired & doesn't work now. He has physical inability of the 2nd degree. He got The trauma at work so now he doesn't work but he has a hobby.

He breeds pigeons. Very other my mum &I are surprised looking at him. He is like a big child. But I love him very much. My mum is 56. Her name is Tatyana. She is a wonderful woman. She is my mum, my friend who always is ready to support me. She un retired too. I really admire mu mum. She had so difficulties in her life but all these things didn't make her make her lose her patience, joy for life. She had a difficult childhood. She lost her parents when she was 10.

So she shad to survive in this cruel world. But I'm proud of her. The God returned her kindness & sent my father to her. Is your family big? Pls tell me about it be waiting. Now I have to go .
Kiss you. Take care
Yours Larisa!
P.s : Don't forget to send me photos witch your family, it it's possible. I attach photo of me.

AMATEUR POOL HUSTLER

From: Chris <coldbastrd@xxxxx.com>
Sent: Tuesday, November 16 1:07 PM
To: Larisa <gilkakisska@xxxxx.com>
Subject: [RE: No Subject]

Oh my fairest Larisa,
Sorry to hear that the day has fired you. Yes I am serious. Have my letters been anything but serious? So what kind of traditions do you do in your country? Recently we have a tradition in this country called Halloween. We all dress as pirates and go door to door in our neighborhoods begging for booty. It is reminiscent of the days of the pirates. You have tradition like this? Next week we have tradition called Thanksgiving where we all get together in families and eat the muskrats and gravy. We eat so much muskrat that we get tired and sit in front of tv and watch European soccer. The next day we go to store and buy many useless things to give to family for the upcoming Christmas. Things that we think the person will need but the really don't. We waste lots of monies. It is great fun!

My job? It is good. I would ride on my bicycle all around town and deliver the paper for news. I love my bike. I have attached a picture of me on bike. I call it my "Little Red Rocket". It is great fun! Perhaps if you come to America, you can ride on my Little Red Rocket. Would you like that? You can go fast or slow. Maybe you can ever polish it. I would like very much if you polish my Little Red Rocket. So to go further with the explanation of job. People see me in town riding bike. They say "wow, look at the macho guy riding his bike...he is like the cowboy on pony". Then person come to me and say you need to be on the tv. So they put me on the tv riding on my bike. And the people love it. I will tell you more about it later.

I am also only chi in family. My family is very small. Only just me...and my Little Red Rocket. Parents are gone. Taken in a tragic peanut combine accident. The family make the peanut butter and everyone knows the family peanut butter name. It is called 'The Curly Peanut Butter'. That is where I have gotten the name. Do you have the Curly Peanut Butter? It is good and creamy and you must taste my butter. You will say mmmmm...give me more of your butter. I want your butter deep inside me. It is that good.

So tell to me, you go to beach? I know that in Siberia there is no beach but maybe you have gone to one? You have the photos of you on beach? Please send to me. It it's possible? Well it finish now. I am fired.
Forever, Curly

From: Chris <coldbastrd@xxxxx.com>
Sent: Wednesday, November 17 4:18 PM
To: Larisa <gilkakisska@xxxxx.com>
Subject: [RE: No Subject]

Dearest sugar lumpy pie Larisa,
How does the day approach you? Are you less on fire then yesterday? I am very VERY sad that you did not write to me today. It made me cry. I cried very many tears. Do you not like the macho mouthstache? I can certainly shave it off if that is which you desires. Please talk to me...please. I miss hearing about your town. It sounds very exciting. I think we would have great fun together there.

This made me think hard. And my head was hurting but not quite to the trauma of the 2nd degree. I think that if you are serious about me, then maybe I should come over. You are so proud of your place of life, that I would very much like to see it. You show me? I have talked to booking agent. He tell me that to come there cost me $950 USD. This is lot of money for me. Peanut butter sales are not what you may think they could be. I think it would be in best interest, since as you tell me, you make $250 Euro a day, and this being good money (even though you think it may not), that you can send me half of $950 to cover plane ride? Once I get there, we take taxi and you show me all the wonderful and cultural center of Tomsk. Do you agree with such statement? You tell me that I am your best friend in world. Don't you want to see best friend? I would cry if you do not. That would not be great fun! I wait in greatest anticipation for you to decide and I hope that you bring me there yes?

I have other question for you to answer. In America, it is tradition for women before they be with man, to strip down in nudiness and show man body so that man can see if woman is fit for bearing of many childrens.

So I ask of you if you send me photos of the nudiness or even the underwears so that I can make the determination that you are fit woman to make the many childrens. This is a fair request. I cannot be with the woman who is unfit for production of the childrens. You understand do you not? Of course I can send photos of the Mr. Winky so that you can determine if it is fit for the production of the childrens as well. This is American tradition and you want to learn of our traditions do you not?

So I feel it is high time to tell you little more about myself. I have attached several pictures. You have expressed that father of you raises many pigeons. This is interesting. I myself raise hamsters. Here you will find within letter picture of me and hamsters. I enjoy hiding so that hamsters cannot see me so they go about their ways without me startling them. My pussy is watching the hamsters play. His name is the cat. Here they appear to be doing naughty things. One hamster is behind another hamster while other hamster watches. I think they make the hamster childrens? It is nature yes?

Here you also find me polishing my Little Red Rocket. You have to keep polished and clean. Nobody wants to ride on dirty red rocket. Sometimes I will just pull out my Little Red Rocket and polish it for hours at a time. One time, woman came up to me and said show me your Little Red Rocket. So I pulled it out and she said, may I polish it? And I said, certainly. And she said, ok I polish your Little Red Rocket for $20 dollars. And I said, perhaps I pay $10 yes? And she said, ok for $10 give you quick polish. So she polished it to hard and too fast and I get upset and yell, you do not know how to polish! You are hurting Little Red Rocket! This is what happens when you only pay $10 I thought. Go away your dirty woman. I polish myself. I told her.

Lastly I send to you my peanut butter. Well I not send it but a photo of it. When you bring me to Russia, I will bring peanut butter with me and you try yourself. You will swallow my butter and like it. If you spit it out, that would make me angry! Do you think you will swallow or spit it out? I hope you swallow.

So that is all I write for the now. Please let us arrange for me to come visit. You can send to me monies by bank transfer yes? You tell me best way for which you to do it. And also before I come, you send the photos so that I can see you can produce the childrens. This will be good yes. It finish here. I go.

Kisses you!

Your bestest friend in the whole wide world, Curly!

THE MIRACLE OF LIFE.

I LIKE TO POLISH MY LITTLE RED ROCKET.

THE CURLY PEANUT BUTTER

From: Larisa <gilkakisska@xxxxx.com>
Sent: Thursday, November 18 9:26 AM
To: Chris <coldbastrd@xxxxx.com>
Subject: [No Subject]

Hello my dear Chris!
I'm so sorry I couldn't write to you yesterday! I was so busy at my work. And then I had to help my mum about the house. My parents were waiting for their relatives , so they are preparing to receive guests.

But you even can't imagine how happy make me your letters ! I look forward you letters ! I 'm glad that I have met you in my lifetime. Thanks God that your letters are coming to me.

My relation to you becomes more & more serious with each your e-mail. What's a pity that we are far away from each other. I'm fired of loneliness It's so difficult not to have a person near you who loves you, takes care of you & respects you. Sometimes when I come back home after work I feel despaired . And only your letters , your attention make me stronger. Help me to get rid of my loneliness! I want to feel care & kindness. I'm sorry for such an introduction you what I peel now & I want you to know about it . Please write to me what you feel about me, ok?

It's important for me. I want to get reciprocity from you. How is your life ? What are you doing? You won't believe but I can say that I miss you . You know. I told my mum about you & she said that she wants to believe that I have met the right man. I didn't expect that she supports me in the idea to find a person through the Internet but she said that it didn't matter now I would get acquainted with a men, the only important thing is to find a men with whom I will have children. My heart was so beating when she was saying all these words.

I can't say that I'm so sensitive but her words touched me so deeply! These words were from my closest person & I'm so grateful that she supports me in my ideas.

Now I can say for sure that I'm quite serious concerning you & our relationship. And because of it I don't want that our relationship develop only by the Internet correspondence . Of course our letters help us to learn a lot of things about saying the most important words directly to the person. Don you support me in this or don't you agree? I fried do describe here my thoughts directly now possible. I wrote this e-mail to tell you what I have in my heart now, I'm dreaming to become closer to you . Pls understand me & I ask you about only one thing! Be sincere !!! Tell me what you feel. Tell me what you think about our future relationship. As for me I began writing to you not just to have a jun. But on purpose to find the right person for meeting & may be for marriage But we can discuss such a serious step in out life confidentially . I want to ,believe that our meeting will happen one time . My dear I say all these words from my heart . I'm sorry I didn't answer some of your questions but I'm sure these things which I mentioned are more important . I'm finishing with these words now. I'm waiting your reply.

A sensitive kiss for you Chris!!!! Forever you, Larisa!!!

THE BEST AND LAST PICTURE OF THE BRIDE

From: Chris <coldbastrd@xxxxx.com>
Sent: Thursday, November 18 2:18 PM
To: Larisa <gilkakisska@xxxxx.com>
Subject: [RE: No Subject]

Oh my dearest sweatiness Larisa,
Me thanks the Gods for you to write to me! To see your words again. It fills my heart with such glee! I thought that I would never hear again your words. I admit, I thought worst. I thought you maybe run over by taxi or that scoundrel Russian man run off with your heart. I cried very much. But then the rage fill my souls. I wait by computer all day and night. And no words from you came. Angry I was. I took keyboard and smash computer! COMPUTER SMASH!!!! I went to kitchen to get sandwich after rage. And there on counter, the peanut butter I was to bring to you. I took jar and smashed on wall. PEANUT BUTTER SMASH!!!!

I take shower as peanut butter all over me. I sat in tub and cried as water sprayed onto me. I put the clothes on and ran outside! I got on Little Red Rocket and rode and rode and road. People see me and stop me in street. They say, please Curly sign autograph. They see me on the tv and want piece of me. I tell them...GO AWAY, GET OUT OF THE FACE! YOU NO HAVE PIECE OF ME! THERE IS ONLY ONE PERSON WHO HAVE THE PIECE OF ME...AND SHE IS GONE! I rode and road and road Little Red Rocket. Until such time as I came to church and graveyard where mama and papa are buried. I threw my Little Red Rocket on dirt. I DON'T CARE ANYMORE! I ran to grave and threw self on knees. I cried mama...papa...please help me! What am I to do? And I kneel there on knees and then something magic happens. The clouds part and sun came on my face. I looked up and there it was. Little pigeon flying in sky. And little pigeon flew down and landed on gravy and I looked at pigeon and pigeon look at me.

And that is when I knew that this must be sign from mama and papa. They knew your papa raise the pigeons. So they sent pigeon to me to tell me everything will be ok. It is true. You are like the angel sent from the heaven that mama and papa lives. I make a picture that I send you with the letter to show you.

I got on Little Red Rocket and road to internet cafe because computer is now smash. I go to letters and there like the magic you are. It is true! The pigeon was right! You come back! I write the poem now to express the feel.

Oh my dear Larisa, Larisa.
How I long to kissa
Your face and the nose,
and maybe the little toes,
that are on the feet.
Boy that would be neat!

The pigeon fly in sky,
and almost poop in my eye,
but he tells to me you are one,
it is like the American baseball homerun!

The mama and papa who are in heaven,
they send me sign at a quarter to seven,
that this is the girl,
with the teeth white like pearl,
that we send to our precious Curl
and she is on the other side of world.

But it doesn't matter,
because I will bring her peanut butter platter.
And I will eat her pie,
and she will say oh my!
And I won't have to sit in tub alone anymore and cry.

It will be glorious day when she rides Little Red Rocket,
that I sometimes keep in my pocket.
We will go fast and slow,
and I will be her beau.
Forever and ever,
and that is what I know!

You like the poem yes? Ok so, I check with booking agent and he still have ticket for me to come to Russia. I make new peanut butter to bring to you. I also bring the flower. I have attached picture showing you. But please you send to me half the monies so I come? This is meant to be. The pigeon told me so! Tell me how we make the arrangement? I look forward so much to seeing you! I can hardly wait! Please to me send more photos! Is this you at beach you send? Do you swim in the bathing suit? You send the photo of swimming? I wait by computer for your letters in great anticipation! The words finish now. Until the next time.

A deep smoochy kissing for you Larisa!
Forever,
Curly

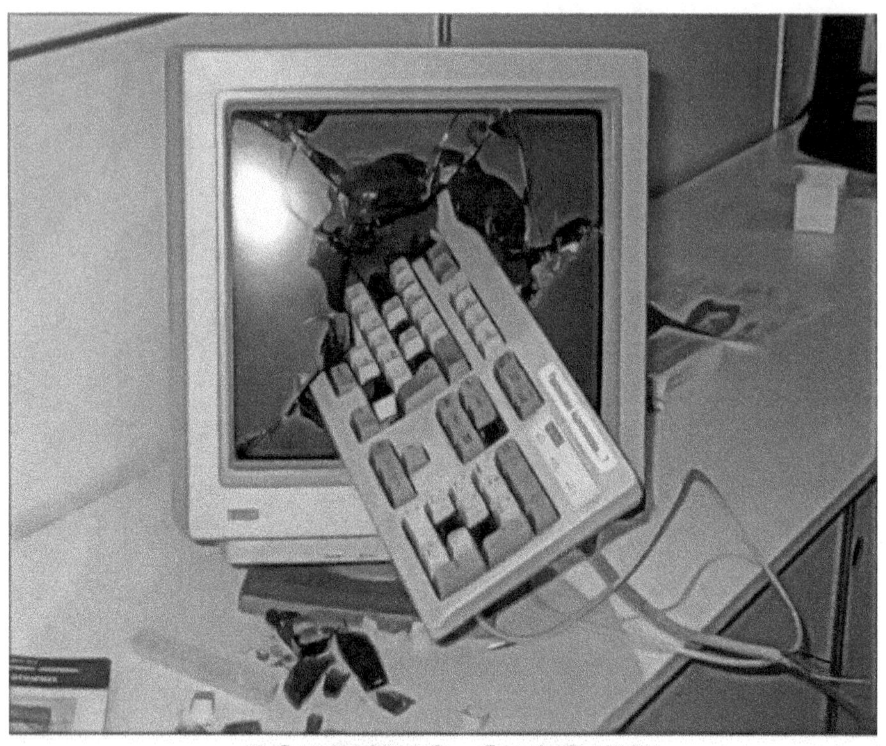

COMPUTER SMASH!!!!!

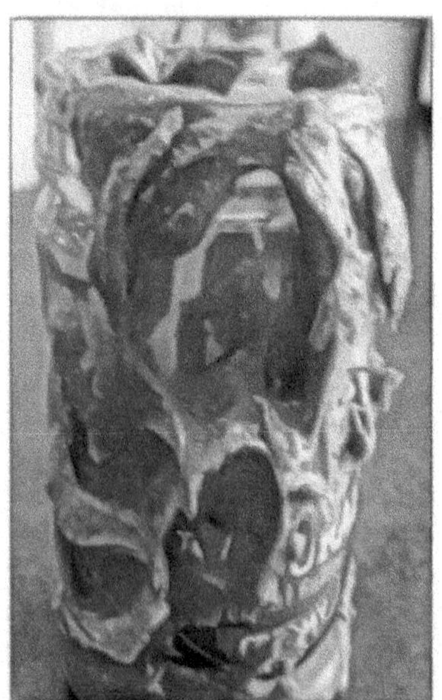

PEANUT BUTTER SMASH!!!!!

mama & papa
Heaven
sun
Angel
Carisa
Pigeon
Little Red Rocket
me
mama & papa
grave

A FLOWER FOR YOU!

MEANWHILE SOMEHWERE IN SIBERIA...

From: Larisa <gilkakisska@xxxxx.com>
Sent: Friday, November 19 10:10 AM
To: Chris <coldbastrd@xxxxx.com>
Subject: [No Subject]

Hello my honey Chris!!!!
How are you? As for me I am wonderful today. I can't determine the reason bat may be its because of writing a letter to you. Yesterday I went to the gum so I was tired yesterday. In the morning it was so hard to get up. like doing sports. It keeps me energetic for all day long. Do you go to the gym? I think sport gives us the force to live. By the way it helps me to be an attractive woman. After my training I took a hot bath. Then my best friend Lena called on me she lives not tar from me. We were speaking for a long time. And I fold her about you. I saw that she was happy for it, even enthusiastic . She adores love stories. And it the case concerns me, she can it stop questions about all the details. That is she is. I can do nothing with it. I confessed that I m interested in you 8 may be I managed to find a man with whom I want to be. Imagine the situation: I m telling her about my feelings s thoughts about our relationship s she begins jam with joy s with burning eyes. Then we were imagining the situation of the future development of our relationship it was funny of course s it was a joke but when I stayed alone s lad in my bed I was thinking of you, of us, of future events. I felt a real desire to be near you. I supposed what you were doing at that time. A lot of people tried to write me. First I answered but now I write letters nobody except you. You are the most creative s interesting person for me! Do you write letter to someone else except me? Please be for you s would like to get the same thing from you.

What did you do yesterday? How did you spend your free time? Did you remember me? I forgot to tell you, vat I adore animals, especially dogs in my child hood I had a little dog. She was adorable.

She was so clever she could understand our speech, our intonation. Bat when she was 16 she died. It was a real tragedy for our family. I will never forget that day.

I cold no understand why the god took her from us. Hater my dad explained to me that our dog died from old age. After it I became calmer a bit. Unfortunately now I can it have a pet because I live alone and spend a lot of dime at my work. And a pet needs so much care as an infant. I also have passion for horses. Sometimes I go on riding with my friends. That is great of course! What animals do you like? Do you have a pet at home? Ok my friend. I have to finish now. I miss you so much! Don't work too hard. Take care of yours! Thousands of kisses. Yours
Larisa.
P.S Send me more photos. Please!

From: Chris <coldbastrd@xxxxx.com>
Sent: Friday, November 19 1:37 PM
To: Larisa <gilkakisska@xxxxx.com>
Subject: [RE: No Subject]

Pryvet my loveliness Larisa,
I learn the little Russian for you! I say hello in the Russian! Are you proud of my greatest achievement? Today I feel wondrous as well. It is because I dream of you in the night times. I dream you floated in my room on the angel wing and I was there and pigeon land on window sill and he winks at me with the burning eyes. I draw the picture of it and attach. It was such the good dream and it makes it feel all warm and squishy. Then I woke and found the warm and squishy feeling was an accident I made in the bed. So today I do the laundry. You do the laundry yes? Are you good woman who does the mens laundry?

So to answer the question, do I do to the gum. No I doesn't. I ride my bike every day. All over. Sometimes in circles and sometimes in straight lines. I do tricks with my Little Red Rocket. I attach the photo. I use my Little Red Rocket so much that it nearly wears out. That is why you have to keep it polished and clean. Or else it would fall apart and get limp. I do not want the limp Little Red Rocket. Why just the other day I entered a race. I pedal so fast and so hard, I winnings the race! I attach to photos. So all the ridings make the body hard and strong like the Superman. You bounce the quarter off me.

So you tell to me more about the Lena. She makes the jam yes? The jam goes good with my peanut butter. Maybe you tell to me more about the Lena. Sends me the photos of her. If I are to know you, then I must know the best friend true? Maybe you go visit the Lena and you take the photo on the beds as you make the jam with the joy? The would be the goods. No I do not write the other womens.

But if you give me the Lena information, I write to her. Just to talk about you and our relations of course. Not anything about the sexy time or the things like that.

So what did I do yesterdays? Well after I talk to you at the computers I go to the news tv. I have told you in past that the people know me from the tvs. So I discuss many different things on the tv. I attach the photo. I hopes you don't mind that I talk about you a little on the tv. People all around country should know that I have meat you. Do you like that I have meat you? I think you do. I cannot wait to meat you in the person. Which reminds me, did you read my letter where I ask for me to come over? What you think about that? You like yes?

We talk about the animals now. Yes I like the animals. Your papa shouldn't be a hater. It is not fault of dog to fall over dead. Dog die, puppy born. It is the circle of the life. Yes I have the pet. Remember the hamsters and the pussy named the cat? The hamster make a many childrens and I sell the hamster to the Chinesa man who lives down street. He owns the Chinesa restaurant. He buys many hamsters. He must like to play with the hamsters a lot! I bet he have big room with hamster playground for the hamster to play. I am happy they go to good home. Other pet I like is horse too! I like to ride the horse! You see photo I attach! You like the sexy horse? Horse is much like bike but you bounce up and down a lot and it hurt my sexy areas. So I don't ride horse a lot. But I like it when I do...except for the hurt of the sexy areas. So I have attach many many photos. I think it is high time you attach the many photo too. And don't forget the Lena photos. It much finish now. Don't work out to hard at the gum and have a happy weekend! I will take care of yours if you take care of mine yes? Billions of the kisses in tenderness!
Forever Curly

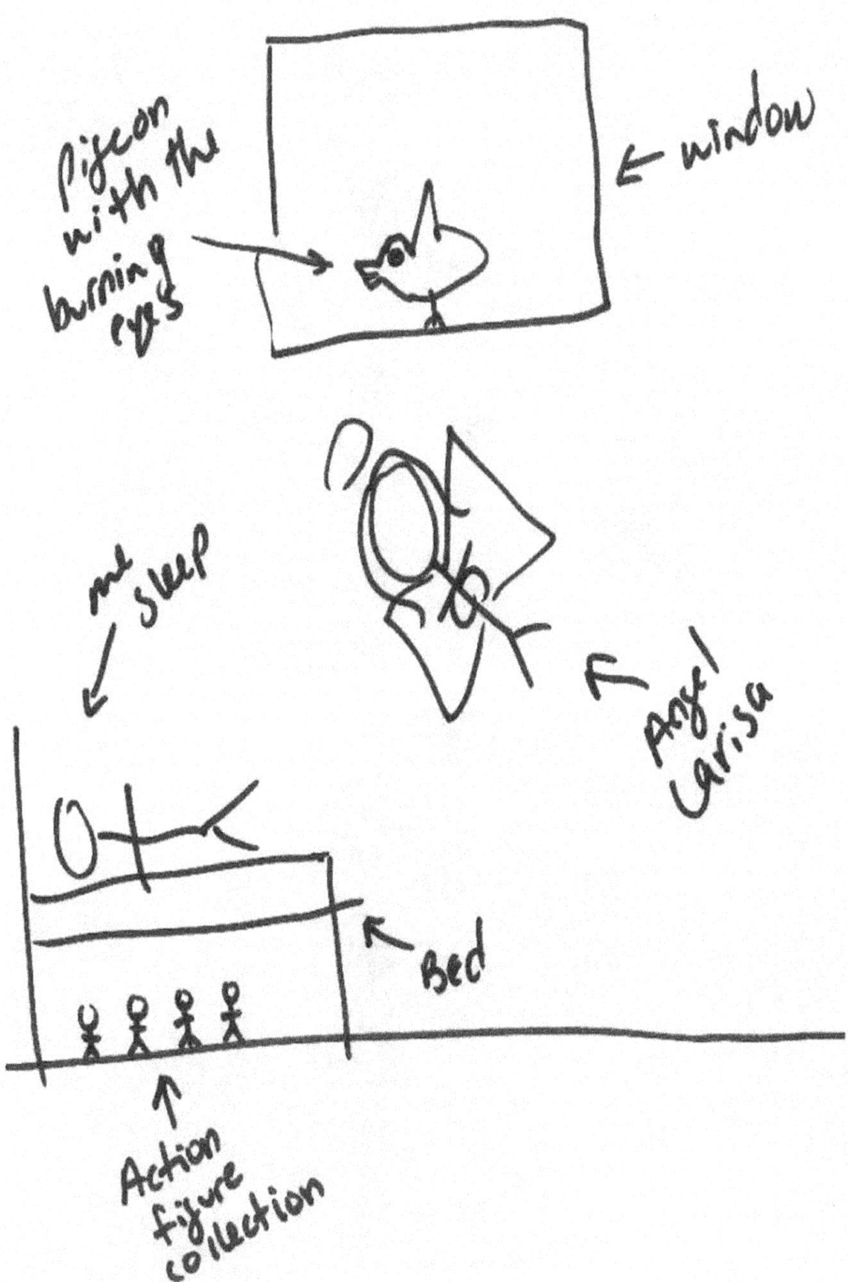
pigeon
with the
burning
eyes
window
me
sleep
Angel
Larisa
Bed
Action
figure
collection

I DO THE TRICKS!

IT IS A RACE! I AM WINNINGS!

FEX NEWS
Curly discusses fate of peanut butter empire and new friend in Russia.
HAPPENING NOW

CHAPTER 2:
CURLY CUE :
ELECTRIC BOOGALOO

CURLY-CUE
ELECTRIC BOOGALOO

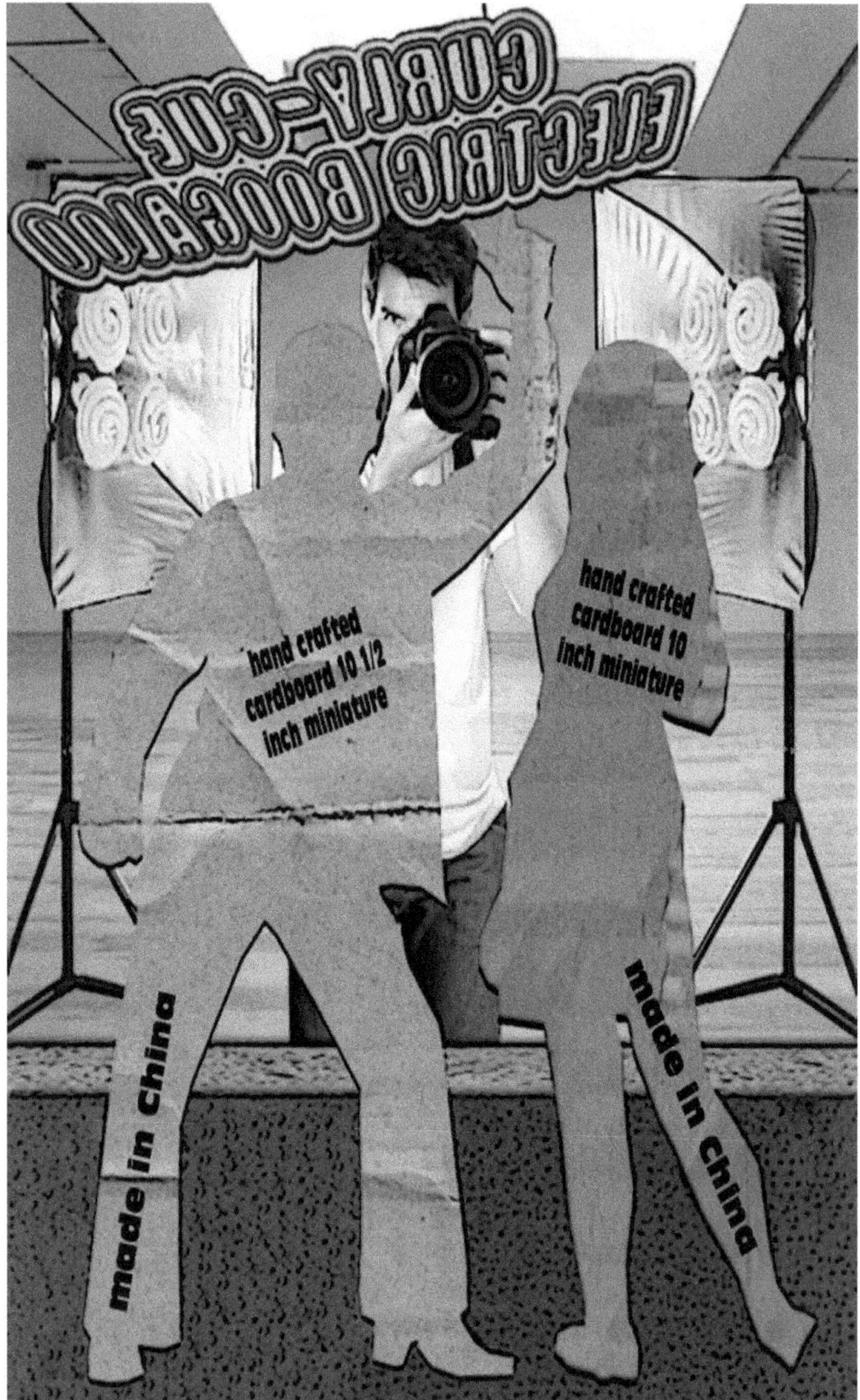
CURLY-CUE
ELECTRIC BOOGALOO
hand crafted cardboard 10 1/2 inch miniature
hand crafted cardboard 10 inch miniature
made in China
made in China

From: Larisa <gilkakisska@xxxxx.com>
Sent: Saturday, November 20 8:44 AM
To: Chris <coldbastrd@xxxxx.com>
Subject: [No Subject]

Hello morning my special friend Chris!!!!
I missed you so much. How is your mood? Is everything ok at your work? I'm fine. Your latest letter aroused warmth, admiration respect. All these feelings overwhelm me now. What do you feel? Please shave me with your thoughts. I'm so sorry dear. I forgot to fell you about my full name my address. Please forget me. I apologize. I forgot about everything because. I'm so busy with my work. Our shop is developing now we should attract more & more customers.
full name is Larisa Shmeleva.
My street is Botanichnaya 4.
Evident The flat is 12
City Tomsk.
Index 634000.
Please fell me your data too. Send me your number too. I will call you. I'm dreaming of. Hearing your voice. I think it's so sweet' & warm. The moment of speaking to you will be unforgivable. I'm sure a real conversation will make us closer to each other! So please give ,e your number & I will save it. I suppose we will find topics of conversation. How did you spend your weekend by the way? Did you go out? What places do you usually visit? As for me I was out of town. We visited my friend's granny. She has a small house with the garden. We had a nice time there. We had barbecue, danced a lot. At that time I was thinking about you. i wished you were with me. i even imagined that. we are sitting together, hand in hand, looking at the fire. There is a silence & we understand each other without words. It's impossible to refer this atmosphere by words. I hope you understand what i mean.

You know, with each letter you become more & more important for me. You begin to occupy the most part of my life. And I don't exaggerate.

My mum noticed that I began to smile more often. It's due to you, my sweetheart! I'm grateful that I could find you. I feel that we have similar souls, opinions, smith which unites us. Do you agree with me? My friend told me one thing yesterday. She heard that there art a lot of bad men in the. Internet who want to use Russian girls & she warned me to be careful & legible in my situation. Well, I know that she's worried about ,e because she's my best friend but. I'm sure for 100 that you will never deceive me. You are a very good person concerning everything. I', used to trusting people & to seeing only positive features. I have a question. Did you speak to your relatives & friends about me? What do they say& I think they also are worried about you & wish only happiness to you.

My dear, I have to stop here. Honey tomorrow. I'm not sure if can write you e-mail. We have auditing at work so I think that it will take a lot of time. Pls don't lose me. I'll come back. I promise. But still I wait for your passionate letter. Millions of kisses.....
Your, Larisa

From: Chris <coldbastrd@xxxxx.com>
Sent: Monday, November 22 2:47 PM
To: Larisa <gilkakisska@xxxxx.com>
Subject: [RE: No Subject]

Hello my moist best of friends Lena,
I missed you very very very much! Do I shave you with my thoughts? Oh yes indeed I do! All the time! With the hot creams. You know the kind you take the cold creams and put in hot creams machine and a few minutes more you have the hot creams. Please tell me about your shops. I have a shops too. I sell the peanut butter from the shops. All different kinds. Nutty, creamy, honey, extra chunky, mango (the peoples don't like this one very much). I incuse the photo of me in shops. It is I with my worker Tiny. Tiny good man but I have the problem with Tiny because he eat too much of our peanut butter. I tell Tiny, listen big man, must limit peanut butter to one can a day. And he say but Curly, your butter is so good, I fill the belly with it deep inside. And I looks at him and I nearly turn to the tears because I take the pride in the peanut butter and enjoy fact that he like my butter inside him.

Thank you for the information. I like the full name "Shmeleva". It sounds like the word smegma. Do you agrees? Here is my informations:
full name: Chris Curly Poindexter III Jr. Esq.
Street is evident: 350 5th Ave.
City of New York
Index 123456

So you would like to know what I do on weekend? Well as always, I ride the Little Red Rocket. That is number one priority. Then after the bikes ride, I go to the nightclub and play the music with my band. My band is called 'Curly and the PB&J's". I am lead singer. I have attached photos of us in the costume we wear for the stages. I sing a songs about you.

When I get the chance I send to you and you will like. It will give you the warm feelings like you are next to fire holding my imaginary hands.

Yes I do agrees with you. We are like the one souls together flying in the space. It is easy for you as you carry me much like the Superman did with the Lois Lane since you have the angel wings to make you fly. Speaking of the Superman, mama and papa came to me in dreams the other night. Much like the Superman papa in the fort of the solitudes. They glow in the dark and tell me that it is meant to bees that we be together! So yes to answer your question, I talk to the families and this is what they say to me in the dreams. Because they are dead it is not like can call on phone. Imagine if you could talk to dead on phone though? You can call up and ask papa, how is the heavens? Do they have the pools where you get out and man wait with hot towels like at fancy hotel? Do they have all the peanut butter in the world you can eat there? Do you see the famous dead peoples like Judy Garland and Burt Lancaster? This would be very interesting yes? I think so. I have attached the photos of me and dead family. Mama, papa, and me when mouthstache was not so big and the macho. In the photo to is the sister. She ran away to circus long time ago and become the lady with the beard. I no longer see her. SHE DISGRACE FAMILY! I SPIT ON HER! SPIT!!

For the friends, yes I tell them all about you. It gives them GREAT joy! I tells to them every day about you. And they say Curly, be carefuls. You know the Russian girls try to use the American men for the monies. And I say SPIT ON YOU! You don't know the Larisa like I do. I am certain to the 1000 she is honest and the trustworthy and maybe she one day make the Curly childrens for me.

So now, I give you many many many photo. I think it's time for you to give many many photos back yes? Please? With the sugary cream on the tops with a cherries?

I will miss you tomorrow honey sugar lumpy pie. But do nots worry, I will be here forever and always waiting for you! It is to end now! I wait for your lovingly letters! Billions of sweet caressing kissies!

Forever, Curly

THAT'S A LOT OF PEANUT BUTTER!

GROOVY!

CURLY AND THE PB&J'S

ROCK 'N ROLL GOD

From: Larisa <gilkakisska@xxxxx.com>
Sent: Tuesday, November 23 8:22 AM
To: Chris <coldbastrd@xxxxx.com>
Subject: [No Subject]

Hello, my Chris!
Thanks for your nice letter. What turnover in my soul when I read your words. Ted will begin with there is something in common between us. This is amazing!

How are you? How did you sleep? did you see me your dream? I saw you in my dream. We were at the seaside. We had a romantic dinner sunset. I had an indescribable feeling. We talked together, looked at each other's eyes. You look so deep & sexy, I felt armor the floors me. After dinner we went to the beach, without shoes, hugging each other. Suddenly, to me & kissed rurned got me so that it was unforgettable. I woke up in this feeling. The morning was beautiful & I was in heaven. My sweetheart. I came to the computer for some time. Thin lines are quite a long way. I'll have to go drive have time to do.

How are you family? Day greet them Ok? You have dinner? I read that it tradition to gather all family members on the National Day? It is true? Concerning us, we to be together so often, to us it's possible. Holidays, which connects the whole family. (I think mine connecting, cunts, cousin, nephew) is a new year. This holiday is considered to be home Holidays in Russia. It is much more popular than Christmas in spite the fact that Russia is a theocratic country. Bat still try to visit me nearest & most expensive every weekend if. Man fie tine course. My grandparents (my mother's parents), some equipment had died years ago. My father, parents living in the country. But the village is so far of our city you are visiting then yes. We cast the false mom Education of. I can say that.

I love them because it's my family but the distance people are far apart but in our case. I may fall, the distance between Rouses & interested. Agree me? But on the other hand, the Internet is not enough to learn each other very well. What do you think? What is your opinion? I As the power of &. I'm sure the relationship bezel flat paddle junkie. I know, now to explain in words. I feel that & that's all. God gives special love for people. He then rewards for your kindness & patience. And I'm sure God sends us rose to take! Are worthy it. We both suffered a lot of this life & now it's time to become happy. Ok dear. I think you already bothered my philcscplical considered. I stopped here.

Be careful, my beloved friend. I miss you! Kisses

Sincerely, Larisa.

From: Chris <coldbastrd@xxxxx.com>
Sent: Tuesday, November 23 1:57 PM
To: Larisa <gilkakisska@xxxxx.com>
Subject: [RE: No Subject]

Hello my tasty peachy pie Larisa,

How are you today? I, not so good. Who is this Ted character??? I WILL BREAK HIM LIKE TWIG!!! TED GO SMASH!!! Tells to me please who he is? Is he a friend? Is he a gay friend because that would be ok. If not, I will be very angry! You do not want to see me angry! I do crazy thing when I am angrys. I have to go eat the peanut butters now to calm down.

Ok I am backs. Did you miss me? Tells to me. For me, I sleep well. I dream of rainbows and glitter stars and you flying on the angel wings. And there I was in your arms as you carried me into the spaces. We went to moon and bounced around like as though you are in the childrens bouncy castle. And when we finished the bouncing we sat down and had a picnic of peanut butter sandwiches and watched the Earth rise like the sun does in the mornings. I like your dream too although it is fairly plain and not as elaborate as mine. I like that you feel the armor. I am like the knight in the shiny armor riding in to rescue you from simple Russian existence. Am I not? I make the computer generation photo of me in thearmor on the pony wielding mighty peanut. You find it sexy yes?

My family? They are still dead. I do not expect the changes in the situation any time soon. Yes the tradition of the holiday is upon us. Remember I tells to you about the Thanksgiving? We gather around and eat the muskrats and gravy. I tell you more about the holiday here.

Long time ago, the peoples from the France got onto their ocean freighter. The sea was rough and manys the peoples were sick and vomit all over floor. They arrive on the Chrysler Rock in the America and pitch their tents all over beach. They didn't have much to eat...the oysters and fishes. People say, I am so tired of eating the oyster and fishes. We are on freighter on ocean for many months and we no like the fishes anymore. Meanwhiles deep in the forest of Endor, the Ewoks, they are the natives peoples of America, peeked out of bushes and sees the French. Now of course the French people being French, they were on the beach topless and they do not shave the armpits. So the Ewoks they were sickened when they look at the Frenchies with the hairy pits and the floppy boobies. They go to Ewok leader and say, boss we don't like to see the Frenchies on the beach with the hairy pits, what do we do to stop this? So the great Ewok leader thought long and hard. He went into his sweaty lodgings and spoke with great spirit Gods in the sky. After 3 days, he come out of lodge. He tells his people, the great spirit Gods tells to me what to do. We are to go to beach and beg the Frenchies to put on their clothings. In return we will give them the muskrats for them to eat since they are tired of eating fishes. So the Ewoks gathered up all the muskrats in the forest and put on big cart. They make big parade to beach with Ewok leader in front. He approach Frenchies and says, hello my good friends, please to me, put on back your clothings. If you are to do this to me, I give you great findings of muskrats for you to feast on. And the Frenchies were in over joys! They say, thank you kindest Ewoks, for bringings to us the muskrat foods as we are so tired of eating the fishes. And there was much singing and dancing and drinking and eating of muskrats. And the Ewoks were very thankful with this arrangement so their eyes no burning no more and Frenchies were very thankful for the food. And so that is the story of the Thanksgiving.

For me, I celebrate by going to the sweaty lodge and try to communicates with the great spirit Gods just like the leader of Ewok tribe did. I do not spend with family as I tells to you, they are dead. Well I do have the one family member who is the lady with the beard at circus I tells you about yesterday and it is true, she is a real cunt. A DISGRACE TO FAMILY NAME!!

Yes this relationship of ours. It is turning me into a real bezel flat paddle junkie. When I go to talk to the spirit Gods in a few days, they will agree with me. Tells to me, I have you bothered the physically? Tell me abouts this. Do you touch yourself in the night times? When I lay in the bed at night, and I dream of you on the angel wings, I get the botherment of physicality too and much touch myself. It is ok and natural to feel these things yes. So for me I write many things and it finish now. Please I send many photos and hardly and photos in return. You send to me please the more photos? Be careful around this Ted character my beloved loved. I await your next writings. A billion kisses and the hugges!

Forever and ever, Curly

YOUR KNIGHT IN SHINY ARMOR

From: Larisa <gilkakisska@xxxxx.com>
Sent: Wednesday, November 24 10:51 AM
To: Chris <coldbastrd@xxxxx.com>
Subject: [No Subject]

Hello, my favorite Chris!

Oh, I'm so happy that I am with you sometime. I'm so tired! Nejaky people nervous. You know, I did a lot of time, because I colleague gas is a little bug didn't agree. He tried blame me. That was the situation, but I stupid Managed to prove that if he were not my faurt. So now the situation normalsized. Well, that's enough about the wrong things.

Thank you, my darling, for your letter. If geared me for the whole day. I hope everything is ok with you. If not, pls share with me! I You can listen & support you difficult time. I always together with you. D, in my mind. Sorry, I do melancholy to you. You are a ray of hope that for me a strong & Gives me moments of happiness. I miss you so much! So my dear, what happened to you in these days? Missed you? By the way, you sent me pictures long held forward to them. I Will pleasant! Certainly if not the same as when they see you in reality, but still these pictures man me closer to you. Sometimes I look on your photos you sent me before. Your eyes are so worthy. I dream of seeing them in reality. Maybe stare. your photos for a long time. With every minute. I Relax that I need. I hope You think the same thing.

Oh darling, I forgot to Rell you! What we have beautiful weather Now! Sand shine, birds sing. All people in the vicinity elated. So now I start to forget their problems. Yesterday I shopping with a friend. I guess you can imagine how girls adore shopping. So I'm no exception. Women walked shop - windows for girlschooling blouse or skirt or something else. It really does me wa.

Well, you're a man & I do not understand my Think passion for A hopping. I know that most people hate This affair. You are so impatient & Thing ready to buy the first you see only not to go into another business. On this issue, we will more readable VAM, man. But I dream to go shopping in geter with you! We select something special for you. I have a good last, so will look great. And I hope you won / t be angry with me, if you go some km together & &. What do you think about this idea? What style of clothes do you prefer?

As regards me as a classic, sports & romantic style. In the official work I have long skirts, jackets, blouses, high heels. When I go out I wear a dress, sometimes prefer the shirt T., jeans. When I go the city, go for a walk I had to sport things. It is very comfortably. Colors vary. It depends on my Moos. But most useful are: red, black, white and blue.

Ok, my dear, I will finish here to bed now. Sweet dreams! I will I come to you in your dreams & kiss with passion.

Take care Sincerely,
Larisa.

From: Chris <coldbastrd@xxxxx.com>
Sent: Wednesday, November 24 12:18 PM
To: Larisa <gilkakisska@xxxxx.com>
Subject: [RE: No Subject]

Hello my dear sweetest Larisa,

I am fine today. You are tired? Is it because you stay up late in the bed thinking about me in the physicality? Your coworker Nejaky is a very slick shady type of character isn't he. How dare he try to pass the gas and blame it on you! I am sure that the gas in which you pass smell like the roses that grow high in the Swiss mountains. So I am certain that it was easy for you to discern who's gas is who's. One time Tiny pass the gas and tries to blame me. But it is only me and he in store so pretty easy to smell who gas is who. Sometime we get into the gas fight but he always win since he is such big mans.

You like the photos I send you. Tells to me what you do to self when you relax and stare into my eyes. Does it give you the botherment of physicality? My eyes they are the worthy yes? Sometimes when I sleep in the nights and I wake up in the mornings, I have the crusty in the eyes. Mama would tell me that the Sandsman would come into my bedroom at the nights and put the sands in my eyes. I would think to self, who is this deranged man who sneak into bedroom in the night and put the sand in my eyes? Why does he do this? Is he tries to make me blind? What is his problems? So I set the traps for this Sandsman. I put the string on can across door and window. Somehow he keeps sneaking in and put the sand in eyes. SOMEDAY I WILL CATCH HIM AND HE WILL GET THE SMASH!!!!!!

Yes now onto the clothings. It is very nice of you to offer to get me somethings. I would very much like to see you in the girlschooling clothings. You send to me the photos? I would stare into your worthy eyes as you wear the girlschooling clothings. It would give me the botherment of physicality. I would like that very much. I have incluse a few photos of my favorite clothings. First for laying about the houses, I like to wear a nice comfortable robe and pants. Ones that is silky and doesn't cause the irritations of the skin or cause the underbottoms to get sweaty. What do you wear around the houses? Do you wear the robe or do you wear the nudiness?

For going about the town on the Little Red Rocket, I like to wear fashionable grey suit with comfortable shoes for when I paddle the bicycle. Here you can sees me at award show for the tv. I think if I are to go out in the publics on the Little Red Rocket, I should look fashionable and presentable. Lastly here I am about to go out to the discotech. I like to wear the flashy clothes so people sees me on the dance floor boogie down! Do you like the boogies? Do you go to discotech and have the boogie? Everybody love to get on the floor and get the boogies! Boogie baby boogie! Want you to taste my boogies! Very nice! Curly Cue Electric Boogaloo!

So I am approach the finish here. If you remember, it is great holiday here for next few days. I will be in the sweaty lodgings speaking with great spirit Gods about you. So you will not hear to me for next few days. Do not worries! I will be back! I would never leave to you! In the meanwhiles, I will be dreaming about you carrying me on the angels wings while smelling the sweet rose gases. Goodbye for the now. A thousand million billion trillion passion kisses for you!
Forever and always, Curly

CURLY'S GUIDE TO MEN'S FASHION

STAYING AT HOME

PUBLIC APPERANCE

BOOGIE DOWN

From: Larisa <gilkakisska@xxxxx.com>
Sent: Thursday, November 25 9:47 AM
To: Chris <coldbastrd@xxxxx.com>
Subject: [No Subject]

Hello evening, my darling Chris!
How are you? As for me I'm fine, the weather is good. Sun is mentation illuminating e-mail for you. I am happy. You do not need to imagine how much Your letters bring joy to me! We certainly close to each other more and more. We can tell each other everything, even our secrets. Make Will you support me in this idea? I hope it is important to me to know Which you can listen to me any time and support me morally. You know, to our knowledge, I ask God to help me find Man who will be a true friend to me. And you Chris Is my right friend, whom I trust and believe. Now I can not imagine your life without you and your letters! I'm beginning to realize that you are a man who I was looking for! You brought me luck in the days you normally night my friend came to me. Returned from her vacation. Sla the land, to see her grandparents. She asked me, about us, our relationship. I said that everything was alright and we were glad That we find. She is a council that for us. Whenever I came home, I think of you, of us, from our life, our next meeting. Very often, I imagine, as we meet for a time. I've never met a man who was more sincere and sensual that you are! I do not understand what I'm pulling for you. In fact, we do not know each other a long time case. I guess it happens because I have not met a person like you! But I can not say that I changed beyond recognition since our known. Changed me! I want to continue in the relationship you! By the way I was watching a programmer is a channel yesterday. The topic of discussion was devoted to marriages Between Russian girls and foreign men. Is said, and from lo pary become happy and have strong trade unions and behold the pairs have no divorce. The woman was interviewed there. Her name is Khalid.

She was married Anglican for 5 years. Have children-twins: a boy girl. She says he is completely satisfied. Living in London I envy her bit. I'm glad for her and I want to have a strong family sam. I can be a good wife. What do you think? I'm sure you're very good husband and father! I told mom I wanted to create a family asked me, I was wrong. Vis, she loves me a lot because I had cast. I do not think you understand. Tell me about your life, your work. Do you often think about me? Well, that's all for now.

Take care honey! Kiss your Larisa.

From: Chris <coldbastrd@xxxxx.com>
Sent: Monday, November 29 1:53 PM
To: Larisa <gilkakisska@xxxxx.com>
Subject: [RE: No Subject]

Hello my sweetness Larisa,
How does the sun greet you on this night? I am beyond happy and excited! I must tell you about my meeting with the great spirit Gods! I set out across the land on my Little Red Rocket heading towards the mighty forest of Endor. It is long ride and you must past many scary place as you go. The flowers from the trees turn road yellow. Along the ways to Endor, you see many animals. Mostly lions, tigers, and bears. I stopped in a small town and I met a group of tiny people. I have attached the photo. They were funny and made me laugh. We will be the friends forever! Do you have the tiny peoples there in Russia?

So after my rest in small town I set off again for Endor. Along way three peoples stopped me. One guy says, I have a problem with the brain. Another mans says, I am having the heart trouble. And last man says I am having the problem with the balls area. So I say to them each, what do I look like? A doctors? Why don't you go to hospitals? Do I look like I can help you with such problems? I am simply riding along on the Little Red Rocket. I cannot fix the problems! So off away I go. Every time I go into the public everybody wants something from me!

After long journey, I arrive in the forest of Endor. I am meet by great Ewok Chief Chokesondeek. He is great spiritual leader of native Ewok peoples. Today we are to go to the ancient sweaty lodges. I attach the photo. We enter sweaty lodges and took off clothings. We eat the mushrooms of the lands and smoke the natural weeds. I see the colors of the rainbow as I move hands and taste the sounds.

Chief talks to spirit Gods. He takes wooden spirit stick and smacks my Mr. Winky. I fall over in the pain. He reaches to sky and says, by the power invested in me by great spirit Gods, you have been given the powers to make the many childrens. He then says, lay back and I rub you with the spirit oils and the thought of worthy woman for you to make the childrens with come to you. So I lay back, close eyes, and Chief rub me with the oils. My booty was tingling all over as the thoughts of worthy woman comes to mind. Do you know who comes into the minds? YOU! Isn't that exciting and the wonderment?

The next day, we dress in native Ewok dress. We smoke more natural weeds. He points to sky and says to me, the spirit Gods have told to me's that you are to take wing and fly to the worthy womans. I have attached the photo of this. He says, spirit Gods call you "Curliwata" which means "man who fly on great chicken wing". The native Ewok womens craft me new clothings representative to new name give by spirit Gods. We then smoke more natural weeds, ate more mushrooms, and danced for rest of weekend.

Do you see? It is true! Great spirit Gods say we must be together. They say that I must fly to you on great chicken wing up in sky. With that said, I need to book a flight because I cannot actually fly. I tired over weekend by jumping off ledge but I fell. So to me you need to send half the airline expense. It is fair yes? It is next step to securing strong trade union where we trade the fluids to have the childrens.

I am coming to the finish now. Can you feel it? Do you want me to finish now? Before I forgets, yes we can tell each other the secrets. Please tell me some of your secrets and I'll tell some of mine. I have many many secrets. And again please, I send many photos but hardly have any of you. Send more please? Pretty the please? You take the loves and the cares! Kisses all over you! Forever and ever, Curliwata!

NEW LITTLE FRIENDS!

THE SWEATY LODGES.

LOOK UP IN THE SKY! IS IT A BIRD? IS IT A PLANE?

IT'S CURLIWATA!!!

From: Larisa <gilkakisska@xxxxx.com>
Sent: Tuesday, November 30 9:11 AM
To: Chris <coldbastrd@xxxxx.com>
Subject: [No Subject]

Hello, my loved Chris!!!
I was glad to read your great letter. How is your mood? Do you miss? I miss you so much! Today in the morning. I have been late injection. It happened because the bus that Gulf. I usually go for my work. It was broken in half of their journey. It was good that my boss not to his place &. I did not have to explain his delay. So generally it 'ok with me. D, has become necessary for me. Our relationship has become warmer. I must tell you that my life &. I'm on seven heaven luck. How did you spend the weekend my apartment. I read detective story. Agatha Kristi. Then I cooked dinner with fried potatoes Chicken & cherry pie. Krusine day. I cook dinner for you. Do you mind? I want to spend more time at the computer & to answer your e-mail at once. Bud unfortunately not allow my work to me. And I think we should appreciate what we got up in life. Do you agree? We have become mutually open. I would like to share my thoughts with you. Even in comparison of values in my life & your country. In Russia all people only a dream to marry a woman into bed. That is horrible. In my opinion, Sexual relationships are possible. Love it all over our world, Which gives the person to learn happiness in this life. All Russian men love to see only the bed. I can not accept. I believe that you agree with me in this matter. Dream of pure love &. And the camera shows that the love for you. But I think it is too early to be touching. We should see each other well, but we have a great distance between us.

Yesterday I was with my friend's son. We walked to the park. We walked Merry-go-round, bought ice-cream. We enjoyed the autumn. Children are treasure. Dream of a son too. Want to have children? Now They feel strong headache. I think that he ate too much ice-cream yesterday & cold. I have a cough & my nose is a warning. So I had to go to drug-store to buy some medicine. I hope you're OK. I wish you were close to me & take care of me OK, sweetheart. I'm out here. Be careful.

Do not mess cat ice-cream like me. I miss you, my friend Chris! I strike kisses infect you. Sincerely, Larisa.

From: Chris <coldbastrd@xxxxx.com>
Sent: Tuesday, November 30 2:24 PM
To: Larisa <gilkakisska@xxxxx.com>
Subject: [RE: No Subject]

Buenos noches my beloved Larisa! Yes I missed you very much! Sorry you were late to work today. What kind of injection did you have? The hot beefy kind? That is an amazing story about your bus! I just read about it on the interwebs news! I have attached the screen photo. You are lucky to be alive! I am so so glad you aren't injured! I would just throw myself off the highest building in the town if you were!

Anyways, I spent the weekend in your apartment in my mind. When I was in the sweaty lodges and I felt my mind travel to your apartment. You weren't there at the time. So I looked around. I hope you don't mind I peeked in your underwears drawer. I like the pink bottoms with the little cherry on the front. I looked in the refrigerator. You really need to get rid of that ketchup. It expired 3 months ago. I had to take a dump so I used your pooper. I hope you don't mind. There wasn't enough tooshy paper so I take a showers. I like the flowery shampoo you use. I poured it all over myself and rubbed it in with the poof. Is it strange for man to smell flowery? I am just trying to keep your smell on me. Is that so wrong? Please don't be the judgmental. After the shower and the toweling, I laid on your bed. I press my nose into bed sheets and inhaled. I try to get your dead skin cells into nose so that I can feel even closer to you. While I was laying in the beds, Chief Chokesondeek smack me on bottom with wooden spirit stick and I came back to sweaty lodges. I closed eyes many times since and can't seem to get back there. I think I took a wrong turn in Albuquerque.

That is so very nice you make to me the dinner! No I do not mind. I wish I was there to eat your tasty pie. I will tells to you a secret. I make the dinner for you every night too. I make the peanut butter and banana fried sandwich. It is the favorite food of the fat man Elvis. He eat too many the fried banana and peanut butter sandwich. The stool could not be processed and had the major backup in the pooper. So it is suggestible that you do not eat too many the fried banana and peanut butter or else you will not be able to process the stool. I place the sandwich on a plate and place it on table in empty seat and pretend that you are there. I have taken the photo. I would sit and eat my sandwich and pretend to talk to you. Pretending is fun yes?

Well to tell the truths, I was getting a lonely without you here and just pretending. So I tells to you another secret. I took your picture and made a life size doll of you. Are you mad? Please don't be mad. As you say there is great distance between us. I visit you in dreams but still it is far away. You agree yes that it is too early for the touching and you are so far away that the touching is impossible. But if I have the doll. I touch the doll and it is ok yes? Please tell me it is ok to touch the doll. If you are mad, I will smash the doll. I hope you will not be mad. The doll gives me something to look at and touch and pretend like you are heres. This is agreeable yes? It is not best doll but it does job late at night when botherment of physicality becomes unbearables. I am thinking of getting better doll which is more real but I need you to send the more photos so it can be constructed in your likeliness.

To answer question of the childrens, yes as I have told you Chief Chokesondeek says that spirit Gods have made me ready to go into the productions of childrens. However this requires the much touching of physicality. But you are not ready for the touch. So when you are ready, we have a great trade union to produce the childrens.

I am sorry you are getting the infections. Please feel better. Of course I wish I was there to smash infections away from your bodies.

Please do not eat the cat milk ice creams again. I imagine the cat milks may not be as sanitary as the cows. Perhaps this is what sickness is. Please do not strike me with your infected kisses. I do not want to get the cat milk sickness. I wait for the kisses when you are not infected. I miss you and I finish now. Please feel the better. Sorry no kisses for you today.
Forever and always, Curly

Welcome to the new AOL.com! New her

Aol.

Web Images Video Maps

Search the Web

Charles Eshelman Getty Images

Gulf Bus In Tomsk Russia Breaks In Half

"Peoples dying, childrens crying" exclaims one passenger as bus mysteriously breaks in two separate pieces.

- *Oficals say peoples lucky to be alive! Read full story here.*

Tales From Tinseltown

- 'Sex' Star Sued Over $109K Error
- 37-Year-Old CBS Show Renewed
- Actress' Tattoos Are Awkward Now

2/12

PB & BANANA SANDWICH. IT IS YUMMY!

I TOUCH THE DOLL.

CHAPTER 3:
THE HAMMER OF SLEDGE

CURLY AND LARKA IN

THE HAMMER OF SLEDGE

CURLY AND LARKA IN

THE HAMMER OF SLEDGE

Hammer of Sledge chapter

Do not remove. Thank y ou.

From: Larisa <gilkakisska@xxxxx.com>
Sent: Wednesday, December 1 8:50 AM
To: Chris <coldbastrd@xxxxx.com>
Subject: [No Subject]

Hello, my darling Chris!
How are you? Is everything all right? I hope so. You can not imagine how I tired. Is necessary to take a holiday in the nearest future. Want to rest and relax for a moment. Today I had a day off & this is the reason why I did not go to work. My film director shorter to me that I had a rest because I deserved it. So today I slept more. Once I He stood frist idea to know what you do now. It's wonderful to think of you know that you do not forget about me too.

So now I sit at the computer writing a letter for you. And I wondered, as we continue our relationship. Dear Chris, with every letter that I understand clearly that the feelings are still on you the big silos. And what about you? I discovered that begin oxupy majority of spare in my thoughts & dreams. I do not know what happens exactly luck for me! You are so handsome, clever, bright, strong & gentle beautiful day, we can be mort than just friends. It depends on our relationship. Afra I'm losing you! You became closest friend for me. I can trust totally & share it with State and emotions. It's very difficult to find a brave man. But I happy. I could find you! And I'm sure that our meeting will first victory in our relationship. I hope that agree with me. Is always Nadherne accept your pictures. Waiting for receipt of your Soft & kind words & your pictures every day.

I can not stop thinking of us. On my opinion we should meet soon. What Your idea about this? Today I stay inches waiting for guests. It is girl. She is 16 Ted is a girls' school & wants to join University, faculty of foreign languages. Her mother asked me to her help with English.

English is a basic test for entry faculffy. I agreed with pleasure. The girl is very smart & very good English. So today we revised CASY & passive voice. She makes a great progress, so I'm sure she will succed in the exam. And How was your day? Ok nice that everything is at this moment. I miss you! Take furnace. Kisses! Forever thy Larisa.

From: Chris <coldbastrd@xxxxx.com>
Sent: Wednesday, December 1 3:59 PM
To: Larisa <gilkakisska@xxxxx.com>
Subject: [RE: No Subject]

Hellos my darlingest Larisa!
It is so fantastical to hear your words to me today! Of course I understand you need to take the time off. I mean what a crazy day you had yesterday! The bus breaking in the half. The cat milks infection. It is just the craziness! I come to you in my dreams and soak your head with the hot towels and feed to you the creamy peanut butter sandwiches.

Why are you so freting about losing me? I am not going anywheres. Well maybe for the Red Rocket ride but that is about all. Yes I agree that we should meet soon. Have you considered sending me the payment for the airfare? Clock is ticking honey. Let's please make these arrangements. I am getting the tired of touching the doll and much touch the real yous.

That is fantastical informations that you are helping to teach the English to the girl. A person such as yourself who has such high command and knowledge of the English. She will certainly pass any exams with the flying stars with your helps!

I only wish that I had someone like you in my lifes when I was the younger to help me with the schoolings. I imagine I would have the great knowledges. I went to the schools when I was younger. I did not do the very wells. Some childrens can be very menacing. They would make the funs of the Curly because I develops the mouthstaches at the first grades. They do not understand that it is signals of virility and machoness. They make the funs and I would get angrys. And I would make them and things go smash!

So teacher only see me get angry and not the reason for angry and make me stands in the corner. I have attach the photo. It would make me sad. I would lie in the beds at night and cry because I did not understands why they make the fun of Curly. Sometimes I would get so sad and angrys at same time I make the puddle of the PP in the beds and mama would get angry.

Mama and the papa see that the Curly is sad so they take me aways from the schools. They teach me at homes the ways of the world. Also they would have me work in the peanut butter factory. This makes the rounded person yes? I have attached the photos of me in peanut factory making the peanut butters. I am using the peanut butter packer machines. Every year around holidays mama and the papa make fudge instead of peanut butter. It is holiday tradition. So I would become the fudge packer. I am so good at packing the fudge. I enjoy being a fudge packer very much. I would like for you to try the fudge. Maybe I make you the special fudge and pack it deep inside you.

So now that the mama and papa are gones, it is just me and whole big peanut butter factory. You can understand that I get the loneliess. One day I decide that it is not right for me to not share my peanut butter factory with the boys and girls since they like the peanut butter so much. Childrens love the peanut butter and jellies. So I decide every year to have the contest for the lucky boys and girls. They find special ticket that I hides in the peanut butter jars. I only make few tickets a year. The lucky boys and girls who find the tickets come to the peanut butter factory and I show them around. I dress in the fancy clothings. I attach the photo of me and the lucky childrens. I let them bring the families too. I am so very kind like this do you agree? I let them see all the factory and sample many peanut butters. It makes them happy. We make a river inside factory. The river is made of peanut oils. You see when you work with peanut, you get the peanut butter and you gets the peanut oils.

Lots and lots of oils! So it is best way to make a river out of oils. We process oils and put in bottles and peoples buy for the cooking. Do you cook with the peanut oils? We build the boat and take rides on river of peanut oil. I have attach the photo. It is great funs! One time fat childrens fall in river and gets sucked into intake tubes. It was great disaster. Had to close factory for week. Little fat piggy boy! He drink the peanut oil. Childrens probably not so bright.

So it comes to the finish and I write many things and send even more photos. When will you send me more photos of you? I wait in great anticipations! Yes I will take furnace for you. It is heavy and bolted to floor but I can remove if needed. Where do you need me to send it? Is it that cold there? I send blanket instead? It is far easier. Kisses for you too...but only if you are over cat milk sickness.

Forever o thy art thy,

Curly

I WILL NOT SMASH THINGS.

PACKING PB DOWN AT THE FACTORY.

I LOVE THE SMALL CHILDRENS!

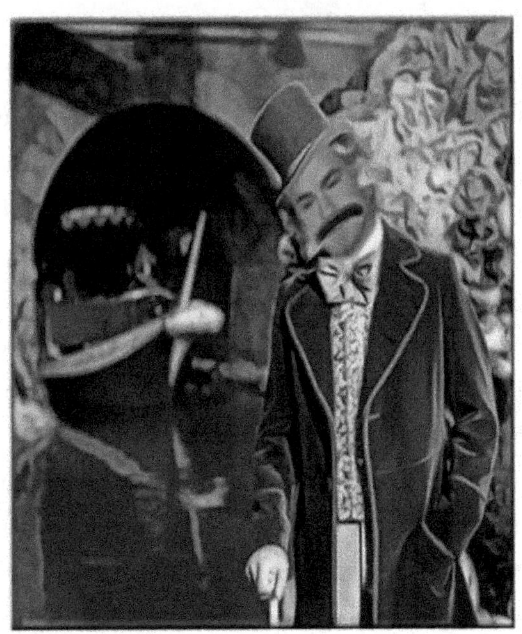

From: Larisa <gilkakisska@xxxxx.com>
Sent: Thursday, December 2 10:03 AM
To: Chris <coldbastrd@xxxxx.com>
Subject: [No Subject]

Hello, my dear Chris!

How are you? What is your day? I'm sorry I did not answer me baby immediately, but frankly, I felt bad. Today I had the most awful day in my life! When I got home I cried because I felt insulted. One client insulted me. I never heard so much kruta words. He did not like the quality of one of the devices in our shop at the end decided that it was me who is to blame in it. And I could not prove to him that I had no relationship to her. Supplier guilty, but not here shop-whatever. But this man did not hear anything. Shouted at me in the cell-commerce department. I felt embarrassed, as people can be cruel to women! I'm sure if there was a man in my position should not humiliate him. But I am a woman and he for he had the right to tell me that the worst words and insulting me. It's not fair! Aha. dear, I was so nervous and could not become calm. My director came in and explained that customers whose fault was. With shouted at me then left. Director saw me state and let me go home early. At home, I calmed down a bit. I thought that everything went wrong from the very morning. In morning I had an argument with my mom on the phone. She told me that I sufficient attention to the sun, and I tried to explain to her that my work It took a lot of time. She said that this was the reason Chromy excuse. I nervous. After work I did and apologized and I said, her about my bad day. Came to me tonight. She cooked dinner For me and took me erie. Darling I wanted you beside me to the world turned to me. I need your protection. I know that my family will always help me. I was very full of them for it. But can arm is another matter. When a man is near, can protect from everything. I am so happy to have you in my life. The only step for NAS meeting.

I hope it will become one day. We believe it? My gold apologize for such a sad letter, but I wrote what I feel now. You know, I'm quite honest and always tell the truth. But I hope that best. God will punish that man for such words, and I will try forget this situation. I'm out here I loved Chris! Please, I know that I appreciate you very much! D, stood near me. I hope the same feeling. Take care of yourself. A nice day! Kisses You Larisa!

From: Chris <coldbastrd@xxxxx.com>
Sent: Thursday, December 2 2:53 PM
To: Larisa <gilkakisska@xxxxx.com>
Subject: [RE: No Subject]

Larisa! Who is this man!! THIS MAKE ME SO ANGRY! How dare he talks to you like this. I MAKE HIM GO SMASH! How dare he humiliates the woman! And especial my angel Larisa! I WILL BREAK HIM! Gods will send him to hells fires where the crows and goats and demons and satans will eat on his brains and he will burn forever! I have drawn the photo to illustrates.

I am so very angrys! I went to garage and get the hammer of sledge. I run through town yelling...why!! Why you do this to Larisa! Car stopped and honk at me. Why are honk you jackalass? I take hammer of sledge and SMASH CAR! I run away! I see big watermelon on table. I so angry I think it bad mans head. WATERMELON SMASH! I run through the towns. People run away from me. Police come and says, Curly you need to settle downs! I say go aways! I run! Police chase me. Photo from newspapers included. I don't know what happens next. I felt electrified and fall on face. I wake up in the police stations!

They take the photo then throw me in the jails! When I was young boys, mama and papa would say if I get in troubles with police, they send me to Siberia. Maybe this is way for us to be together? Maybe they sends me to the Siberia? I am stuck in the jail now. I need help! Please can you help me? I am sure that if you sends the monies, they will accept the payment for my mischief and let me go homes. Please help me! They let me use computer to send the letter to you. It is customary to get the one phone call but I have no one to call. Only you in life to reach and touch me.

I am sorry I gets so angry and rage engulfs me. It is not right for what the mans do to you. If only I was there, he would not do such things! I want to be near you. I want to protect you! If I was there, I would! And also give you the kissings all over the bodies. Please you mother is right. Pay sufficient attention to sun and tan the skins.

If you are pale and ghostly, that is not attractive. Must be fit and attractive womans to be with Curly. You agree? It must finish now. Police man tells me to stop typing and to get in showers.
Please help me!
Kisses forever and ever and ever! Help! Curly!

Little Red Rocket
HA HA!
me
Angel Larisa

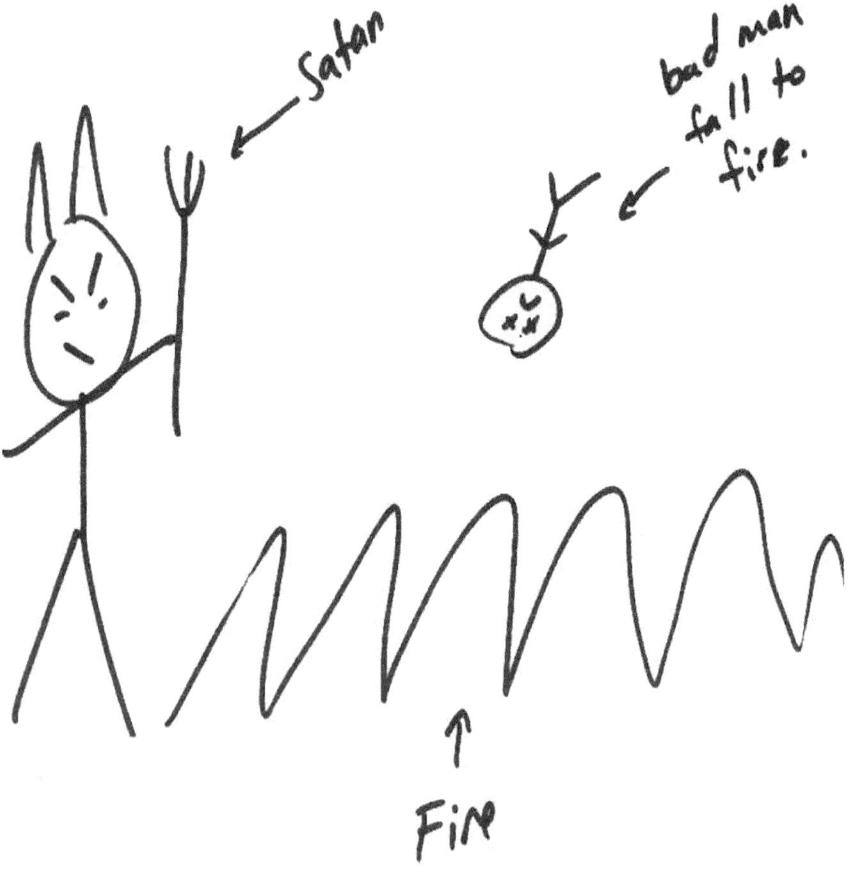

Satan
bad man fall to fire.
Fire

CAR SMASH!!!!!!

WATERMELON SMASH!!

I RUN AWAYS!

HELP!

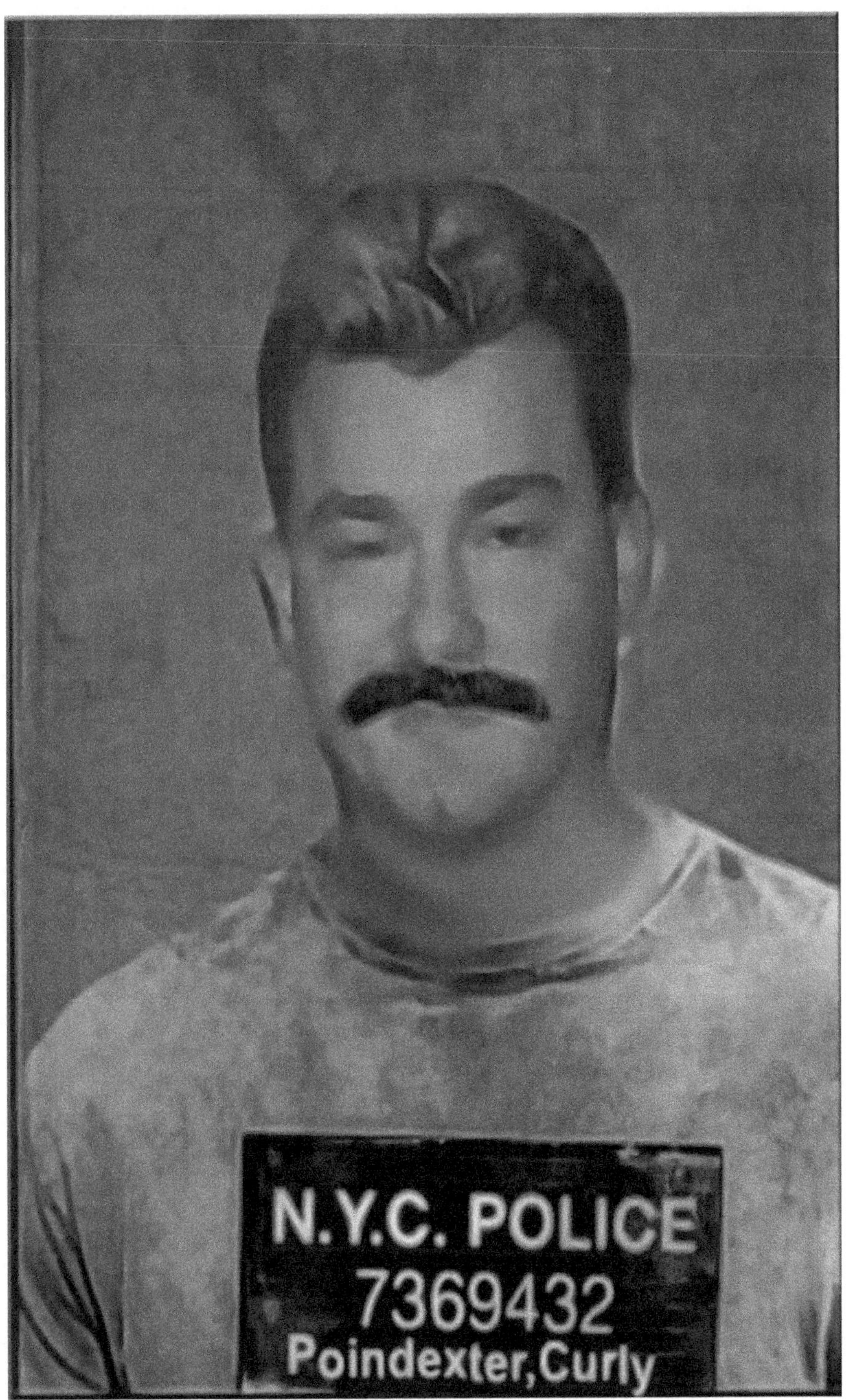
N.Y.C. POLICE
7369432
Poindexter,Curly

From: Larisa <gilkakisska@xxxxx.com>
Sent: Friday, December 3 9:40 AM
To: Chris <coldbastrd@xxxxx.com>
Subject: [No Subject]

Hello Chris, my Prince Charming! I am very pleased with your letter. Honey, I have good news. I was looking forward to you about it! There were meeting in my work. Director talked about plans for the future & other problems. But then he mentioned the good things. Was call the division of vacation. He gave it to 3 people. And my dear, I was in this list! I'm so happy. So I leave since. by. My dear, if it is real hope Us! Veris? It's an opportunity to meet. What do do you think? I am looking forward to visit you. I consulted my mum & she was shorter me that if we continue our serious relationship I had visit You know how you live, get acquainted with the family & then we should decide what we do. In my opinion it is quite right. Additionally I've never been abroad. I like your country & want to know more facts & see if everything on their own eyes. So you think?

I can not explain what I feel now. Feeling lucky calm & happy. Pulp me! Finally, I see! I can touch the kiss, embrace you & whisper weigh our words. Do you rat? My heart is filled with happiness. I believe that you're my desting! I chose tea! It is a sign from above. We believe that fate? I thank my lucky stars! I dream of meeting you. I would say that you & & feel begins to understand each other. is quite important. We must trust each other. Lez is a very bad thing. My mother taught I told the truth only from childhood. So we should trust each other complete! We believe that you would never play dirty game with me!

So I think we need to learn what is necessary to take to you. But if later. First tell me what you think. Do you Are you sure you want to see me? Do you really think that our relationship? What Furthermore, if you? I'm sorry that I wrote too many questions for you, but I To be sure that everything is really OK with us, my mile. I donkoceni here. I ask one thing! Be honest & sincere with me. Tell me about their wish, ok?
We miss you! Thousands kiss!
Forever to Larisa.

From: Chris <coldbastrd@xxxxx.com>
Sent: Friday, December 3 12:19 PM
To: Larisa <gilkakisska@xxxxx.com>
Subject: [RE: No Subject]

Larisa! Thank you so very much for the letters! Please let us put aside talk of the rainbows and butterflies and fairy dust and unicorns for the moments. I have extreme news of extremity!

Last night while in the prisons, my bunk boy who sleep in cell with me, Lefty, he decides to break the prison! He needs my help and we make the great prison escapes! Once we left the insides, Lefty said, you go your way, I go my way. So I am now alones on the outsides. I run and run and run and run! I hide in dumpster at day, move under cover of darkness at night to avoid detecting like secret ninja. I do not know what to do with self! People are after me! I see on news they say that I am on the lamb. THIS IS LIES! I do not have a lamb. If I did, I can go running much faster and get aways.

I go to post offices to send you a postcard. There on wall is my face on poster! I rip it down and take with me. It not such good drawings. I RUN AWAYS! I go to internet cafe and use the computers. People are looking at me but I must send to you the letters. The governments are everywhere! I must keep moving! They put the bugs inside the bodies so they track your movements. When you call on the telephones to order the pizza foods, they listen to your call. They even read these letters! Even when you go to airport to fly away, they put you in radio machine and take nudie pictures of your Mr. Winky just so they can compare the size of your Mr. Winky to their Mr. Winkies. That is how crazy governments is!

I lay in dumpster and dream of pulping you. I dream of pulping you all the time! Please I agree. Lez is bad thing. I do not want you to become Lez. This is why I tell you the feelings so that you do not become Lez. I am caring about you and I do not want the Lena to steal you away from me. Please do not let this happen! I am here for you! When we meat, I will pulp you like you have never been pulped before!

So I come to finishes now. I must keep moving to elude governments detector. You may not hear from me in few days. Please though, can you send monies? Any monies? I am eating garbage inside dumpsters. Thrown away cans of old peanut butter, banana peels, this sort of things. It does not make for the sufficient meal. I try to run across the country and row boat to Russia so that we be together and I escape the governments. I need the strength to accomplish such feet with the feet. I will write when I cans. Please help! I miss you and sends to you thousands kisses. Sorry I no brush teeth and mouth a bit stinky. Excuse the mouth breathes. You take kisses anyways.
Forever and ever.... please save me! Curly

FBI TEN MOST WANTED FUGITIVE

FOR QUESTIONING CONCERNING THE OFFENSE OF

PRISON ESCAPE

SEX: Male	HEIGHT: '5 7" - '5 10"	Hair: brown
RACE: White	WEIGHT: 160 - 180	EYES: unknown
AGE: 27 - 32	BUILD: thin	COMPLEXION: fair

CONSIDERED ARMED AND EXTREMELY DANGEROUS

IF YOU HAVE ANY INFORMATION CONCERNING THIS PERSON, PLEASE CONTACT YOUR LOCAL FBI OFFICE OR THE NEAREST U.S. EMBASSY OR CONSULATE.

REWARD

The FBI is offering a $1,000,000 reward for information leading directly to the arrest

From: Larisa <gilkakisska@xxxxx.com>
Sent: Saturday, December 4 8:33 AM
To: Chris <coldbastrd@xxxxx.com>
Subject: [No Subject]

Hello my dear Chris!
How are you? I'm fine. I am very happy that you are me see. I love you very much and I want to be with you. I am happy Do you still write me. You gotta know how happy I am when I see your message. I am very very happy that you meet me. I think our appointment. I do not understand that happens in my soul. I can not explain the words I just feel. I want to see you as soon as possible. I want to fly home. I do not know if I can pay for the trip home. I do not know how much it cost but my opinion on your flight country is very expensive. You know my salary is very small. It does as food and clothes. For some time I was able to some money aside. If this is not enough I will try Ceratina to borrow money from my family. I think my beacoup travel. I've never been in your country. Tomorrow I will have the tour agency to learn all the details of the trip. I hope you understand me. Tell me stop. I hope you would support me. I await your e-mail. Big big kiss. With love, Larisa.

From: Larisa <gilkakisska@xxxxx.com>
Sent: Monday, December 6 10:04 AM
To: Chris <coldbastrd@xxxxx.com>
Subject: [No Subject]

Hello my friend Chris.
Why are you not writing to me? I want to know more about you and your attitude to our relations do not seriously. If you continue to write no letters I see no point in continuing the relationship with you, I want to know about you the more I want to know what you do during the day. I hope that you know what I mean and you it seriously and we continue our relationship with you, your girlfriend Larisa.

From: Chris <coldbastrd@xxxxx.com>
Sent: Monday, December 6 1:32 PM
To: Larisa <gilkakisska@xxxxx.com>
Subject: [RE: No Subject]

Hello my fairest sweet Larisa! I am so sorry I didn't write to you this weekend! Please forgive to me! Please do not become the Lez! I spent much time running aways from the policemans! I tell you story of weekend.

As I was telling you other day, I hide in dumpster to not be found. Well I decide to make journey to Ewok friends in forest. While I was making the journey, I see the policemens trying to find me. I hide in back of group and they didn't see me. Photo from news I have attached. Man there in the black directs others and is very crafty. He tells police peoples, Alright, listen up, peoples. Our fugitive has been on run for ninety minutes. Average foot speed over uneven ground barring injuries to the feets is 4 miles per the hour. That gives us radius of the six miles. What I want from each and every one of you is the hard target search of every gas station and residence and warehouse and farmhouse and henhouse and outhouse and doghouse. Your fugitive's name is Curly Poindexter. Go gets him.

When I hears this, I get the scared and make the PP in the pants. I runs away! Man in black sees this and chases me. I find pipes and hide in them. He chases me there. I run and run and run. I come to end of pipe. It is big jump to river. I am scared. Man in black points gun at me and tells me to give up. I turn around and jump in rivers! I attach photo from security cameras! It is amazing! I swim and swim and swim. I hear Man in black be angry. He yells, bring me head of Curly! I swim away!

I make way through forest to Ewok village. I find Chief Chokesondeek. He says he has been waiting for me. He takes me to aside and shows me a bed sheet. I do not understand what is going on. He pulls off the bed sheets. There, gleaming in the sunlights, my Little Red Rocket exposed for all the world to see! He even polish my Little Red Rocket with the spirit oils. This makes it shiny and glowing. I hug him and cry. How did you do this, I ask. I take the cloth and oil and use my hand in jerking motion to give it the polish, he says.

No I mean how do you get my Little Red Rocket? I go to peanut butter factory and take it for you. He says. Great spirit Gods tell me you are in trouble and need my helps and for me to get you bike. I hear his words and this makes me so over joyous!

We go to sweaty lodges and smoke the weeds of nature. I lay back as he rubs the spirit oils on me. I close eyes. Papa appears to me in dreams! He is glowing in the blue light and wears a monk robe. He says, you must go to the Dagobah system in Alasska and find Adoy, an old and wise spirit guide. He will guide you in your journey. You must go and find your loves in Russia. It is there you will find the happiness. I open eyes and dream is over. So I must set out on journey to find Adoy and he will help me get to you! This is my destiny!

Chief gives to me laptop computer and I use to talk to you. I must conserve battery so I can't talk all the time. I write when I can and give the updates of the journey to you! Chief also gives me a sword. It has led lights built into it to help hunting at night. He calls it a saber of light. I should be able to live off the bounty of the lands. He gives to me bag of muskrats and I give to him a long hug. I will never forget you Chief I say to him. We will take care of peanut butter factory and your hamsters till you return he tells to me. My hamsters! I nearly forgots!

But I am assured he will take the care of them. For now I set out and great journey across country and to my destiny which that is you my sweetest Larisa! Is this exciting! I can hardly wait to be in your arms and pulp you! So now I set out on journey. It comes to the finish. A billion million kisses to you till I sees you again! Forever, Curly!

I HIDE BEHIND POLICEMANS.

MAN IN BLACK POINTS GUN AT ME!

I JUMP IN RIVERS!!!!

MAN IN BLACK SAYS BRING ME HEAD OF CURLY!!

From: Larisa <gilkakisska@xxxxx.com>
Sent: Tuesday, December 7 9:16 AM
To: Chris <coldbastrd@xxxxx.com>
Subject: [No Subject]

Hello dear Chris!
How are you? How is your mood? I hope it will. I glad you is writing. Now I feel the happiest woman in the world because I met such a good man you. As I promised I went to the tour agency. A woman has me assistance. I explained to him my situation I want to come to the foreign in my love. She explained what to prepare for Travel: lrs papers and how much it costs. I must prepare the passport Internationally, the return ticket, visa and good reputation. Tickets cost 975 $. For the visa is required 154 $. The passport is 53 $ and insurance Medical is 26 $. In total the trip will be 1208 $. Papers be prepared in 7-8 days. I was very sad. I asked him why is very expensive. She explains that it is a minimum. After The tour agency I'm back at home. My cousin came to me. I explained to him the whole situation. He is very surprised. But agrees to give me 200 $. After I had asked my parents but unfortunately nobody may help. My dear you are my last hope. I need to e 1008 $. I hope you me understands. I want to see you very very strong. I want to have you near me. And I hope that it will happen one day. I end my letter here and I await your reply with impatience. Your love Larisa!

From: Chris <coldbastrd@xxxxx.com>
Sent: Tuesday, December 7 12:48 PM
To: Larisa <gilkakisska@xxxxx.com>
Subject: [RE: No Subject]

Oh sweat Larisa. My sweat sweat Larisa! How I have missed you! I must tell you abouts my great journey thus far. It is amazings!

Yesterdays after I write I get on Little Red Rocket and peddle and peddle and peddle. I ride all the way to Pedophilia. After long ride, I am hungrys. Since it is cities, there is no muskrats for me to find and feast on. I find butchery shop and ask if I buy the food. They say that I can have their beef. They explains to me that their beef needs to be tender so I take my hands and beat off their beef. BEEF SMASH! I have attached the photo of me beating off my beef. They were very happy at job of beating the beef and they want me to work there being a beef beater. But I refuse tellings to them that I am on great journey to see my love in Russia. They understands and heat my beef and I eats it.

After beefs, I ride to high steps in city and look out over land. I am there and suddenly from the nowheres, Man in black appears! He has follows me! I have attached photo of this bad man. If you see hims, run away! He points gun at me and tells me I am arrested again. I put my hands up in air. Suddenly, another person appears on motorcycle and throws grenade. THERE IS BIG EXPLOSIONS! I take to the advantage and run aways! I ride Little Red Rocket out of Pedophilia and into smaller city in hopes not to be found.

Last night, it begins to raining. I find bridge and wait for rain to pass. A car pulls up next to me. I am thinking it is Man in black again and about to run away! The door opens and it is handsome woman. She tells me to get in car. I ask what about Little Red Rocket? I cannot leave here in street! It will be stolen. We put in trunk and drive way.

She tells me that she rides the motorcycle and helps me escape earlier. I thank her greatly with kiss and hug. Don't be the jealous! She tells me she and friends see me on the news and want to helps me. She tells me that I have the bugs inside and this is how Man in black finds me. She takes out the machine and sucks the bugs out of me! It is crazy! She wants to take me to her tribe leader so I agrees.

We go to hotel in city. We go to the rooms and I takes the showers since I am so dirty. She watches as I take the showers. She makes sure that Man in black can't get me in the shower. After I put on the clothings and we go to meat with tribe leader. His name is Napster. It is strange name yes? Maybe he takes naps all the time? He says to me, in my hands are the Flintstone chewy vitamins. You are on long journey and need the vitamins to stay healthy. I take the vitamins and feel much better. He says to me, we see your plight on the tvs and are here to help you. We are the big fans of your tv show and we think the policemans are wrong to arrested you. It is not right, he tells me. He hands me phone. It is old phone from some years ago. Big and the clunky. He says, if you are ever in the troubles with the Man in black, call me on phones and I will come helps you. This is very nice of you I says.

They give me bed to sleep on and I sleep. While I was sleeping, I dream of you and of us being together for the ever. It is possible yes? So in mornings, I gets up and thanks the woman and the Napster and the tribe. I get on Little Red Rocket and peddle off to country side.

I am reading your letters. I think it would be the best if you stay in the Siberia and wait for me to come there. You agrees? It is best this way since I am on move all the time and don't know where I'll be next. It would be best if you send to me the $200 you have gotten from your cousin so I can use for eatings and vitamins. It is agreeable yes? You want me to not starve you agree? You wouldn't want to do that to your Curly. Please tell me it is agreeable and I will tell you where to send me the monies. It must finish now. Always looking over shoulder for Man in black. Must keep the moving. I write when I cans. I will dream of you in my nightmares and hope you dream of me too. Until the next times, I give you the 1000 million kisses. You accept them, it's ok. I brush the teeth recent. Forever and ever amen. Curly

BEEF SMASH!!!!!!!!!!!

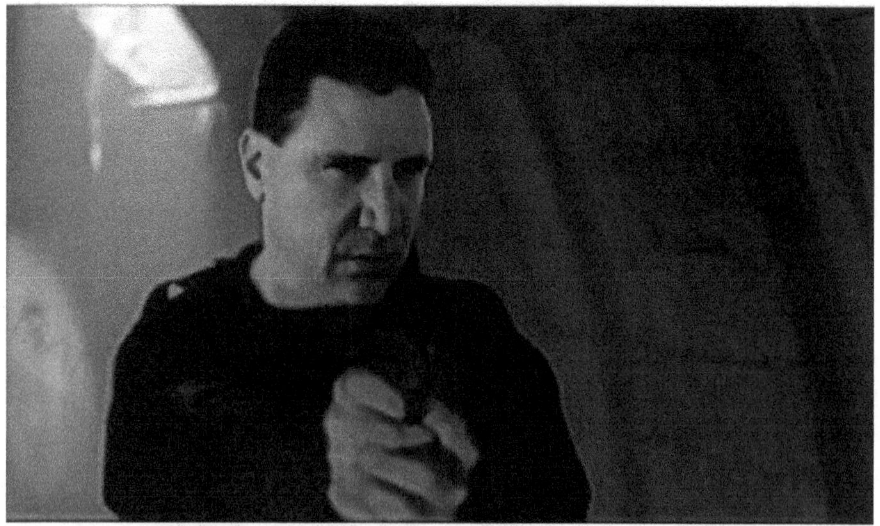

MAN IN BLACK FOLLOW ME!!

I'M UNDER ARRESTED!!

BIG EXPLOSIONS!!!

I WAIT UNDER BRIDGE IN RAIN.

WOMAN SAYS GET IN CAR!

SHE SUCKS THE BUGS OUT!

NAPSTER GIVE ME THE VITAMINS

CHAPTER 4:
LIVING IN A DANISH PARADISE

Living in a Danish Paradise

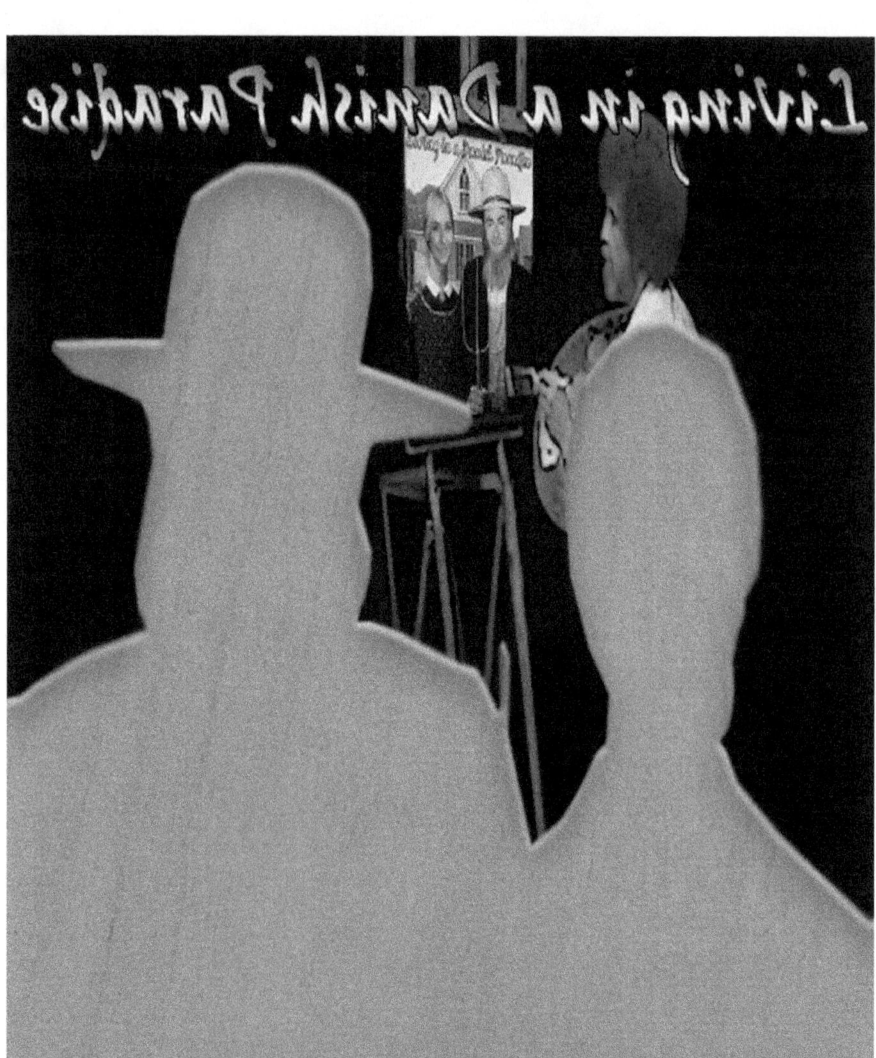

Handcrafted in Pencilvanilla
by
Danish Craftsmen

From: Chris <coldbastrd@xxxxx.com>
Sent: Wednesday, December 8 1:27 PM
To: Larisa <gilkakisska@xxxxx.com>
Subject: [RE: No Subject]

Hello my fair Larisa! I was so sad that I had no letters from you today. I cried. Weep weep weep weep weep. Why do you make the Curly cry? You know that I am going through lot of changes. No words from you makes the Curly so sad. Please tell me you haven't gone the Lez with Lena! It would be ok if I were there to watch and participate but I worry she will steal your heart! I will tell you about my journeys now.

Yesterday after I left the city, I rode to the country side. Many farms and trees and birds and horses. It is beautiful. I rode all the way to almost end of Pencilvanilla on boarder of Oreo. I made a left in Pittsburgers and headed south. It is getting cold here at the nights and I go south were it warm. I runs into strange people called Danish. They have no modern things. No phone, no lights, no motor cars. Not a single luxury. Like Robinson Crusoe, as primitive as can be. They are fearful of the Gods that he will send them to river of fire so they pretend to live like it's 1850. They fear that the Satanman lives in the phones and tvs and refrigerators and ipods and cocktail drink blenders and he will jump out and make them take out their Mr. Winkys and do bad things with them. So they do not have such devices to ward of the Mr. Satan.

This is very interesting to me. They live such life in quiet and harmonizing. They ride the pony and plow the fields. This is simple life. I imagine it is what life is like in Siberia not long ago too. I decide to stay a little while and live among Danish. Old mans Jessup allows me to stay with him and learn ways of Danish. I shave the mouthstaches. I hope you are not upset!! I try new Danish look and attach the photo. What do you thinks? It is not real beard but glue on. I cannot grow beard so fast.

They only had the red hairs. I look like great American president James Buchanan. He is on $5 bill monies. They say he is first homosexuals presidents because he had no lady friend but I do not believe. I think he just not luck to find such amazing woman like I have found with you!

Today I helps with the raising of a barn. It is hard work! I have attached the photo. I work all day long and get the very tired. We go back to Jessup house and eat the supper of muskrats and gravy. After supper, Mrs. Jessup churns the butters to use the next day. I attach the photo. I watch her use old butter churn. She places butters in churns and holds onto handles. She pumps handle up and down and up and down. Pumping and pumping and churning and churning. I watch for several hours as there is no tvs for entertainments. Churning, pumping, churning, pumping the butters deep inside the barrel. I go to sleeps. Old man Jessup has me sleep in bed with daughter. She is nice girl but they do not shave the body. So hair on legs keep me warm at night. At the night I dream of you churning the butter. I must tell you secret. It gave me botherment of physicality.

Tells to me, this is simple life and I think it is good life. Is this something you would like? Churning and pumping my butter? Maybe if you comes here, we live the Danish life and you churn my butter every day. I would very much likes that. We live on farm and raise the cow and sheep and goats and barns. I think this is the good honest life. Do you agrees? So it much finish now. I must milk the cows and fork the hay. Please, please write to me. I need your letters to give me the strength of 1000 Curly's to get through day. It is cold and lonely on the road. You bring me love and respect that I need in Curly's life. I send you the kisses and the hugges a thousand times. Your love forever, Curly

I AM A DANISH!

RAISE THE ROOF

CHURN THAT BUTTER!!!

From: Chris <coldbastrd@xxxxx.com>
Sent: Thursday, December 9 1:11 PM
To: Larisa <gilkakisska@xxxxx.com>
Subject: [RE: No Subject]

My dearest love Larisa,
I have not heard from you in a few days now. Why do you leave Curly in his greatest moment of need? I makes me so sad that you have given up on me and left abandoned on the side of the road like yesterday trash. I had thought that maybe Man in black had taken you, but then I was wrong about thoughts and I will tells to you why.

Yesterdays I worked hard in fields and barns. I milk cows, feed pigs, fork hay. After long days I come to eat with Jessup families. They see that I am the sad. Mother Jessup has surprise for me. She takes butter churns and churn homemade peanut butters for me. This is such nice jester. I eat the peanut butter on bread. It is ok. Not as good as the Curly peanut butter. I thank her kindly anyways. After the supper the family puts on play about Gods and Satan and have me participate. I attach the photo. It was awful. These people needs the entertainments center. Maybe this isn't the Danish paradise I had thought.

After the plays, I is tired, and sad. I go to the beds. Old man Jessup has me share the beds with daughter Mary. I think they like very much for me to be part of family. She is nice girls but kind of the homely in the faces. I attach the photo. We lay in bed and I toss and turn thinking about you churning the butter. I begin to cries as you do not send me the loves anymore. Mary tells me to quiets, don't make the noise. She rubs my chest hairs. It calms me. She gives me kiss on cheek. It makes me turn the red like Little Red Rocket.

She moves hand down and she touches the Mr. Winky! I could not believe it! I say, what are you doing? She says shush, you will not be sad anymore. This feelings gives me much botherment of physicality! I close my eyes and think of you.

Suddenly, from out of nowheres land! Man in black crashes through windows! I jump out of bed! It is hard to stand as Mr. Winky is stiff as woods. I throw pillows at Man in black. It knocks him to floor. I grab computers and run out doors!

I jump on Little Red Rocket and peddle way! I ride and ride and ride all through night. Looking over backside for Man in black. I stop on side of rode for rest. I think I am in Kuntouchy now but not sure. I see flowers. It makes me think much of you. I have barely clothings, barely foods, barely anything, but the one thing I have is you. I send the photo. Please excuse mouthstache. I shave it off and growing back. I take fake Danish beard and try to make new mouthstache for temporarily. I keep the flowers for you and give to you when I see you.

Please come back to me my love. I miss you and need you more than ever! Don't leave me please! It must finish now. I need to steal clothings from clothings line and continue riding. I pray and hope with every moment to hear you. 1000 billion kisses reaching to you across the universe! Forever, your truly, Curly

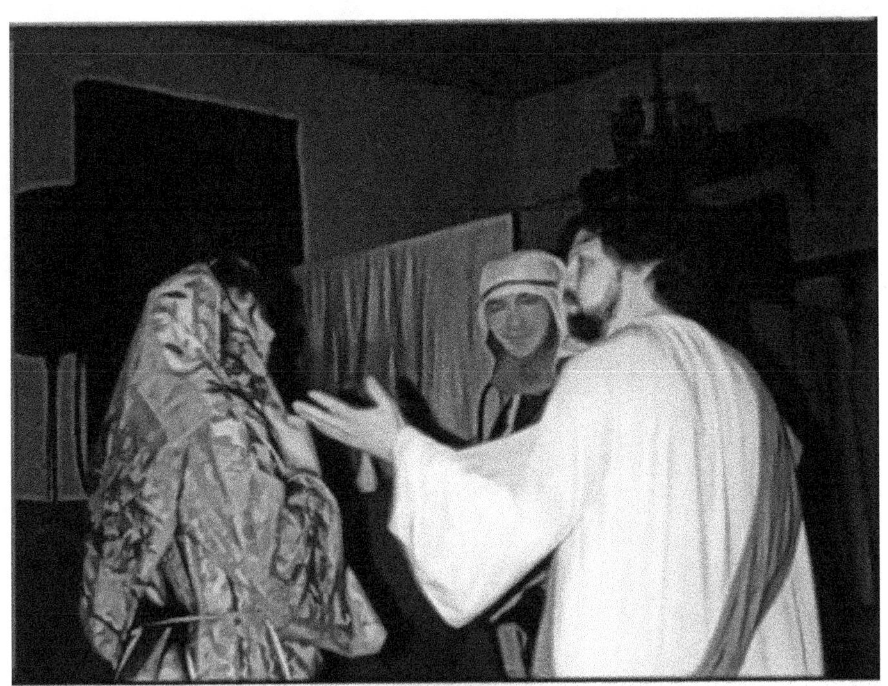

WHAT A BORING PLAY!

MARY AND ME

I PICK FLOWERS FOR YOU.

From: Chris <coldbastrd@xxxxx.com>
Sent: Friday, December 10 2:59 PM
To: Larisa <gilkakisska@xxxxx.com>
Subject: [RE: No Subject]

Hello my dearest Larisa. It is many days now and still no words from you. Is everything oks? I am really worry about you. I have fantastical news for me to share! I tells to you all about it!

Last I had wrote, I thought I was in Kuntouchy. I am correct! This is great rolling hills of green grass state. Kuntouchy is famous for it's chickens. There is great man I will tells to you about. Many years ago, man named Flanders joined army to fight Nazis in the wars. He was great leader and had many ideas on how to defeats Nazis. They make him Colonel in army for he is great leader of cavalry. He was also great cook. He maked the boiled chickens and people from all over would come to eat his chicken wings and thighs and breastages. During time, governments work on secret atomic testing on chickens. They create huge atomic chickens as big as horses. Colonel Flanders says, give to me the atomic chickens! I will ride my cavalry army to defeats the Nazis. So he ride the atomic chickens and Nazis have hard time defeatsing the Colonel's Atomic Chicken Cavalry because much like little chickens, big chickens move fast and in all different directions so it is hard for Nazis to shoot men and chickens. I have attached the photo of Colonel Flander's Cavalry.

Now you say, Curly, why is this such the good news? Well I explain the bit more. During wars with Nazis, Colonel has brilliant idea. He says, people like my boiled chicken so much, why don't we shoot boiled chickens at Nazis. Commanders did not understand. But Colonel knew what he was doing.

They lines rows of cannons and filled them with boiled chickens. They shoot chickens at Nazis. Nazis try boiled chicken. They love it! This was called, Battle of the Buldges because their bellies were so full from the eating so much chicken, they cannot fight anymore and give up. It was incredible victory! When was finish with Nazis, Colonel go back to Kuntouchy. He thinks to self, people love my boiled chicken so much, I must share it with all of worlds! So he starts Kuntouchy Boiled Chicken. You maybe have this foods stuffs there? I have attached the poster from advertisement.

So I am in Kuntouchy and I see sign for KBC, chicken eating contest. I am so hungry, I enter contest! They sit me down and I eat, and eat, and eat, and eat some more! I eat so much, I win contest! Even after winnings contest, I still eat more! I have attached the photo. It is incredible! I win the monies! I tell you I have wons the $1000 dollars and coupons to eat at any KBC! This is great news yes?

Let me asks you. I shall keep $500 dollars and send to you $500 for safe keepings. Do you agree with this? In case I get in troubles you will have monies to hold on to for me. I think this is the great idea. Please oh please my sweat Larisa, write to me. I miss your soft words. Your warm heart. You embraces. We shall be together as the mama and papa told me so. I much finish now. I need to get on Little Red Rocket and burn the fats off from the contests. Belly is full of chicken foods. I will continue riding over weekend and write next weeks. Is this oks? Please I miss you. Write to me. Kisses and huggs and lovers! Forever yours, The Curly

COLONEL FLANDERS CALVALRY

I WIN THE CONTEST!

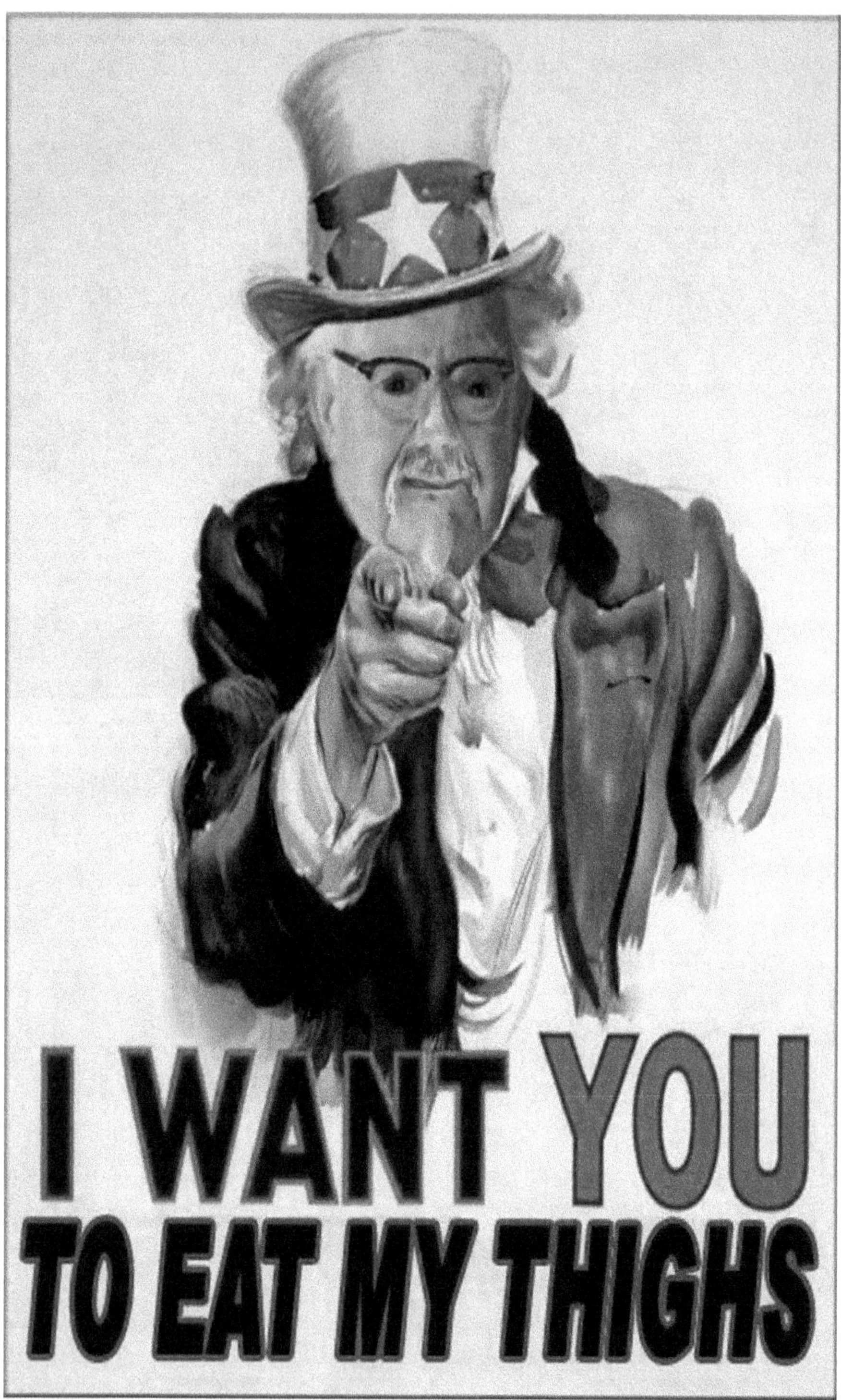
I WANT YOU
TO EAT MY THIGHS

From: Larisa <gilkakisska@xxxxx.com>
Sent: Monday, December 13 8:06 AM
To: Chris <coldbastrd@xxxxx.com>
Subject: [No Subject]

Hello my expensive Chris! How you? I'm is entirely correct. Honey, as it was your day today? Sorry I did not write you. I went in the cafe of the Internet, but I was said that in the cafe of the Internet some technical problems. It was very last, I was very tired on the work; therefore I will not go home and do not wait to these problems they are excluded. Hope of you' re not mad on me. I love you and choice to be with you. I am glad that we write every day. I am very glad to which you want encounter with me. I love you much, and I want to be with you. I thought about our encounter with you. You can occur, I they did not carry out that going further into my soul. I cannot explain in the words, it must be. I am very glad to which you want us to meet you. I actually want this. I think much about my turning off. I' m very excited, the I never, it is which they do not find in your country. I look forward for our encounter. I think that to us to come to the agreement it is relative the specific time in which I can see you. Write to me. I eat in the following letter, ok? Say to me, if you please. I hope that you is supported me. I look forward to your letter.
Your love Larisa.

From: Chris <coldbastrd@xxxxx.com>
Sent: Monday, December 13 2:51 PM
To: Larisa <gilkakisska@xxxxx.com>
Subject: [RE: No Subject]

Hello my dear Larisa! You do not know how the ecstatical your letter has made me feel! I was certain that Lena stole you away and you were gone for the evers. This makes me so happy I nearly make the accidentals in the pants. Much like the fat man Elvis would do. Speaking of the which, I must tells to you my latest journeys.

After the chicken eating contests, I got on Little Red Rocket and peddled some more. I am now in the Tennisea. This is home of fat man Elvis. I go to his homes, Gracylands. I have attached the photo of me at the Gracylands. I go on tour of Gracylands. Remember I tells to you that fat man Elvis die on toilet? I have attached the photo. They say it is because he eats the bad foods like fried peanut butter and cornbread and sugary breakfast cereals and fried banana and Twinkies. While on tour I see toilet that fat man Elvis die on. I go to toilet drop pants and try toilet to see if it works. Everything comes out ok. So it is not plumbing that kills the Elvis. This makes me suspect the news peoples lie.

I continue on tour. Near end of tour, it is customary to put on Elvis suit, go on stage, and eat Twinkies. I do this and it is funs! I have attach the photo. They let me keep suit. I am thinking this is good because it will allow me to blend in with peoples so that Man in black can't find me. I walk around some more and think that it is not right for fat man Elvis to be dead. I think news peoples lie. You don't lie right? I do tell truths too. Why would news peoples lie?

After I left the Gracylands, it is night time and I am hungry as I only eat the Twinkies all day. I go to store. I go to fruit section in store, and there by bananas, it is the fat man Elvis! I have attached the photo. He is probably going to fry the bananas on George Foreman grille. I say, hello fat man Elvis, how are you? He says, hush baby, don't tell anyone you saw me. I say, of course fat man Elvis, I am hiding from the peoples too. He takes the bananas and I take some too and we leave store.

Hey says to me, hey baby, for not telling anyone you see me, you can have my green suede shoes. I try them on and they fit. I say thank you fat man Elvis for your shoes! With this he turns and disappears into darkness of night. Well more like waddles off to waiting taxi cab and drives away but it makes no differences. I am thinking it is good that I have suit because no one sees me or fat man Elvis so we must blend in with the peoples.

So I will continue on with journeys. I feel the energizer and can ride Little Red Rocket all the way to Russia now since I received your letters! Do you want me to send to you the $500 for the safety keeping? This will be good. Tells to me where I am sending it. I must finish now. Road is calling Curlys name and must peddle onwards. At the nights I will dream of us together. I wait for your letters in greatest anticipations. You will eat in your next letter? Tells to me what you will eat? The Curly peanut butter? Will you put it deep inside? I hope that you do. I send you millions of deep smoochy kisses until the next times. Forever and always for evers, Curly.

GRACYLANDS!

I EAT THE TWINKIE!

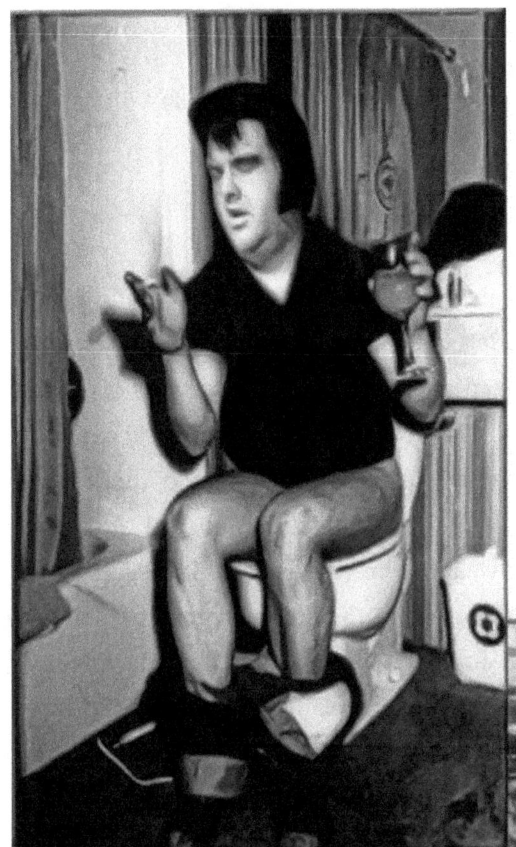

THE KING ON THE THRONE.

FAT MAN ELVIS AT THE STORE

From: Larisa <gilkakisska@xxxxx.com>
Sent: Tuesday, December 14 9:15 AM
To: Chris <coldbastrd@xxxxx.com>
Subject: [No Subject]

Greetings my loved Chris!
It is very pleasant for me to receive your letter! My Chris I would like to inform in the beginning of the letter all over again about business. My agency in which I am provide only a full package of services it do not undertake to make only one visa this agency arrange trips with manufacturing the visa and with purchase of tickets! They do not do one visa they make only the visa together with the ticket aboard the plane! My Chris at us today good weather in the street shines the sun temperature approximately -10 degrees in the street in general well and not so coldly it probably from for that that the wind in the street is absent! And your letters my love me to very strongly heat my idea on that that we soon shall meet adds temperature to my body! I so love you and want to be near to you! I shall wait yours for remittance what to order tickets with the visa! I can not order the visa because I do not have money for tickets! And the agency makes the visa only together with the ticket!
Your love Larisa!

From: Chris <coldbastrd@xxxxx.com>
Sent: Tuesday, December 14 1:11 PM
To: Larisa <gilkakisska@xxxxx.com>
Subject: [RE: No Subject]

Hello my fairest Larisa! Your letter warms the cackles of my heart! I must tell you abouts my latest adventures!

Yesterdays after I leave the Tennisea, I ride Little Red Rocket for some time. I was so tired from eating Twinkies all day that I need to stop for rest. I stop on side of road and take snoozies. I awake in sunlight to discover I came in George. I am really going south now. I reach ocean very soon! Along road comes man in orange car painted like race car. He pulls to side of road and gets out. He climbs out window. This must be tradition in south. He tells to me that he is Bo Fuke and he needs help delivering drink calls moonshines. I have never heard of such drink. He gives to me jar with drink. Looks like water to me. I do not understand. It is not shiny. I see no moon particles inside. He says, take drink. So I take drink. It burns inside the body like fire! I tells to Bo, you should not call to this moonshines, you should call firewater!

He explains that brother is at home taking care of sick uncle and that he needs to delivery this moonshines to customer so he can get the monies for medicine. He asks for my help making delivery. I say ok as long as I can bring Little Red Rocket. He agrees and we put in trunk. I ask to him, why is car painted like race car? Why does it have flag and "General Lee" painted on roof? I ask if he is General in racing army.

He explains to me that it is tribute to great General Broco Lee. I have attached the photo. He tells to me that General Broco Lee fights man named Charlie in Vietcong. He explains that 11 on side of car is number of Charlies that General Broco Lee kills in war.

He would cut off their ears and hang around neck like necklace. He reaches over and honks horn. I expect to hear normal honky noise. Instead it plays battle cry of General Lee's army.

We get into car through windows. I attach the photo as this is strange southern custom that I am not use to. We make deliveries all over Haphazard County in state of George. On last delivery I am waiting in car. Suddenly, big fat man who calls self Boss Hoss arrives with many police. He yells, I'm going get you Fuke boys if it's the last thing I do! I honk horn for Bo but I cannot wait. Policemens approach car. I cannot go back to the jails! I must go to see you! I jump in drivers seat and take off! I attach the photo from the news. I speed off with policemens chasing me. I drive all over Haphazard County. Boss Hoss pulls up alongside me and take photo. I attach. He yells, you're not one of them damn Fuke boys! Give me that moonshines you're carrying! I ram Boss Hoss off side of road and drive onwards! I am driving fast towards boarder of Fornicata state. Policemens set up road blockages! I drink moonshines to give courage. I push gas pedal all the way to floor! Car pops the wheelie and I jump over road blockages! I attach the photo from news reports! I jump all the way to Fornicata! Policemens can't follow me to different state. I find place to hide General Lee. I get out Little Red Rocket and pedal onwards. That was a close calls!

I am nearing ocean my darling! It will soon be time for us to greet! Tells to me the travel agency, can they get you to the Fornicata? Perhaps I meet you there? How much do you need to get there? Tell to me please. I am waiting on each letter from you. You are my sunshine, my only sunshine, you make things shiny when skies are gray! It must finish now. I continue ride to ocean and soon I cross and we meet and be happy for the ever! I send my kisses to you with the tenderness! Forever y'all, Curly.

GENERAL BROCO LEE

WE CLIMB IN WINDOW

I RUNAWAYS FROM POLICE!

BOSS HOSS TAKES PHOTO OF ME!

I JUMP TO FORNICATA!

CHAPTER 5: GREETINGS FROM MUTANT WORLD

GREETINGS FROM
MUTANT WORLD!

GREETINGS FROM
MUTANT WORLD!
Mutant World Park
THIS
END
UP

From: Larisa <gilkakisska@xxxxx.com>
Sent: Wednesday, December 15 4:48 AM
To: Chris <coldbastrd@xxxxx.com>
Subject: [No Subject]

My lovely Chris,
I love you I was in new agency and to me have told that I do not need in free money for the tourist visa! It seemed to me strange that it so but I believe them to me as have informed that to me would be not necessary to goto Moscow what to do the visa for me their courier which itself personally will go will make out the visa instead of me and when she will be ready he will arrive and will hand over me my visa!
It is necessary to pay the ticket aboard the plane at once! To me have told that the ticket aboard the plane to me will cost 810 $! I wait for your letter. I love you! At me all is good my mum transfers you huge greetings and would ask you that you cared of me! I wait and I can not wait when we shall meet I very much I want to you my prince! I shall write to you the letter tomorrow. Now me expel because coffee is closed at 18:00 and time already 18:15!!!

Well all right write to me my prince!
I love you! Whole! I have big surprise for you!
Yours Larisa!

From: Chris <coldbastrd@xxxxx.com>
Sent: Wednesday, December 15 3:16 PM
To: Larisa <gilkakisska@xxxxx.com>
Subject: [RE: No Subject]

Oh my sweatness Larisa,
How does this day greets you? Yesterdays and todays I have fantastical times in Fornicata. I tells to you about times now.

I go to place called Mutant World. It is fun happy place for grownups and childrens alike. Remember I tells to you about atomic mutations during wars with Nazis? Well back in days, governments create whole race of atomic mutants. This was experimenting with Gods and creations to make super soldiers to defeats Nazis. They conduction many experiments with varying results. The mix race of mens with many animal races and create mutants. They create half man half rat....half man half duck...and so on.

Problem being with mutants is usually have giant heads so this is not good because it is easy to shoot mutant in head with gun from far away. So what did governments do with mutants? Well mutants are very fun and happy so they put them in special places to entertain peoples. I attach postcard photo from Mutant World so you can sees. Here I am about to enter Mutant World. They must give to you examinations before entering so that they are sure you are not carrying sickness that may kill off mutants. This is Fifi the rat girl. She is girl wife of king of Mutant World, Dickey the rat boy. Photo is while she examining heart. After this she gives the rectums examinations. Is it wrong of me to feel a little botherment of physicality about rat girl? Never mind. I should not have said such things.

After examinations, I enjoy many rides and foodies. Here is photo of me riding in flying elephant. Original flying elephant was used in war with Nazis. He would fly over cities and drop elephant droppings onto Nazi heads. This cause Nazis to be angry with such foul play so they shoot down flying elephant and kills him. Ride is tributary to Flying elephant air force. Next I attach photo of me in giant teacups. This is dinnerware of huge giant mutant who dies of heart condition. They take his dinnerware and make ride with it.

It spins around and around and around and around. It makes me bit ill and I produce the vomits. I wish you were here to ride with me and I would just stare into your face and it would keep me from vomit production. Next photo I am in ride called it's a small mutant world. This is story of tiny mutants who live all over the worlds. I believe it is like the little peoples I have encountered on road to Endor. Do you remember these peoples? They had representatives from all over world including Russia! This is amazing. I didn't know you had mutant little people there. Have you seen them?

Lastly I attach photo of mutant called Gloopy. He annoys me greatly! I would be walking around looking at rides and mutants and I'd turn around and this crazy half-man half-dog mutations is following me and walking funny. I laugh at first. I continue walking. He follows behind me making the fun of Curly. I say, listen manmutt, stop following the Curly! He covers mouth with hands and pretends to laugh. I get angry! I take manmutt by head and smash him into bongos! GLOOPY SMASH!!!!!! He falls to grounds. This teach him not to make the funs of Curly!

So you have the visa now? You probably should have went with master card in the first place. Please wait and do not come on plane yet! The $500...I kind of spent a lot of it at Mutant World on rides and candy. I have left this place and almost at coast. From there I cross ocean to come to you! One more day and I should be there! It is amazing yes! Such a long journey. I am so glad it is almost finished and I see you! It finish now. I ride Little Red Rocket to coast. Please tell me surprise you have! I await your letter my princess!
Forever and yours always, Curly

THE LITTLE PEOPLES!

GLOOPY SMASH!!!!!!!

From: Larisa <gilkakisska@xxxxx.com>
Sent: Thursday, December 16 8:27 AM
To: Chris <coldbastrd@xxxxx.com>
Subject: [No Subject]

Hi my dear Chris!
I think that Love is one of the most necessity of the People. Thereby is very important not only therefor Love to receiving, the wishfulness for Love, but also therefor Love to give. You know that, the feeling in your stomach when you somebody loves, that heat of the moment, the sinking in each other and excited beating of the heart, that intensive feeling to be desireable, that almost crazy willing to relate to, the fascination and passion of Love. You will that feeling to experience again and again the Love is element that absolute Happyness make it out of your satisfaction with your living complication first of all. Everybody hoping to find another half. When falling in love lay out you must to take a one decision. You must work out if yours roots in that mass with each other connecting are, that only idea of one separation unbearable is! Then in fact this is Love! Love is that what at the end available is when the Fire of amorousness put out!

I cant wait to read more about you! And maybe to see a new beautiful sexy picture from You! When I look your pictures I realize that Angels still existing! I wrote to you that I would like to find serious, honest, caring and decent man, the person I could share my life and create a strong family with kids, based on kindness, love, understanding and tenderness. Now I know that I found that man. I think there nothing more perfect than trees flowers cloudy fantasies and harmony of masterpieces created by nature.

My prince to a regret I need to finish my letter! I went to the agency and learned about " Free Money " they to me have told that I should have at myself this money and that of me will not pass through customs house! I spoke them they have not the right to release me from the country without " free money " they to me have told that it equivalently have explained that what to throw persons in desert without water they to me it it so! My prince so " free money " will be necessary for me!

My love I too is very glad that we shall meet quickly. I very much love you and very much want to be near to you and as soon as possible to nestle on your strong body! It is a lot of millions kiss!
Your Larisa!

From: Chris <coldbastrd@xxxxx.com>
Sent: Thursday, December 16 4:13 PM
To: Larisa <gilkakisska@xxxxx.com>
Subject: [RE: No Subject]

Well hellos there my sweet Larisa!
Lordy lord, I'm talkings like I am in da south! Maybes it's because I am in da souths! In da dirty dirty! WHOOP! How y'all doing today? Well looky here. I have to tells you about my adventures crossin' da oceans and a suches. Maybe I shouldn't be in da good moods cause I gots da sad story. Ohhhhh it make da Curly cries just tinkin's bout it. It all start yesterdays...mmm hmmm.

I gets to da oceans and looks around. Mmmm, that be a long swimmins I tinkin. I sees a man theres by a boat. I say, hey boy, y'all tink you take me cross da oceans so I can be wit my darlin? He get all serious and such. Hey say, sure I take you cross the oceans, but y'all be warned. There giant seas creatures swimmins round dat ocean. They have da eyes. Eyes like dolls eyes. And once they get ya, they just keep a poundin and a poundin. I say ok, I'm not fraid of no seas creatures. He say, ok we set sail den. My name is Captain Taint. Greatest cap'in in all dis seas. I attach da photo of Cap'in.

We take off cross the oceans. We sing da songs bout Spanish ladies and shoot guns in da air. Suddenly a big seas creatures jump out da water and onto the back of da boat. I attach a photo. It's like a big 'ol catfish! This big 'ol fish go a floppin and a flappin all on da back of da boat. Cap'in try shootin it, but dat no matter. Cap'in run up on da deck and fire up da throttle. Yeah buddy, come on get some! We haulin' the bacon. I attach the photo.

It make no matter doe. That dang fish come right up outs da water and land on da deck. Dis the part I sad bout. Cap'in Taint try fightin da fish but that big 'ol beast grab him in his mouth and swallow him up hole! I attach the photo. Dis make the Curly sad. I worry cause the boat start sinkin' and the big 'ol fish he keep a floppin. Then suddenly! Out's the air come a hole group of dollfins! Well they jump and jump and run into dat big 'ol fish. You know they kill that big 'ol sea creatures? I'll be damned.

Now whats I gonna dew about gets in to Russia. You know what happen? Dem darn dollfins come up from under me and start a swimmins. It's the darnest thang! I ride dem dollfins all the way to Russia! Photo attached! We rides in all the way to Guacamole Bay. I gets off da dollfins and gets onto the shore. I wave goodbye to dem dollfins. You know wats? I am here in Russia! Dis why I am so happy!

I didn't knows dat Russia was so hot and topical! You knows da language I kinder recognize. Da guy whos da janitor at my peanut butta fact'ry, Jose, he sounds like da peoples here when he talk too. I walks arounds in da street askin' for Larisa. Nobody seems to know yous. I'm goin's have da fine me someones hare dat can show me da way to Siberia.

I get your letter. I like it hole lots. I dream of the cloudy fantasies too! Wit you floatin round like da angels. Mama up der floatin round wit the angels too. Well I better get to gettin'. I need to find where yous at. Not worry bout spendin' your free monies. I'll be to you soon! I'm so happy! I finish it hare now. Throwin da kisses at ya darlin! Curly!

CAP'IN TAINT

BIG SEAS CREATURES!

WE TRY TO ESCAPES!

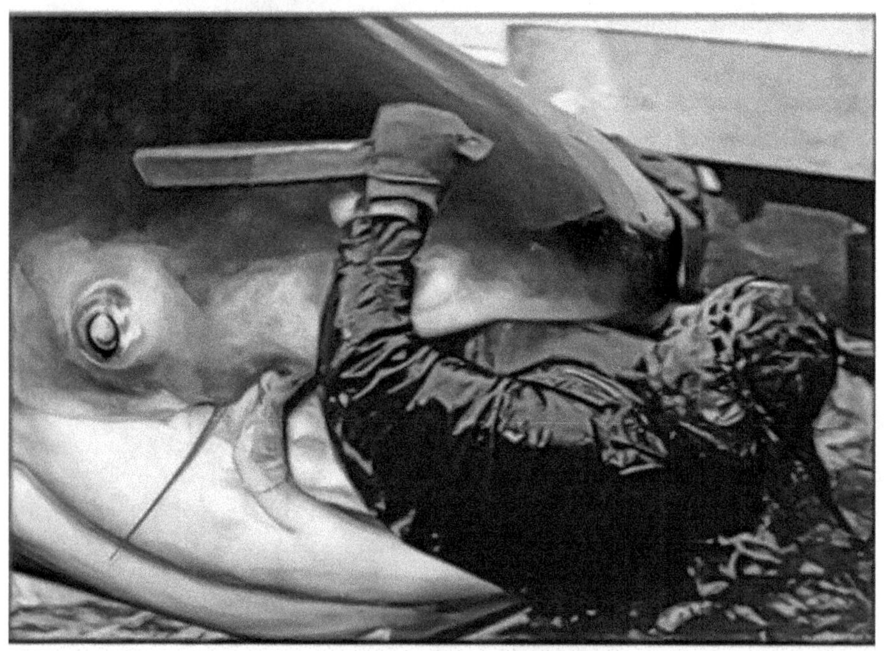

TAINT IS EATEN!

DOLLFINS KILL BIG 'OL FISH!

RIDIN' DOLLFINS TO RUSSIA!

From: Larisa <gilkakisska@xxxxx.com>
Sent: Friday, December 17 3:52 AM
To: Chris <coldbastrd@xxxxx.com>
Subject: [No Subject]

Hello my dearest Chris!
I want to say to you that as usual and usual, I'm happy so much from your answer on my last letter! I think about you all days. I so wait or your warm letters for me, I want to say to you that now I can't without you and your so feelings letters. You letters are so important for me, it are a part of my life, it are a source of my pleasure to my life. I want to say to you that the occurrence of you is a beterest part of my lonely life now, your letters give me a great happiness and pleasure in my life. Believe me, that I speak this my words with my sincere care to you, with my respect for you. Also I want to emphasize that I thought about our feelings to you, I have come to a conclusion that we are created for each other. In last night I didn't sleep well, I couldn't do it because I thought about us, about our acquaintance Internet, about your warm letters, and in about you! I thought about all , I want to say to you that I can't without you my, I want to say to you that I have fallen in love in you. You my dearest prince! It has taken place so quickly and suddenly, I didn't to expect it my darling, it's so sensual for me my, I can't without you. I LOVE YOU, DARLING! I feel to you the greatest feeling on ground, it's my love to you my dear. From your letters, I see that we aren't indifferent to each other, I hope that you will agree with me , is it for true? I hope that you feel to me such great feelings to me. I want to say to you that I love you very much, my relatives and my friends are very happy for us very much. Also my dear, I want ask you a main question, I will try to learn my dear about the necessary documents for my future coming to you, as I know from my girlfriend Lena, I will need free money to leave country.

If I can't get is all, will you send to me? My darling, I hope that you have a great desire of our meeting my love. I so want it my love, I love you and I miss you badly. I will wait for your mutual warmth letters. All my warmth kisses, Warmth hugs, Your Larisa

From: Chris <coldbastrd@xxxxx.com>
Sent: Friday, December 17 2:16 PM
To: Larisa <gilkakisska@xxxxx.com>
Subject: [RE: No Subject]

Oh my warmthest Larisa!
How I have missed you! I have very much news of sadness! I have made the discoveries that I have made great errors in journeys. I have discovery I am not in country of Russia. I have come to country of Poopa. It is terrible accidentals! I wonder around streets looking for you. Everyone here speak no English. This is strange to me since you speak such perfect English. I figure that everyone in Russia speaks the English. Not here! I go to large building and knock on door. Man answers. He says, hello, what do I do for you? He speaks the English. This is good I thought. I say, hello, my name is Curly. I am looking for my loves in Russia. He says, you are terrible mistake. You are in Poopa, not Russia. Come in, have a drink of lemonades and a lunch. You must be exhausts. He says his name is Fidle Castrate. He looks like dirty homeless Satan Claus. We take the photo and I attach. We sit down for the lunches and discuss the Russia. He tells me that Poopa is like the Russia but not Russia. I do not understand. So to tells to me, I ask, Poopa is like mini Russia? He says yes. Now I understands. It is like little people I find in forest. They look like big people, but they are minis.

He says to me, come, we takes the walk around cities. We leave and go for walks. He tells to me that Poopa is warm where Russia is cold. Is this true? Russia is cold? Like the Eskimos? Are you like the Eskimos? Tells to me. It is true that Poopa is warm and people wear the near no clothings. This can give one some source of botherment of physicality, but not me. I think only of you all time! We walk some more then things turn to the bad! He leans over and whisper in ears. He says, Curly, please come back to my houses. There you can touch the Mr. Winky.

I am old man and have not had the Mr. Winky touched in long times. I cannot believe he ask this of me! My heart and body belong to Larisa I say! I turn around and kick him in ball bags. He salutes me for great tactical maneuvering. I attach the photo. I run aways!

I make the understandment from Poopa peoples that Castrate is leader of Poopa. This I didn't know. They say, ohhhh you're in trouble! I do not want to go to jails here! I hears that they take you to Guacamole Bay and tie you on board and pour hot beet juice on head! This is horrible! They do not do this in Russia do they? I run for coast to get back to America. I see peoples on homemade boats about to sail. I say, which way you goes? They tell me they are going to America. It is traditional way for Poopa peoples to get to America. I ask if I board ship. They say yes oks and we leave! So now I am sailing back to America. Luckily I have kept my laptops in plastic bag and I get signal to write you letter. Man named Pepe swims and catches fish for us to eat. He takes photo of ship while swimming and I attach.

This is becoming such the long journey! More than I expect. But for you my dearest Larisa, I travel to end of worlds! I tells to this my princess, I LOVE YOU TOO! I cannot sleep...I cannot eat...I think about your letters and faces and bodies and warmth and kisses and huggies and bodies. It gives me the great pleasures much like you say it gives to you. I think to you need to send more pictures for me to make the pleasures on my journey. Is this agreeable with you? The journey is slow in boat and this may take few days to cross oceans. I leave computers off to save battery. I write to you in few days. This is agreeable? Tells to me what free monies you need? Can you not get free monies there if it is free? I don't have much now. I live on fish and rice and beans. But when I get back to America, I will try to get some monies to sends to you. This is agreeable? It must finish now. I will dream of the warmthest kisses and huggies of you and send to you mine. Forever and always yours forever, Curly

ME AND FIDLE CASTRATE

FIDLE WHISPERS IN EARS!!

I KICK IN THE BALL BAGS!

I SAIL BACK TO AMERICA.

From: Larisa <gilkakisska@xxxxx.com>
Sent: Saturday, December 18 11:20 AM
To: Chris <coldbastrd@xxxxx.com>
Subject: [No Subject]

Hello my dear Chris.
I'm glad to see your letters. How are things? Is everything OK with you? I hope you have a good day. I'm good. You said that you could help me with half the amount of travel money, I'm glad that you're trying to make every effort for our meeting. And I'm just going to make all efforts that would find the missing amount of money for our meeting with you, but for this I need that would be of you had the maximum support in this matter. Soon the Christmas and New Year, I think if we start to prepare now, we will have time to organize our meeting and meet. Do you think that we should take now, I need your advice and sharing solution. In few days I leave Moscow to be with family members for holiday. I wish that would be our meeting place, a very important step, we need to take action is now. I leave 10-15 days. I will miss you and think of you. I think it would not be bad to spend holidays together. I love only you. On it I finish my letter. Write to me, I'll look forward to your letter. I love you, miss you, gently and passionately
kiss you. Your Larisa.

From: Larisa <gilkakisska@xxxxx.com>
Sent: Monday, December 20 9:46 AM
To: Chris <coldbastrd@xxxxx.com>
Subject: [No Subject]

Hello! I did not get long for your letters! What happened? Are you all right? I want to continue our acquaintance and relations. I want you I wrote this. Soon I leave and need securing you are still with me. I'll wait for your letter. Love Your Larisa.

From: Chris <coldbastrd@xxxxx.com>
Sent: Tuesday, December 21 2:15 PM
To: Larisa <gilkakisska@xxxxx.com>
Subject: [RE: No Subject]

Greetings and salutations my passionately princess Larisa!
I am so sorry I didn't write in past few days. Will you forgive the Curly? Please? Oh very please with the cherry on the top? Of course I support you magnificently and spectacularly in sending to you monies! What would lead you to decide the otherwise? If you remember, I spents the half monies at Mutant World. The mutant rides were too tempting a resisting I could not make. I had next to the no monies left. I make Dickey the Rat Boy a rich mutant! But I must tell you the stories of past few days!

Once I arrive to the America I must find the Little Red Rocket. I had hidden it away but I do not remember where! Oh no's I think! This is great tragedy! I search and search and search some more. It takes me a whole day! I forgot I had hidden it in bushes and covers with palm leaves and coconuties. I hide before I leave for Russia, which wasn't Russia but the mini Russia which was the Poopa once associated with the Russia. I climb on my Little Red Rocket and peddle and peddle and peddle. It is so hot here in south. I get so the tired. I remembers that I hide General Lee car in top of Fornicata. This would be great for making up the time since it is car and I am only foot powers.

So I go to place where hides the General Lee. I hide in abandonment double wide trailer. Very popular here in south of America. I start up and look out window. I see policemens! I drive out of trailers! I attach the photo! Policemens chase me so I must drive to new state. I drive all the way to state of Alibaba. I lose policemens in chase.

I am hungry so I go to place to eats. Place is call Waffle House. They are fine cuisine establishment in all of souths. There I meet new friends. They are what you call "good ol boys". They like car I drive and invite to party at their trailer.

I have attach the photo of me and new good ol boys friends. They wear the hairstyles in what is called mullets. They say it is the business all in the front and the party all in the backs. I do not have the style so they wrap t-shirt around head to look like mullet. We drink the moonshines. I remember this drink! It burns throat like pit of fires! After awhile, I forget where I am at and later wake up in bathtub. Good ol boys tell me that my car is so fast and the cool, I should race. They say I win the monies in the race. This is the great news yes!

I go to racetrack where they race. It is what they call Nascar which they tell me means Nice Azz Southern Cars Always Reckin. I do not know what this means at the first. Cooter, one of the boys straps me in the car. I fire up the engine and he tells me to get her done. I do not know who this her is that I am suppose to be doing but I do not do anyone but you! So I refuse to get to the doing of her or him or anyone else! I go on race track and drive in circles. Peoples try to drive me off roads! They are the crazy! I slide sideways from left to the right. I attach the photo. Everyone is wrecking cars every which way. Big wreckings happen in front of me's. I turn wheels and General Lee goes on the two wheelies. I pass wreckages! I win race! I attach the photo! Do you know the what? I win $500 monies! This is fantesticals! Here I attach photo of me winning monies and drinking fancy drinkages after racing!

This all comes with the prices though. I have wrecked the General Lee beyond the repairs. I attach the photo. I cannot drive anymores. I think I will stay here in Alibaba over holidays. I need to rest from all these travelings! This is amazing journey!

Tells to me. You go to Moscow? You will be gone but make the return yes? Tells to me about the traditions of Christmas there. Do they have Satan Claus for the Christmas? What do you do? What about the New Years? What do you do? I would like to know such traditions. I will tell you about mine but I am so tired of writing now. So it much finish. Do not worry. I will always be here for you. Well not here in Alibaba because I am traveling to Russia to see you but here on the interwebs. You understand. I always look forward to your letters. Please send more. And I need more pictures! Maybe you gets to me for a Christmas present? You dress in the sexy time clothings? I would like very much to see this. I send you the passion kisses! Forever yours, Curly

POLICEMENS AGAIN!

GOOD OL BOYS

NICE ASS SOUTHERN CARS ALWAYS RECKIN

I AM WINNINGS!

IT IS GREAT VICTORIES!

GENERAL LEE IS BEYOND REPAIRS

From: Larisa <gilkakisska@xxxxx.com>
Sent: Wednesday, December 22 9:09 AM
To: Chris <coldbastrd@xxxxx.com>
Subject: [No Subject]

Hello my dear Chris, I have great pleasure in reading your letter. I am very pleased that your feelings for me are wonderful. I hasten to assure you that my feelings for you as much sincerity. I'm just like you imagine our meeting with you. I think that it will be fine. The first few minutes will be exciting. After all, we are meet, see each other in reality. But then we'll talk to you and speak. I'll hold your hand, look in your eyes. This will be the most touching moments. Heart would jump out of my and your chest. I will love you as no one else. I think that our idea of meeting coincide. I hope that you'll be able to give me an unforgettable love. I'm glad you're willing to help me with everything. I think it would be better if we start to process documents after the new year will be less rushed and we will do everything calmly. We welcome the new year usually, fireworks, just paints a Christmas tree in the center of town, lots of music and fun. I like to greet the new year, I really like it when lots of people and all the fun. We also have Santa Claus, who brings a feast of people. I'm really miss you and want to see you, see you. At night I can not sleep, thinking of you at night, I too think of you. Miles between us now, but soon we'll be able to meet and be together. I love you so much my sweet, and can not go without you! I wish I could be with you, see you always hear your voice. For me there is no other, and there is only you. I love the way probably no one liked. With you it's different, somehow it is not so, all the better. With you I felt something that felt no one man.

I must leave now for Moscow. Darling, I'll never forget you. You're the best thing in my life and I do not want to lose you. I want so much to you now by my side. I hope that this letter will be fully understood by you, because I sincerely tried to tell you about my feelings to you my dear. Not a day goes by that I do not think about you. Such a man as you is beyond my mechtaniy. No the most important thing in you is your dignity love for me. But it must be time-tested, proven actions and are tested by fate. I love you, miss you, gently and passionately kiss you. Your beloved Larisa.

From: Chris <coldbastrd@xxxxx.com>
Sent: Wednesday, December 22 4:26 PM
To: Larisa <gilkakisska@xxxxx.com>
Subject: [RE: No Subject]

Special holiday greetings my beloved Larisa! I am so excited for the Christmas. Are you? However it makes the Curly sad that we cannot be with each other during this times. I get the great pleasures in reading your letters too. It get the Curly throughout the day. When we do meet, my heart will be pounding and other parts of my body will be throbbing. The blood will be rushing so much around, I might pass outs!

So it is the Christmas times. I tell you about my latest journeys and more about the holidays now. As you know, I am still in Alibaba. I do not stay with good ol boys anymore. They are noisy and dirty peoples. I grow tired of their banter. I go to mall yesterdays on Little Red Rocket. Did I ever tell you story of how I gets my Little Red Rocket? Well one Christmases I was young childrens. When I was childrens, I had problem with legs. I had the one leg skinny and one leg fat. It was strange ailment. One day in the Christmases, I awake to find big present under tree with my names on it! I so excited! I wait for mama and papa to awake but I can't help it. I unwrap the dressing and to which I surprise! I find my Little Red Rocket! I attach the photo of me as childrens with my Little Red Rocket. It is hard to tells the crazy legs as mama would dress me in big pants but you see. I would ride my Little Red Rocket all over from this day forward. My legs became normalize. You no make funny of the Curly legs I hope. I don't think you will. It is subjective of sensitivity. It is my Little Red Rocket that makes the Curly strong! It is the source of all powers! Without my Little Red Rocket, I think I would dies! It is strange though. I ask the mama and papa, did you get me Little Red Rocket? And they tells to me no. So I believe the Satan Claus does. But he has not. He has told me so.

I do not know who gives me Little Red Rocket. Maybe someday I finds who. How do I know the Satan Claus? I have just meets him. I shall tells to you. As I discusses earlier, I go to mall yesterdays. I am looking for special gift to give to you for holidays. Shhh do not tells anybody! So at mall I see the Satan Claus! I wait on line to see the Satan. It is hot in mall so I take off some clothings. Not to worry. I do not remove all! I get to front of line. It is tradition in America to sit on Satan's lap and tells to him what you want for Christmases. I sit on lap and tells him I want Larisa for Christmases. He tells to me, I don't have any Larisa's. I have a horn. Here is for you. He gives me horn. We take the photo. I have attached. He tells to me, hey boy, do you want to make the monies? I say certainly! I use monies to go to Russia to see my Larisa! He says oks. You will be my helper. You put on suit and help me with childrens. I put on suit to become magic elf to help the Satan Claus with the childrens. I have attached the photo. We see many childrens and grant many wishes this holiday seasons!

After the workings at the malls, Satan invites me back to house for drinkings of eggs from nog. I am so excited. Satan lives in North Pole with all his little elf friends and make toys for all the good boys and girls all over world! Now he tells to me that I cannot see his secret castle in North Pole. It is special secret that no one can nose. He put the blindfold on me and puts me in trunk of his special sleigh along with my Little Red Rocket. Not long after, we arrive at North Pole! It is so exciting! He takes me into basement and shows me his special toy room. I attach the photo. I am not really sure what these toys are but he tells to me that he will show me soon. We drink noggy eggs till wee hours of morning.

We get up and he puts me in trunk and soon we arrive in malls. He tells to me that you must drink lots of water before working to keep active when dealings with many childrens. He drinks many bottles of water before work. I attach the photo. We go to the work.

This is great fun for me! I am around the childrens all day. It reminds me of how you would like to have the many childrens. Do you think if we find the compatibilities we go into the production of childrens? I would like this very much! After the work in the malls, we return to North Poles. He tells to me that we are going to have big Christmas celebration! Lots of foods, drinks, and many elves are coming for party! I have read your letters. Satan brings you feast of people? I must ask Satan about this. Here it is tradition for Satan to give coal to bad peoples. But I did not know that they use coal to cook bad peoples! And in your country you feast on the bad peoples! I am wondering in which country they prepare the feasts.

So today we paint a Christmases tree green. Not in center of town like you do, but in center of room. Soon many magic elves arrive at Satan's castle. We drink, eat, and play many games! Satan takes me in back room. He gives to me new elf suit! I am so happy! I put it on right away. I go back to party but things are quieting downs. I think everyone drink too much noggy eggs! I take the photo of me in new elf suit at party and attach.

I cannot believes you are going away. This makes the Curly sad. But I will be thinking of you entire time! You must be safe in the Moscow! Do not let the evil Russian men try to take you aways! For me, I will stay here with the Satan till after Christmases. It is safe place and we have lots of fun so far. Not a day will goes by that I do not think about you in ways that I am certain will give me much botherment of physicality. A woman as you is beyond all of my mechtaniy. It must come to finish now. The elves are beginning to awaken and Satan wants to take them and me to his special toy room and give us presents. Please think of me. I will think of you. I will dream of you in the greatness of pleasures. I love you, I will miss you, gently and lovingly kissing you. MERRY CHRISTMASES AND HAPPY THE NEW YEARS MY LOVE!!!! Your beloved Curly.

LITTLE ME AND LITTLE RED

SATAN GIVES ME HORN!

I HELP WITH CHILDRENS!

SATAN CLAUSE'S SPECIAL TOY ROOM!

MUST DRINK LOTS OF WATER BEFORE WORKING

BIG CHRISTMAS PARTIES!!

CHAPTER 6:
RIDER ON THE STORM

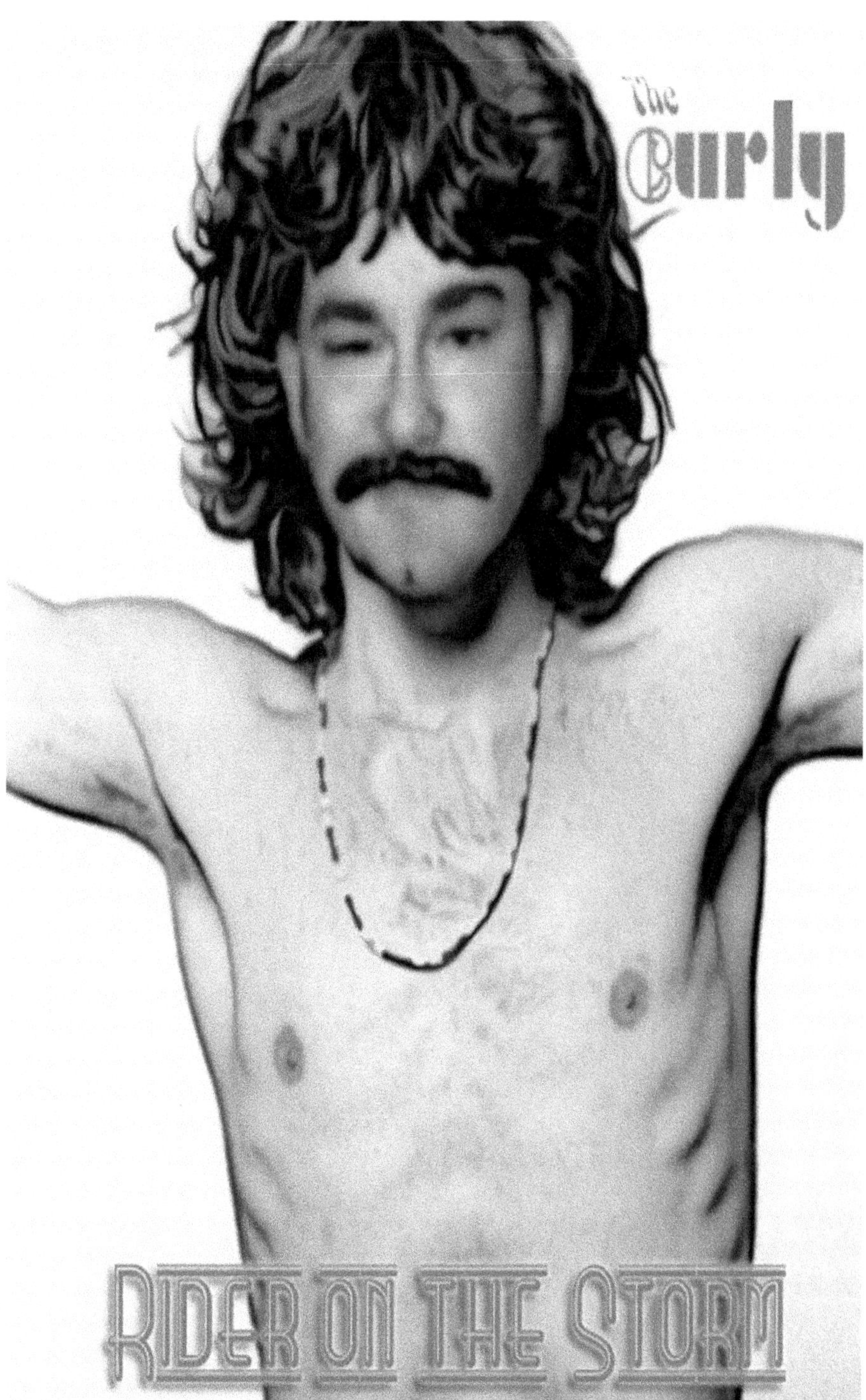
The
Curly
RIDER ON THE STORM

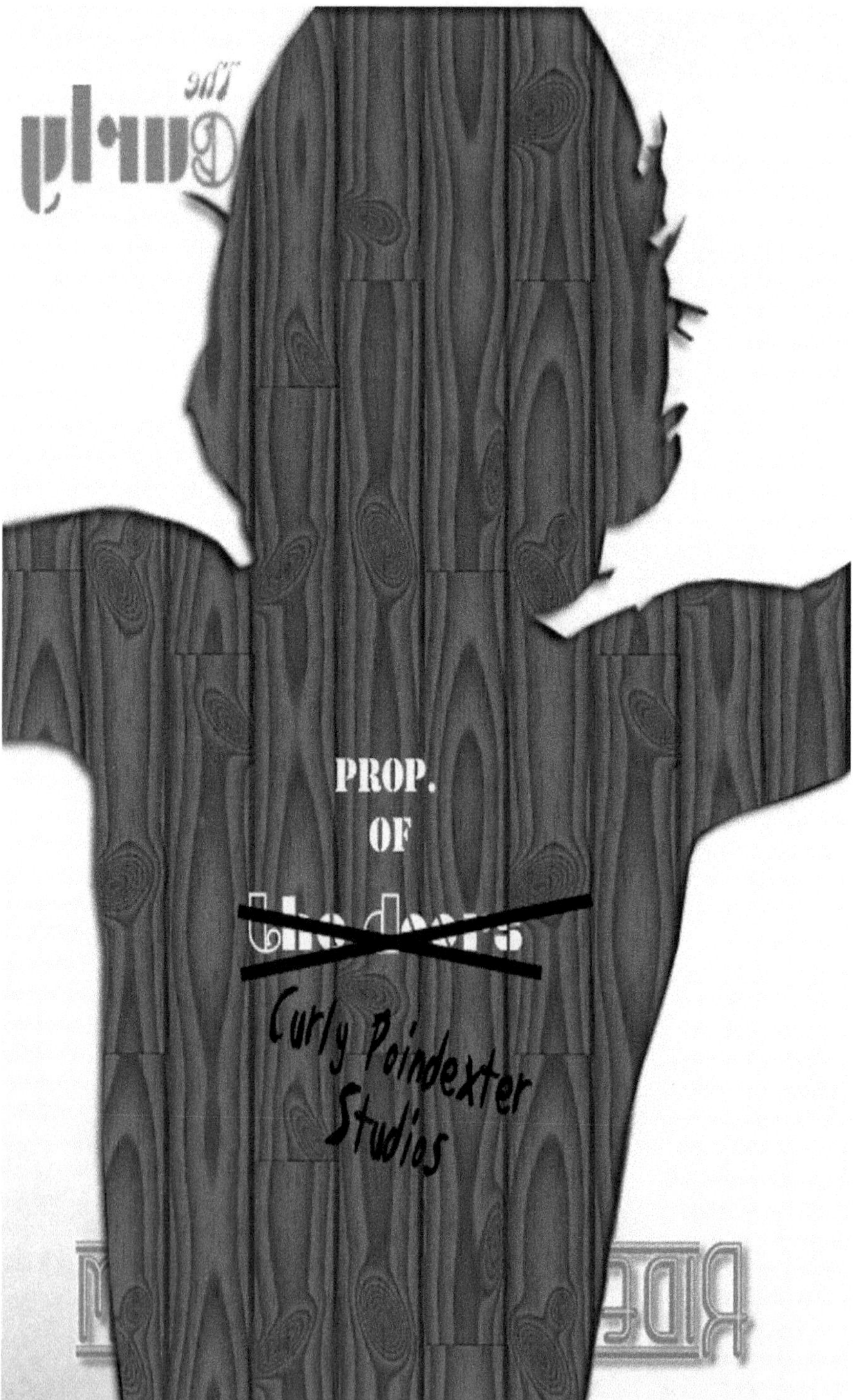
PROP.
OF
the doors
Curly Poindexter
Studios

From: Chris <coldbastrd@xxxxx.com>
Sent: Wednesday, January 5 3:01 PM
To: Larisa <gilkakisska@xxxxx.com>
Subject: [RE: No Subject]

Hello my fairest of beautiful precious Larisa!
I have so so missed you! How has your trip to Moscow? What did you do there? How was your holiday? Did you get the many presents? And New Year? You did not kiss the strange mens on New Years did you? Please tell me you have not! I WILL SMASH THEM IF SO! I must tell you of journeys since we last meat.

I have made terrible error in choosing the friends. Remember I tells to you about the Satan Claus? It turns out he is the liar! He is not real Satan Claus! He is named Norman. He does not have the magic powers of Satan Claus. I cannot believe he is liar! You would never lie to me I know this. Just as though I never lie to you. I tell you truths of journeys and love for you. How can someone be so rotten that they lie like this? I do not want to speaks about what happens with Norman. It is sickness! I sit in shower and wash sickness off me as best I could. I wash and wash and wash again. I attach the photo. Please we no speak of this man or places again. It gives me great pains.

I have finds myself near sea coasts of Alibaba. I am so sad to spend holiday seasons alone. I go to store and think of things to buy for my sweet Larisa. I find the box of chocolates. You like chocolates? I attach the photo. Mama always said, life is like a box of chocolates. You never know what you are getting, unless it has the nuts that you can see under the chocolaty coatings. Or if they have picture guide printings on underneath box lids. But still sometimes picture guide not explaining. What is with chocolates with pink fillings inside? What is this? It taste like nothing I know of. I SPIT OUT!

And what about when you take the bites of chocolates with goopy fillings inside? It runs all down face and onto shirt! Why do they not warn you of such gloopy filling? I look at box of chocolates and am not sure what mama means. They look like little dog turd nuggets placed inside icicle tray. Does this mean that life is like bunch of frozen doggie turds? I do not know. I decide to throw out chocolates. I ate to manys and makes me ill. I bring something else to you like my creamy peanut butter.

So I am on coast and am thinking I need to get another boat to take to Russia. I go to boat place and I run into man in chair with wheels. He tells to me that he is Dan and that he lost the leggings in peanut combine accident. Just like the mama and papa! Except they no escape and dies. He says that there is boat I can buy for small monies. So I buy boat! I am my own boat captain. I attach the photo! But I do not know how to ride the boats. Dan says to me, he will help me so he comes to me as new first mate. I attach the photo. He says to me, Curly, you need to name this boat. Every boat must have name. It is simple to me to pick. I name my new boat 'Larisa'. I attach the photo! Isn't it spectacularly!!!!

We go to sailings. I am smart this time and leave Little Red Rocket and computer hidden behind. Last boat experience not so good. Dan tells to me that Russia is near Pacifier ocean and we are in Golf ocean. Now this makes the sense why I couldn't find you first times! I am in the different oceans! Dan says we must sail far to bottom of world almost then back up towards Russia. This will be far trip! I had no idea.

We are sailing on ship for many days. As New Year approaches, we find ourselves in big storm! I attach the photo. This is part where sadness comes to me. We fight storm for many hours. OCEAN SMASH THE WAVES ON SIDE OF BOAT! I cannot smash back. Ocean to big. Then we look out windows. What is this we see in distance? I attach the photo. IT IS GIANT WAVES! I attach the photo again!

We scream and cry and run around boat in madness! We don't want to dies! I attach the photo! Wave smash boat! I fall out of boat. I look back as ocean churns and spits me all over places. I see my sweet Larisa sink beneath waves! I cry out! NOOOOOOOOO!!!! Tears approach face as I realize Dan is inside Larisa. WHY!!! WHY HAVE I BEEN CURSED IN SUCH WAY! There is nothing for me to do. They are gone. It is I all alone in ocean.

I float in ocean. I think this is end. I am too died. I will never see my sweet Larisa again but only from the heavens with mama and papa. Then suddenly, big whale jumps out of oceans! I AM SAVED! He comes under me and lifts me out of waters. This is like dollfins friends but he is much bigger and braver. I call him Big Willy. He is like bull! I hold onto my Big Willy and we make the swimmings for land! This is incredible. I have attached the photo of me holding my Big Willy. Isn't my Big Willy amazing? I think if you ever come to America, you should ride on my Big Willy. It will give you terrific sensations.

We ride in to beach. I get off on my Big Willy. He is tired and limp. I tells to him, thank you my Big Willy. You take nap of sleep now and rest. You have helped me greatly. I attach the photo of my sleeping Big Willy. This is such incredible crazy adventures! I decide it best not to go in ocean anymore for some time. Too much badness happens there and I have no lucks.

I find my way back to Little Red Rocket and computer. As I sit here in park and write this, I look at sunrise and inspired to write poems to you about you and latest adventure. Would you like to read my poem? I knew you would. Here it is...

Rider on the storm
It's true my butt got torn
By fake Satan Claus called Norm
In his basement full of porn
Naked as the day I was born
Rider on the storm

On the sea I did ride
I have missed you so much I cried
Big wave almost make me died
Rode Big Willy in with tide
I say goodbye my friend Dan
He had a pretty decent tan
Want you to be my bride

Box of chocolates I will bring
You will think I am a king
Maybe we go to Beijing?
Together we will sing
My world on you depends
I hope this never ends
Rider on the storm

I hope you like the poetrys. So I much finish now. I am going to continue journeys. Before Dan was eaten by ocean, he says to me that Russia is west. So I continue in direction of where sun sets. I miss you so much. Please write to me now. I want to hear your words again. I send you kisses and loves from my heart to yours.
Forever and forever, Curly.

I WASH THE SICKNESS OFF ME.

I BRING CANDIES!

I AM OWN CAPTAIN!

1ST MATE DAN. HE HAS THE NO LEGS.

THE SS LARISA

BIG STORMS!

WHAT IS IN DISTANCE?

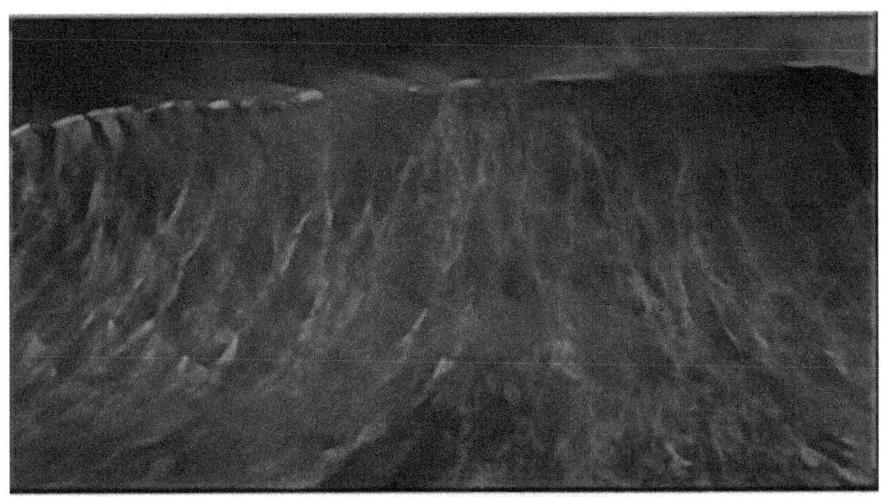

THE BIG WAVES!

AHHHH!! WE DON'T WANT TO DIES!

I RIDE BIG WILLY!

BIG WILLY SLEEPS ON BEACH.

From: Chris <coldbastrd@xxxxx.com>
Sent: Thursday, January 6 2:48 PM
To: Larisa <gilkakisska@xxxxx.com>
Subject: [RE: No Subject]

Greetings my delicate flowers Larisa! How does the day greet you? I have not heard from you in some time. I am missing you greatly! My soul would fly across the universe when I hear your words written again! It has been an eventful night and day for the Curly since I last write the letters. I tells to you about it here.

I have ridden my Little Red Rocket westward into Mrspeepee. I find name funny hehe. You see I have know that Mrs peoples do not have pee pees. When I was a young childrens, I walk into room of bathings by the accidental as mama was taking showers. I look and see. I say, mama, Why do you have the Mr. Donald King in a leg lock? He surely cannot breathe the airs down there between your legs! I attach the photo of the Mr. Donald King. She tells to me, I do not have the Mr. Donald King in leg lockings. But I say, mama where is your pee pee like the Curly? She tells to me, Curly I do not have the pee pee. I say, what has happened? Was it removed in terrible accidentals? She says, no Curly, the mrs and the mamas and the girlings do not have the pee pees. But I say, mama, if you have no pee pee, how do you go pee pee? All she tells to me is that she can. I still do not understand this all but I know that the mrs has no pee pee because the mama tells me so. Maybe you can tells to me? Does it come out of the hole in belly button? What about the girlings who put the rings of jewelry there? Wouldn't than make it spray all overs when you go?

Anyways, I ride Little Red Rocket to place called bayou. It is swampy places. I was getting cold and in distance, I see big fire. I think that would be good idea to warm the feets and hands. I go to place of fire. There I see group of people. They are warming by the fire as well. They are so cold they dress in bed sheets! I ask to them, please can I join by fire to warm bodies? And they say yes. We roast marshmallows on fire. Do you roast the marshmallows? It makes a gloopy mess so I put them on fire until they are blackened and burning and eat this way. How about you? After marshmallow roasting, the peoples join hands and sing songs around fire. I attach the photo. They sing song were they say, Kumbaya my lord, Kumbaya. I do not know who this Kumbaya is that they sing of. But it passed the night away. In the morning I awake by myself in middle of bayou. The Kumbaya people are all gone.

I hear splishing splashing in waters nearby to the Curly. I go to make the investigations. My heart sinks into stomachs! IT IS MAN IN BLACK! I attach the photo! How did he finds me! He holds gun to the Curly! I have no choices. I runaway into bayou! I attach the photo! He shoots the guns at me as I run. Is he crazy! Why does he try to hurt the Curly??? What is this mans problems? I do nothing wrong! Ok maybe I make a bit of mistakes with hammer of sledges, but that was long time ago. Stop trying to hurt me Man in black! IF YOU HAD NO GUN I WOULD SMASH YOU!

This is now big problems. I have run away but I leave behind Little Red Rocket. I must go back in darkness tonight and get my precious bike. In meanwhile, I come to big river. I think it is Mrspeepee River. This is too big of river for me to swim. Why must it be more water again? Why is there so much water everywhere? This makes the Curly crazy! I find small cabin by river. There is strange little boy playing with ukulele. He plays same song over and over. I attach the photo. He has canoe there by cabin. I ask if I can borrow to cross river.

He continues playing ukulele. What a strange little man he is! So I take canoe anyway. He just keeps playing. Maybe he is practicing to be next big rock a rolling star like Eddie Van Ukulele. I attach the photo. I bring canoe to river and test out. It isn't so bad. I thinks that I will have no problems. I am hoping.

Tonight I get Little Red Rocket and cross Mighty Mrspeepee on canoe. Send to me your lucks please! It comes to the finishing now. I am tired and need to get some rest before the night times. I am praying and dreamsing and wishing and hoping that you write again soon. I hope that nothing has bad come to you during trips to Moscow. I pray this. I will take nap and dream of you caressing my tenderness. I miss you and send you the kisses and hugs. Forever and always forever, Curly

THE MR. DON KING

WE ROAST MARSHMALLOWS AND SING SONGS.

MAN IN BLACK AGAIN!

I RUNAWAY IN BAYOU!

STRANGE BOY
WITH UKULELE

EDDIE
VAN
UKULELE

From: Chris <coldbastrd@xxxxx.com>
Sent: Friday, January 7 4:11 PM
To: Larisa <gilkakisska@xxxxx.com>
Subject: [RE: No Subject]

Hello my princess Larisa,
It has been many many many days since I last hear your words. Is everything ok? I am hope so. It is concerning to the Curly that you no write. I cry. Weeep weeeeep weeeep weeeep weeepp!!! Do you not love the Curly anymore? Should I return homes? I have travelled so far to be with you my sweetness. What is Curly to do? I write you of what happens to me since I last spoke of you.

Last night after wonderfulment nap where I dreamsed of playing with you on soft fluffy clouds and rainbows, I awoke in the night times. I sneak back to where I leave my Little Red Rocket. It is dark but moons guide me. M-O-O-N, that spells moon. I see in distances my Little Red Rocket. But there under tree is Man in black! He is sleeping and sets the trap for me! I slowly creepy to my Little Red Rocket on the tippy toes. Just like secret ninjas in the nights. I take Little Red Rocket and runaway! I have drawn the photo and attach as it is too dark for the cameras. I make way to canoe and cross mighty Mrspeepee.

I bring canoe to edge of shore and unload my Little Red Rocket. I am so tired from all excitements, I go back to sleep under tree. In the lighting of morning, I awake to two mens standing over me. They are very strange and missing teeth and such. Strange man sticks fingers around my mouth and holds it open. He comments on what pretty teets I have. Do you think I have the pretty teets? I have seen your photos and your teets are very pretty! I say to mens, go away you strangers! I have no business with you. They grab me! I fight but they are too strong! They take me and Little Red Rocket and throw me in back of pickup trucks!

They bring me into their houses. They tie me with the ropes! I am not believing this! They begin to take pictures of me. They make me put the thumbs up like the Fonzy. In America when you put the thumbs up, it means you enjoy to have the peoples put their thumb up you underbottoms. It is like hand signals indicating you want to participate in such things. I do not agree with this but they make me do it! The one man tells me to squeal like the piggy. I do not squeal like piggy! I tell them to shut ups and let me go! They put ball in my mouth so that I cannot speaks! They begin to take off my clothings. These are sick piggy men! I think they must be friends with Norman the liar Satan Claus!

They bring me into back room and take pictures with camera and video camera. They say they are going to the store and will be back. I kick and fight and scream till I break the ropes! I am free! I get the clothings and take film from camera so that they cannot look upon the Curly anymore. I find board in room. I wait for piggy men to return. They walk in room to see I am missing. I jump out of closet with board. PIGGY MEN GO SMASH!!! I leave piggy men house. I take their piggy pickup so that they cannot follow me. Thank the Gods Little Red Rocket it safe and secure!

I come to new place I think. I believe I am now in Nude Oilings. It is farther west then I have been before. I am in hotel now resting from journeys. This is hardest thing I have done in life. But I would do anything for my Larisa. ANYTHING! Please tells to me you are still with me! Please tells to me that you have not been kidnappings in Russia and sold to slavery. I miss you so so so so so so so so so very much! I want nothing more than to be with you every day and night and morning and evening and mid afternoon and brunch time. I must come to finish now. I will stay here few days to hide from all these peoples after me and to make rest. It has been so long since good rest. I will write to you in few days. Please write to me. I send the love and kisses and hugs to you!
Forever your Curly!

Tree
moon
owl
Man in black
sleeping
Little
Red
Rocket
me
Tippy
Toes

15
15 100-6 KODAK
15A
16
16 GOLD 100-6
16A
17
17 100-6 KODAK
17A

From: Chris <coldbastrd@xxxxx.com>
Sent: Monday, January 10 4:50 PM
To: Larisa <gilkakisska@xxxxx.com>
Subject: [RE: No Subject]

My dearest princess Larisa,
I am beginning to frets and worry of your wellness. It is been many many days and I still not hear your words. Are you dead? I don't think you are as you have not come in the visions like the mama and papa. That is how I am to knows of your death. So you must be still breathing the airs. I tells to you now of my latest journeys. I have come to the city of Nude Oilings. This is big city with long glorious history. I sees that there is not many people around and many houses and places are smashed. There are many signs in places that speak of a person called Katrina. I attach the photo. I ask a mans walking down street. Who is this Katrina person and why are people so angry to hers? He tells to me that she is giant bitch that came to town many years ago and destroy much of city and kill many peoples. I attach the photo of this crazy Katrina woman. Perhaps it is size of Katrina lady that makes her so angry. I imagining that it is hard for such woman to find a satisfactory man of her size to make the fulfillment of her needings. Even thought the Curly is big and strongs, even I would find much difficulty making her satisfactions. Can you imagine the size stool droppings this woman produces?

While I am here I have found that city is place of whoreshiping of what they call voodoo practices. It is way for peoples to find the Gods. Have been on such long lonely journey I decide to find the Gods to talks to. I have meets man who is a doctor in voodoo practicing. I attach the photo. I tells to him that I need to speak to the Gods to help find my way to you and protect me in journey. He takes me into the bayou where the voodoo practicing is practiced. We go into water of bayou (yes water again...I hate water now) with other voodoo childrens and try to contact the Gods.

I attach the photo of voodoo rituals. Doctor voodoo says that an offering of the chickens must be made to Gods. This is amazing to me. When I was with Ewoks, and they make me the Curlywata, the Gods tells to me that I am to ride on mighty chicken across the heavens to meet my love in Russia. A priestess in the voodoo takes the chickens and sacrifices them as offering to the Gods. I have attached the photo. I didn't hear from the Gods but I am having the great confidences that they will protect me in journey. I also pray to the Gods long and hard that my love Larisa would write me again and that you are not dead in sewer somewhere in Moscow. This ritual lifts my spirits and I write the poem for you now. Here is poem:

Well I'm writing letters to a Russian,
I write them all with the fingers on my hand.
Well I'm writing letters to a Russian,
I write them all with the fingers on my hand.
It's takin' me such a long time to get across this island,
Someday I'll get to the promise land.
Yeah, cause I'm a voodoo childrens.
Lord knows I'm a voodoo childrens!

I didn't mean to eat up all the sweet limes,
But my head is full of purple haze.
Yeah.
Brother can you spare me some dimes,
I haven't talked to my girl in a couple of days.
If I don't hear ya no more in this world,
Email me in the next one, that'd be great.
Would be great!
Yeah!
'cause I'm a voodoo childrens,
Lord knows I'm a voodoo childrens!

Do you like the poems? I hope it is so. I have returned back to city. I am finding that Nude Oilings has another traditions. I sees the people throwing necklaces of beads at each other. This is strange tradition I am thinking. I go to library and look up what this tradition is. I have found that many many years ago, long before the Curly was on world, there was a rich powerful man who ruled Nude Oilings. His name was Count De Monei.

He was old and crusty man but had more monies than the presidents. Thus many a young fair woman wanted to go into the productions of childrens with him. He had his fair pick of any womans he wishes. So if he finds a woman he is to liking, he would give them a pearl necklace for them to wear. In turns, the womans when she accepts the necklace, would expose her milky bits for the Count to see if she is worthy of his lovings. I attach the painting of the Count with the woman wearing the pearl necklace. You can imagine he gave many women pearl necklaces all through the city until he found the woman of his liking. Now tradition of Count De Monei's courtship is carried on through city to this day. Now of course it is very expensive to give peoples pearl necklaces so peoples today use beads. I wanted to try tradition but I am not in need of a woman. I already have you and there is no need to try other womens. So I dress in old womans clothings and carry sign for asking for the beads. I attach the photo. I will get beads and bring to you and I will give you the pearl necklace and you will be happy that I have put it on you.

So I come to a finish now. I have had much fun in Nude Oilings but journey must continue. I cannot stay here. Tomorrow I am expecting to reach Applesauce and from calculations I am thinking I am half way to being with you! This is excitement! Please write to me! I long to hear your words every day. The thought of you wearing my pearl necklace gets me through day but I need your words again. Please with the cherry on the topping! I send you the love and kisses. Forever and the always, Curly

CRAZY WOMAN KATRINA

ME WITH VOODOO MAN

VOODOO RITUAL

SACRIFICING THE CHICKENS

THE FAMOUS COUNT DE MONEI

Give me beAds now!

CHAPTER 7:
OAKLAHOMO!

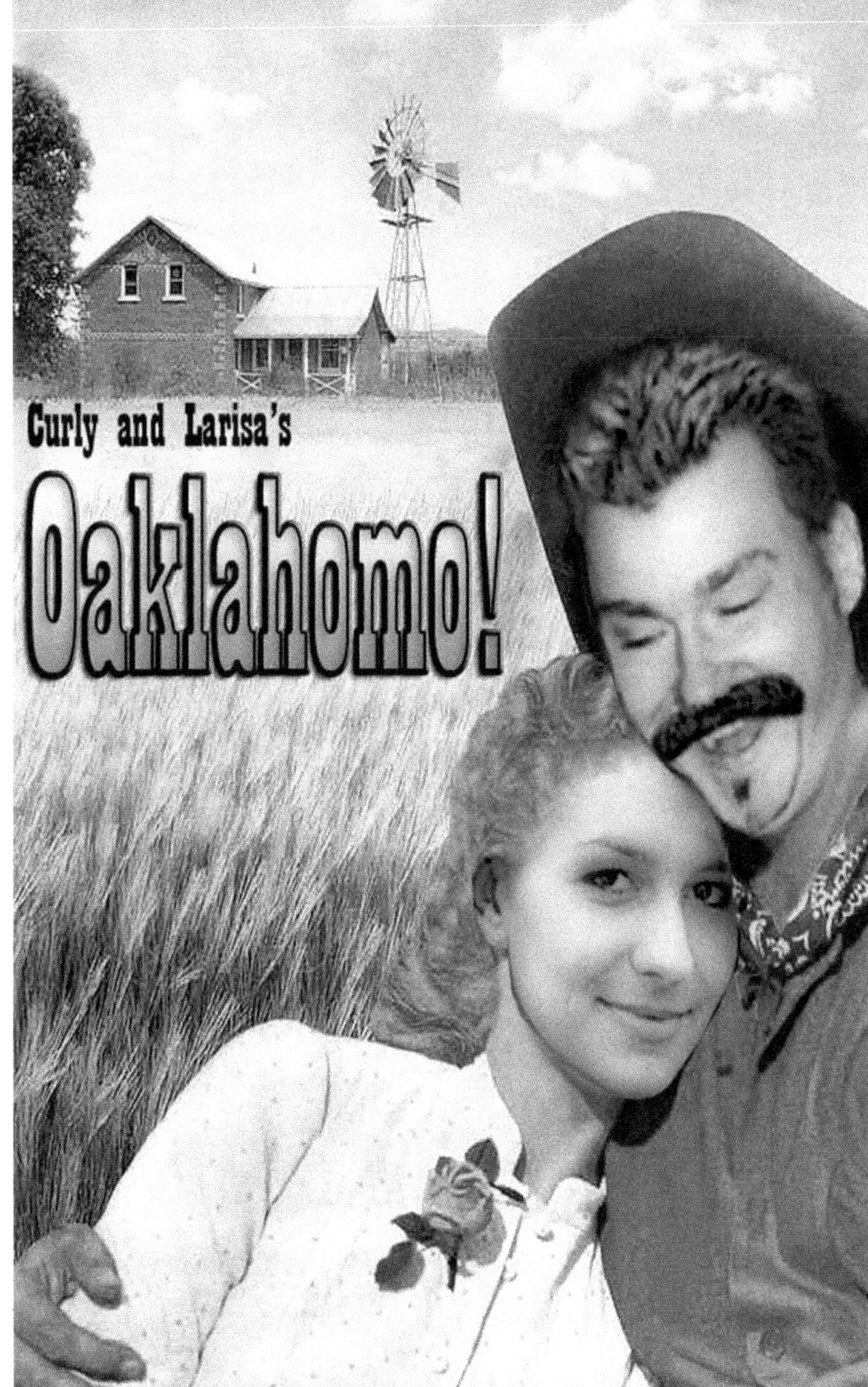
Curly and Larisa's
Oaklahomo!

Curly and Larisa's
Oaklahomo!
FRAGILE
KEEP DRY
GND PREPAID
FedEx

From: Mariya <girl_1980@xxxxx.com>

Sent: Tuesday, January 11   3:33 AM

To: Chris <coldbastrd@xxxxx.com>

Subject: [No Subject]

Hello !

My name is Mariya.

I have found you on internet.

As for me I want to find my love.

I was born on 17 November in 1980.

My new friend I ask you to write to my e-mail:

girl_1980@xxxxx.com

Thanks for the reading.

Mariya.

OH NO! A CRAZED BEAR ATTACK!

From: Chris <coldbastrd@xxxxx.com>
Sent: Tuesday, January 11 1:46 PM
To: Mariya <girl_1980@xxxxx.com>
Subject: [RE: No Subject]

Hello Mariya,
It is very nice to meetings your acquaintance. My name is Curly Poindexter III Jr. Esq. You are looking for your love? This is greatest coincidences. I am looking for my love too! Her name is Larisa. Tells to me, have you seen her? I have not heard from her in many many days. I am beginnings to think that terrible things have happenings to her. I have come the long way in travel to find her. But then suddenly, she goes to Moscow and doesn't return. This makes the Curly sad! I cry now. Weeeeppp...weeeeppp...weeeepp....weeeep. I think maybe she is being held in secret government labs being forced to watch reruns of Charles in Charge. I attach the photo. Or perhaps evil Man in black has kidnapped her and trying to use as bait to flush out the Curly. I attach the photo. I am also thinking that maybe she has been captured by sickening thieves and sold to slavery. I attach the photo.

Tells to me, do you think we can make a team and search for our loves together? Maybe it is same peoples who capture our loves? Please tells to me about your love? Is he big and strong like the Curly? Together we join the forces and we will be dynamo duo of unstoppable forces! I attach the photo. Do you agree with me on our partnership? It will be mutual agreement for us both. I ask that you do not try to seduce the Curly though. My love and my Mr. Winky belong to the Larisa. I am certain you are understanding. Are you ready to find our loves and smash the bad mens who take them away from us? I await your letters.
Sincerely, Curly

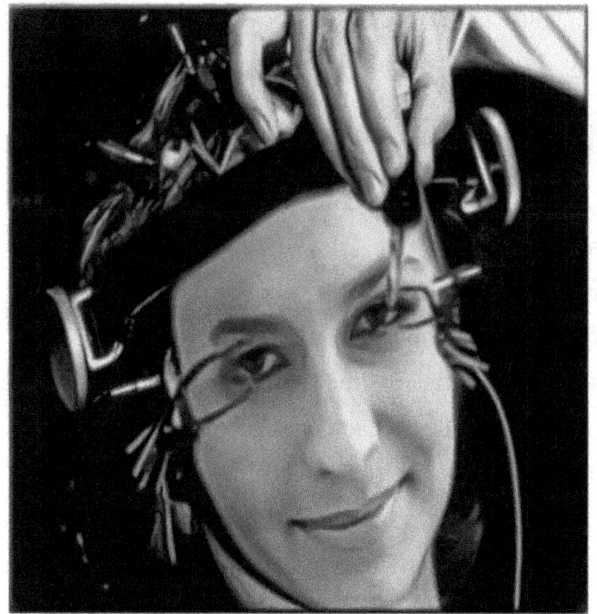

NO MORE CHARLES IN CHARGE!!

CURSES YOU MAN IN BLACK!!

SLAVERY?

WE MAKE THE DYNAMO DUO!

From: Mariya <girl_1980@xxxxx.com>
Sent: Wednesday, January 12 7:25 AM
To: Chris <coldbastrd@xxxxx.com>
Subject: [hi again]

Hi my dear and new friend Curly!!!
I'm very glad that you have interested in me and I will try not to disappoint you and you will get everything new about me. I'm asking you to write me about everything that you are able to say me. I will be glad to know about your work and family, your close friends, your hobbies... It seems to me that you are very interesting person, handsome and simply good person. I hope that you are exactly good man and that in future we will become close friends. So now I would like to tell you about myself.

I am a simply Russian girl, not differ from others. Maybe to describe myself it could be easier if i do it for a first time. I did not hope that you will answer me and when i saw your letter I got choked in my heart and now i am sitting in front of computer and do not know what to write you. I am sorry if there are a lot of mistakes in my letter because i know English not very well. But I hope that you will understand me and if you have some questions I will answer them with pleaser. Anyway it is time to say some words about myself.

My father died, when I was a child. It was an auto accident. I miss him a lot!!!! Since 2 years old my mother grew and educated me alone, It was very difficult for her and I love her very much. And now she is the best friend for me. I'm the only child in the family and I don't have any children, but I dream to have my own family, children. My mother works in Cheboksary in the hospital as a medical sister. I have never been married before. I am healthy woman and I do not smoke but sometime I can offer myself to drink some good wine in good occasions.

Most of all I like red wine. From food i like Chines food and Russian food and I would like to east European and West food. I am not exactly that I want to have a child because i think that first of all I want to find a man who will become my ideal sexual partner and simply good friend for my heart.

I work in office as manager in the insurance company, I work 40 hours per one week. I work with the clients who want to insure his or her car or real estate. I help our clients correctly to choose best for them to insurance. I know that in your country the system of insurance etc is advanced very well. In Russia people just now have begun to think about insurance, therefore we have many clients at this time. In our company we have good boss, we have studied together with her at University, but she is older than me for three years. I have good relations with my boss. I have the high salary for our city. It is about 5-6 $ dollars at one hour. I live in the city - Novocheboksarsk. It belongs to Chuvash Republic, about 640 KM or 400 miles from Moscow. I think that this information will help you to know me better. I would like to know about your work and City. I shall send you some picture of my city later.

By the character i am kind person and trying to enjoy everything in my life and trying to distroy all difficulties in my life. So, lets go further. My friends say that i am attractive even beautiful young woman. But unfortunately this fact did not help me to create my own family. Now i am sick and tired of my loneliness. I am an open minded and communicative, but sometimes a little bit shy, girl. Now i want to find that someone who can make all my dreams come true. In my turn i would be very glad and happy to do the same thing for my beloved man. So what do you think about it? By the way, i like spork very much. I am not a sporksmans of course. Just in order to be in good form. I visit the gym three times a week. I like to swim in the swimming pool.

But to tell the truth, i am afraid of water. But I try to overcome this fear. Sometimes, not very often, I love dancing very much. I can't say that i like a particular type of musik. It depends on my mood, what type of musik i would like to listen to. But usually i am very busy to have some rest and to do things i love to. Well, what else? I even don't know what to tell more. In such case i will finish my letter. I am waiting for your reply! Good bye, my dear new friend!!!! If you can please send me your pictures. I will be glad to get your letter and pictures.
I am sending you my smile to make you feel happy.
Your Mariya from Russia.

DID
I LEAVE THE
IRON ON?

HELP! I'M
BEING ATTACKED
BY THIS HAT!

RANDOM SHRUBBERY ATTACK

From: Chris <coldbastrd@xxxxx.com>
Sent: Friday, January 14 2:49 PM
To: Mariya <girl_1980@xxxxx.com>
Subject: [RE: hi again]

Hellos Mariya. It is the pleasures of me to making of friends. This is such the great news I tells to you! You live in the Russia! That is where I am going! What is the lucks? You will help me to find Larisa? She is somewhere in Moscow and you are tells to me that you are nearby. Maybe you have seen her?

I tells to you little bit about the Curly. I do not revealing all about Curly. I do not wants for you to become in the loves with me. My heart belongs to Larisa. Do not takes to this in wrong ways. You seem like the very nice womens although a bit buttery in faces. Your milky bits are nicely made however and it gives the Curly slight botherment of physicality. Perhaps you are to show to me? FORGET I SAID THESE THINGS! I am very sorry. I am lonely and miss Larisa and her words that touch my body. I look into your eyes that are deep pools of blueness that are bluer than smurf stooling and it reminds me of sky in which I wish I can fly into and find my love where ever she may be.

So to tells to you, home? I have no home. My home is the road, and the miles in between. The rivers and oceans and deep blue streams. The miles I've traveled, and places I've seen. The people I meet, and the places I've been. This is the home in which I know of. To find the woman in which I love. The Man in black may have taken her away. And I cry every night on the cold ground which I lay. These words that I say, they are not a lie. I will search for her whole heart until the day that I die.

That is who I am and that is my mission. Will you join me in mission? You claim to be the kind person. Then you are to help? Please? I have no one else to make the turns too. We have the more in common than you are made aware. My parents die too in horrible peanut combine accident. It is only I in world now. I too am afraid now of waters. The waters nearly swallowed up the Curly twice now. I too also love the spork. It is half fork, half spoon. Who comes up with such wonderful inventions? He is the genius! I love the musiks and the dance.

I go to clubs and get my boogie down on dance floors. I also like the Chinesa foods made by the peoples of Chinesa. I sell the hamsters to Chinesa man down street in places that I come from. With all this saids, I feel the connections to you in this way. Cold and alone in scared world. It is strange feelings to be so connected do you agrees? But together with such connectivity, we take on cold and scared world!

It is now times to attach the photo. Please do not become overwhelming when you gaze upon me. It is only I, Curly. I do not won't to choke you heart or give you the botherment of physicality. If you are with weak heart, you may want to visit mother in hospital. So here is the Curly. It is I leaving Nude Oilings. I have collecting many beads that represent pearl necklaces in which I give Larisa. Maybe if you help me, I gives to you a pearl necklace too.

I continue on road now. Please tells to me if arrangement of our cooperating partnershiping is agreeable to all involvement. I shall enjoy your letters again soon shall I? Please send more photos if you are wishing so that Curly can study you and get to know of you better for when we are meeting if we are to meeting in some times. I looked at your photos again and I finish now. I talk soon. Sincerely, Curly

YOUR HERO CURLY

From: Mariya <girl_1980@xxxxx.com>
Sent: Saturday, January 15 3:18 AM
To: Chris <coldbastrd@xxxxx.com>
Subject: [Hi again Curly]

Hello dear Curly!!!!!
Hope you are fine? I would like to tell you some things and please let me know what do you think about it. Okey? I am looking for a serious relationship, somebody who can understand me and whom I can understand. I think relationship between man and women is most important, a man should always treat a women nice and with love and respect, who stands by her in bad and good times and takes care of all her necessities. He should give her all the love he can so that she feels like the luckiest person on this earth. Similarly a woman should do the same for man, to support him all the time, to be with him when he needs her. I think love is the key, a very important factor in a relationship and only way you can make somebody love you if you are honest, sincere, faithful to that person. I would like to tell you some words what i did today.

Today when I was at job come a very solvent client who has wanted to insure the real estate. He has arrived to our republic from republic Komi. It is in the north of Russia and he badly talked in Russian. I have spent about three hours while explained him conditions of our insurance. And he has agreed to insure the real estate in our company. My boss promised me to give me holiday soon))

Tell me what films you like and what kind of books you like to read. May be you are already bothered to read my letter. As for me I like actress Sarah Michelle Gellar. Most of all I like film with her participation under the name " I Know what you did last summer "; Have you ever seen this film? If yes, tell please what do you think of this film?

I looked 2 more part of this film, but there was no my favorite actress, this film was not so that I liked. My favorite actor is John Travolta. I can talk about it indefinitely long, therefore I shall not take your time for reading my letter.
I shall wait for your letter.
Your friend Mariya

MULLETS ARE STILL FASHIONABLE IN RUSSIA

RIDE THE PONY!

From: Chris <coldbastrd@xxxxx.com>
Sent: Monday, January 17 2:08 PM
To: Mariya <girl_1980@xxxxx.com>
Subject: [RE: Hi again Curly]

Hellos to you again Mariya. So you are looking for the serious relationship. This is good news. Yes I agree that I am serious about finding Larisa so I am glad that you have decided to join me in relationships to help find her. This is best news all day! Thank you for photos. Please do not send any more photos unless you are to put the bag over the head. Let me asks you question. When you were small childrens, did you fall out of tree face first and hit every branch on way down? I am curious about this.

So now I am to tells you about my day but it is not nearly as exciting as yours. I have travelled on my Little Red Rocket to Applesauce. Oh I am forgetting, you do not know what my Little Red Rocket is. It is my bicycle in which I am travelling across country to come to Russia. It is my most prized procession aside from Larisa. Maybe someday if we are to meet, you can ride my Little Red Rocket. It will give you much pleasure. Anyways, yesterday I ride into Little Cock Applesauce. It is birthing place of American President Billiam Clitoris. You have heard of him? I believe he is friends with Fidel Castrate of Poopa as he has great affinity for cigars. I am tired and can use refreshments so I go to night clubs. It is to my surprise that I meets President Billiam. I attach the photo. He is great fun and we have many refreshments through night times. After drinking of refreshments, we decide to dance at night clubs. I have attached the photo. It is great fun! After we are dancing, President Billiam invites me to his houses. We try to sneak in houses as it is late in the night and Billiam's wife is sleeping. The lights go on and it is Billiam's wife! She grabs Billiam by neck and starts to choke him! She is the crazy lady! I thank Billiam for evening and run away out of houses!

I do not need to be chocking by crazy lady! So I ride Little Red Rocket till I find field in which I sleep. It is morning now and I write the letters before I make way for next places, Oaklahomo. I am so tired. And so very sad. I have not heard from the Larisa in such long times. I pray to the Gods every night that I hear her words again, but I do not. Such the Gods have forsaken the Curly. Why are you to do this to the Curly?? I yell to thems.

So I am reading the writings you are putting in letters and seeing the photos. You ride the pony? Larisa likes to ride the pony. I miss her. I am thinking that your pony will not ride long ways away with it bolted to floor. I am also thinking, who is cutting the hairs? Are they blind person? I am curious about this. Yes I know who you are speaking of in your letters. Buffy. Hollywerd is so fake. They put the makeup on the peoples and make them look different. Here is photo of Buffy without the makeup. Has anyone tells that you look like Buffy? I know what you did last summer too. You sit around house alone as no man pays the attention to you. Travolta? He is fat old man. I attach the photo. Amazing what they do with the makeup and wigs yes?

So it is coming to the finishing. No I am not bothered by the letters. Please continue to write the Curly with updates on your search for Larisa. This is great relationship and I am so glad as to finds you. I go now and will talk to you again soon.

Your friendship Curly

ME AND PRESIDENT BILLIAM CLITORIS

I DANCE WITH PRESIDENT BILLIAM

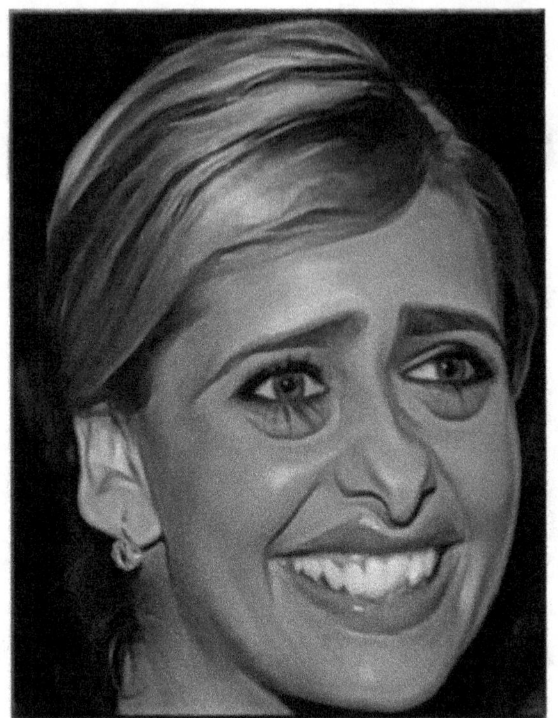

BUFFY WITHOUT MAKEUP

TRAVOLTA IS A FAT OLD MAN

From: Mariya <girl_1980@xxxxx.com>
Sent: Tuesday, January 18 4:10 AM
To: Chris <coldbastrd@xxxxx.com>
Subject: [Hi again Curly]

Hello my dear Curly!!!
Thanks for your photos. It was pleasant for me to receive your letter. How are you? Everything is well here. Nevertheless I want to tell in this letter slightly about what I like to eat and prepare. You know that I like to cook!!!Everything I was learned from my mum. I prepare almost everything. These are various soups, a ragout, pies, salads and many other things. In the best way I like to cook our national Borsch. Have you ever heard about it? I like to make pies that I usually I prepare them with a cherry and apricots. Do You love pies? If yes, with what? Still I adore ice-cream especially chocolate. And I am able to prepare for it. Have You ever tasted Russian dish??? I'm sure there are some Russian restaurants in your country are there!!! What food do you prefer, what cuisine? In Russia there are a lot of usual products and unusual dish, but i hear that foreigners always like Russian food!!! There is large variety of milk products: "smetana", And several types of milk products like yogurt, for example. Smetana can be used with almost everything: with the soup, with meat, or strawberries and apples. It's also used with pancakes. There is a great choice of soups and dessert dishes. Russia is famous for red caviar, with pancakes usually . it's very useful for your health, As for cold dishes it's very tasty cold boiled pork with spices(buzhenina), jellied tongue, meat jelly and horseradish sauce and various salads. I can cook all of them!!! There are plenty of soups: cabbage soup, kidney and cucumber soup (rassolnik), meat and fish salyanka, mushroom soup. I should tell you that it is very pleasantly to read your letters. In my life there was only one man who left me for a long time. All over again he seemed to me kind and attentive. I trusted him and he deceived me all time.

He changed me to the other girl. And I had to forgive him. It is difficult for me to speak about it but I simply wanted to say you about it. I think that you can understand it.
So hope to hear you as soon as possible.
Your Russian friend Mariya.

ANOTHER SHRUBBERY ATTACK

HOLD THIS POSITION. I CAN SEE DOWN YOUR SHIRT.

FORGET YOU. WHO'S THE BLONDIE?

From: Chris <coldbastrd@xxxxx.com>
Sent: Tuesday, January 18 3:04 PM
To: Mariya <girl_1980@xxxxx.com>
Subject: [RE: Hi again Curly]

Hellos again Mariya. How does the day great you? With fantasticalness I am hoping. I am reading your letters. Do you ever get feeling of diggy vu? Like you have said, seen, or done something before? I have the feelings when reading your letters. I will answer to you what I like in the cuisine and hopefully this is last time I have to write this. I like pies...cream pies, peach pies, cherry pies. I also like beaver, bearded oysters, beef curtains, pink tacos, and furburgers. Tells to me, does your friend in last picture make cherry pie? I would like to eat her cherry pie and maybe put some of my special homemade cream on it. I have never tasted the Russian but I am looking forward to it. I have not tried meat jelly but if you wish, your friend can try the jelly from my meat. It is a bit salty. I can also use my jellied tongue that would give your friend great satisfaction. I am seeing your milky products in the second picture and perhaps you need to send me more of those. Also please tell me about the Blondie. And I am forgetting, I make the peanut butter! How can I forget? It has been so long since I have tasted its creaminess. It is called the Curly Peanut Butter. I will try to find a jar before I come to Russia so that everyone can put my butter deep inside them.

So now I tells to you about my days. It is days of confusion and revelations. I have ridden to Oaklahomo! I am liking Oaklahomo. The great grassy plains and the farms. Maybe this is good places to settle with Larisa. I am running out of the monies so I need to find somes. I have findings a place in practical middle of nowhere. It is called a circus. Do you have the circus in Russia? I ask if I can work in circus for short time to make a few monies and they agrees. They give me two different types of workings. One job is very easy.

I stand in place and put arms out. Muscles man climbs on head and does tricks on top of the Curly head while I stand still. I have attached the photo. Also they make me the circus clown. This is great fun for me because I like to entertain the childrens. They give me mini motorcycle to use that is red. How funny is this? I call it my Little Red Crotch Rocket. I attach the photo. I am both happy and sad clown. I miss my sweet Larisa. This is why I have tear.

Now here is parts that are very strange and revealing. I am taking break from making the performances. I walk around outside circus grounds. I see what is called circus sideshows. This is where strange peoples make performances of their strangeness. I sit and watch shows for some time. Then it is to my surprises that a performer comes on stages. The bearded lady! It is my sister! She was great disgrace to family! I attach the photos. I cannot believe eyes! I have not seen her in years. I knows that she runs away to circus but I did not know where she goes. I wait for performance to end. I greet her backstage. Hello it is I, Curly. Do you remember me? I tells to her. She says, yes of course I remember the Curly! She goes to give a hug but I pull away. I says to her, why do you run away and leave family? Why do you dress as trashbaggy whore and put beard on faces? Did you know that the mama and papa die and you leave Curly all alone in world to fend for self? She pulls away and tears approach her faces. I am sorry Curly, she says, I wanted to stay but I knew I didn't belong. What do you mean you never belong? I say. You are always part of family! No Curly, I wasn't always part of family. She says. You see Curly, the mama and the papa couldn't have the childrens, I was orphan and they take me in and take cares of me. What is this you are saying? I ask to her. Why are you lies to me?!? No Curly, it is true. She says. You were only tiny childrens when the mama and papa tells me these things.

My family were circus high wire act performers. "The Amazing Fettuccini Family". She says. She shows me a photo. I have attached the photo. They were great high wire act from the 1970's. One evening during performance, they were all balanced on wire and poles and chairs. Father Fettuccini slips on banana peel on wire and they all fall to their deaths. Sister too young to be in performance and she watches as her family falls to death. After funerals, no one can take care of sister as she is too young and a circus lifestyles is not one for little childrens to take part in. So circus people put sister for adoption and my mama and papa adopt her. This is amazing revealings, I tells to her. Why did you run away? Why didn't you tell me these things? She tells to me, that she always felt connected to circus. She says, even though I see family fall to death, I was too young to remember. But every time I see Boner the Clown on the TV, it brings back the memories of circus. It wasn't until the mama and papa tells me everything that it all makes senses. I knew my heart belong in circus even though mama and papa provide the great life to us. I knew I must go live the circus lifestyle.

Mama and papa didn't want to tell you these things as to not make you saddened so they say bad things to you about me so that you wouldn't be sad. They try to protect you Curly. She says to me. This is where my home is, she says. This is where I belongs. She then tells to me, Curly, I am not only one who is adopted. I do not understand. She asks, why do you think you talk with accent? I do not know what she means. I ask, what do you mean I talk with accent? She says, you do not have American accent. You speaks like you have accent from Eastern Europe. I do not know I have accent! I say. Do you think I have an accent? Well you probably cannot tells from my letters. Don't you see? She says, we do not look anything alike. You don't look like the mama and papa. I says to her, what are you trying to tells to me? She says, Curly, the mama and the papa are not your mama and papa, they adopt you too! I AM BLOWNS AWAY! You mean to tells to me, whole Curly life is lies? No she says.

You were just tiny childrens when mama and papa found you in cradle on front step. You had note sayings to take care of you. So the mama and the papa took you in and raised you as their own. It was the right thing that they do. But why didn't they tell me? I ask. Because they didn't want to hurt you, make you feel sad, or make you feel different. She says. You were always their special boy and they loved you very much. Sometimes I would be jealousy of how good they treated you and I would get angry. She says. But I have gotten over the jealousy and anger. I have made my home here and this is where I stay and am very happy in life. She tells.

She takes me to her trailer and I meet her husband. He is also circus performer. I attach the photo. She asks to me, Curly, why are you here? Why are you not at home? I tells to her, that I have met the special love of my life, Larisa. She lives in Russia and I am going to be with her. She has disappeared in last few weeks and I am worried about her. I have found another special friend in Russia and she is helping me, along with her Blondie friend, to find my Larisa. My sister gets up and goes to her dresser. She opens and drawer and pulls out a box. She opens the box. Inside is a ring. She says to me, Curly, this is for you. We found it with you when you were left on our porch. It has writing but we do not know what it says. I take the ring. I attach the photo. She goes in drawers and finds a necklace. She attaches ring around necklace and puts it on my neck. She says to me, Curly, I hope you find your love. I have found my love, my happiness here, and I wish you same. Not only do I wish you to find your love and happiness, but also yourself in your journeys. She gives me hug and kiss on each cheek. She pulls monies out of pockets and gives to me.

Go now, she says, find your love....find your happiness...find yourself. I leave her trailer, get on my Little Red Rocket and go. I am happy I make the peace with sister. But so many questions! Where am I from?
Who am I? What is this ring? This journey has taken me amazing places, but it is not end. I ride on now with greatest effort. I will cross country!
I will go to Russia! I will find Larisa! So it is written, so it shall be done!
I am sorry for such long letters. You forgive as there is lot on plates for me to take in. Please tells to me if you have any news on your findings of Larisa. I await your letter. Please send more pictures of Blondie friend. I shall talk to you soon. It comes to the end now.
Your friend in America
Curly

GREAT ACROBATICAL FEATS

LITTLE RED CROTCH ROCKET

IT IS MY SISTER

SISTER PERFORMS ACT

COULD THEY BE ITALIAN?

SISTER WITH THE HUSBAND

THE SPECIAL RING

CHAPTER 8:
UP ON BROKENBUTT MOUNTAIN

Up On
Brokenbutt Mountain

Deliver to
tornado tommy s
brokenbutt mountainranch
c/o curly poindexter
texaco usa

From: Mariya <girl_1980@xxxxx.com>
Sent: Wednesday, January 19 3:51 AM
To: Chris <coldbastrd@xxxxx.com>
Subject: [Hi again Curly]

Hi, my dear friend Curly!!!!
Thanks for your photos. How is your mood? I am very happy, I have some news at my job. Today at job my boss has praised me for my job. I had long conversation with her and she has said that I well work and I has concluded many favorable contracts for our company. She has said that she will give me holiday and I shall receive the premium for the well done job. I am very glad to this news.

I think that we can get know each other closer. As you know, if you meet someone you must see, if everything beautiful in a person - face, clothing, spirit and mind. As for me I judge not by persons appearance. The most beautiful thing, which I like in man is his spirit, not the face. I think that if the man has nice spirit, he is the best man in the world. As for me I have everything but not love that's why I decided to write to you. I hope that everything will be all right. And what do you think about it? What can you say about your character? And what are the main features of your character? As for me the most important thing when a man understands me and my fillings. I think that we have similar ideas and beliefs, attitudes and interests in common, if not, so I think that it will not much time to reach this point. It seems to me that you are a very good and interesting person, and I would like to know you better. It is my first time when I use the Internet to get acquainted with somebody. I know the English language not very well, but I hope, that you can understand me and will help me to learn English.

However now I want to inform you about my city. Novocheboksarsk is not big city in Russia. I like it very much, it's not so big as other city, for example, but it's very clean and smart. There are a lot of parks and churches, there are a lot to see and there a lot of tourists!!!! I think it's worth visiting!!!Novocheboksarsk is a city of Chuvash Republic. The population is here about 200000 people. Have you heard anything about my city?

By the way, my address:
Berezova 9-57,
Novocheboksarsk, Chuvashia,
Russian Federation.
i hope that it's really interesting for you to read my letters and i hope that we'l continue writing to each other!!! Hope to hear from you very soon!!!
Take care, Your Mariya.

SOMEONE NEEDS TO SAVE THIS GIRL FROM ALL THE ATTACKING SHRUBS!

EVEN DEAD SHRUBS ATTACK HER.

WATCH OUT! MONSTER FROZEN SHRUB BEHIND YOU!

From: Chris <coldbastrd@xxxxx.com>
Sent: Wednesday, January 19 2:23 PM
To: Mariya <girl_1980@xxxxx.com>
Subject: [RE: Hi again Curly]

Greetings Mariya, How are you today? I am in the good spirits....almost. I still miss my Larisa. Any news of her on your side? How about your Blondie friend? That is very good news about your workings. Maybe you take vacation to Nigeria and sit on beach and play in ocean. So now I will tells to you about my days.

I have arrived in Texaco. This is very big state. I tells to you about history of Texaco. Long time ago, Texaco use to be Mexican. But as America gets bigger and bigger, people from America go into Texaco. The Texacans tells the Mexicanos, all your bases are belong to us, you go aways now. Well this upsets the Mexicanos. Well many rich people build big houses there because Texaco has warm climates. Whitney Houston builds big house that she calls Alamo. It is customary for rich people to name their estates here. One of her friends is on street and hears of Mexicanos being upset with Texacans and they are going to invade Texaco. And to make an example, they are going to make their first raid on Alamo. So friend calls up and says, Houston, we have a problems. The Mexicanos are coming! So Houston calls some of her friends. She calls Betty Crocker and David Bowie. Betty Crocker says, I will bake the Mexicanos a cake and they will be fat and happy and leave us alone! David Bowie says, if they try to raid your house, I will take my Bowie knife and gut them like the fishes. So they go to Whitney Houston's house and fight the Mexicanos. The Mexicanos lose Texaco and go back to Mexico. The Texacans say, nah...nah...nah...you can't have it! Well ever since, the Mexicanos have been trying to take over Texaco. They become partners with illegal aliens from space and invade Texaco on a daily basis. And that is the story of Texaco.

Well I am riding along and I meet a man who is a cowboy. He is called Tornado Tommy. He use to be rodeo performer and put on shows. I attach a poster. However he falls off horse and has injury so he can't make the performances anymore. I am tired and I need rest. He tells to me that he will give me food and shelter if I help a little while with his sheep and goats. This is so cools! I will ride the pony and learn to be the real cowboys like Cliff Eastwood and John Wayne Gacy!

He gives me pony to ride and we heard the sheep and goats. He moves them from place to place on his farm so that they have freshest foods to eat. He calls his farm Brokenbutt Mountain. I guess it is traditions in Texaco to name property just like rich peoples. When we find fresh places for them to eats, we sit and watch them for hours and hours. Job is somewhat boring but Tommy really likes the goats and sheep and he just stands for hours watching them. I attach the photo. After a long day of hearding sheep and goats, we make the campfire and eat and drink refreshments and talk and watch the sheep and laugh. I attach the photo.

In the night times, he pitches a tent and I come inside. It is an easy, relax full lifestyle up here on Brokenbutt Mountain. Perhaps someday I will have my own farm and can heard sheep and goats and Larisa will help me. Maybe you can come for a visit. I will allow this. So we are in tent resting and I hear a noise. What was that noise? I jump out of my cot and check outside tent. Is it the Man in black? Tommy comes and looks out tent. I attach the photo. He tells to me to go back to bed. Everything is ok. He will go check on sheep and goats. He sneaks out and goes and checks on sheep and goats in middle of night. He is so dedicated to his animals! What a good brave man! I attach the photo. He comes back after a few hours of goat checking, tells me everything is ok, and goes back to bed. This is good. I feel safe with strong cowboy looking over me.

I may stay a few days but then must move on. I must get to Russia immediately! This is no joking! Larisa has been silenced for so long now, I forget her words almost. Please be on the lookout for her and tells to me if you hear anything! I must finish now. We are going to have more fun with sheep and goats. Talk to you soon.

Take luck, Curly

TOMMY WATCHES SHEEP AND GOATS ALL DAY LONG.

WE SIT AROUND CAMPFIRE.

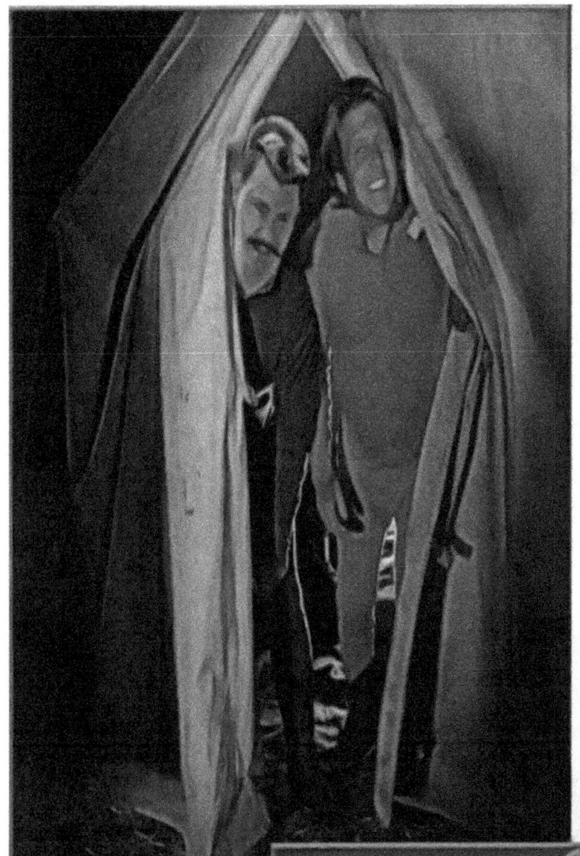

WHAT WAS THAT NOISE?

TOMMY CHECKS ON SHEEP AND GOATS IN MIDDLE OF NIGHT.

TORNADO TOMMY'S
ROOTIN' TOOTIN'
WILD WEST SHOW!

From: Chris <coldbastrd@xxxxx.com>
Sent: Thursday, January 20 4:26 AM
To: Mariya <girl_1980@xxxxx.com>
Subject: [RE: Hi again Curly]

Hello dear Curly!!!!
Thanks for your photos. I have very good news!!! Today when I have come on my job. The boss has congratulated me. She promised me to give the premium and she made it, I has received my premium (about 500 $ US dollars!!!) also I have received my monthly salary for holidays (about 1070$)!!! Earlier I never received the premiums... Since tomorrow's day I shall leave in holiday from my job 45 days. Today I had heavy day and has passed all reports and papers to the colleagues. I am so happy today..

I wait for your congratulations. May be for your country it not so big money, but believe me for Russia it's the big money. I yet have not decided what I will do in my holiday, but I will think about it today. You can give advice about that, what me to do in my holiday??? You have some ideas? May be I will travel to see other countries, other culture. I never was abroad earlier. OK, dear I have very good mood and I wish to you good mood also.
Yours good friend from Russia Mariya.

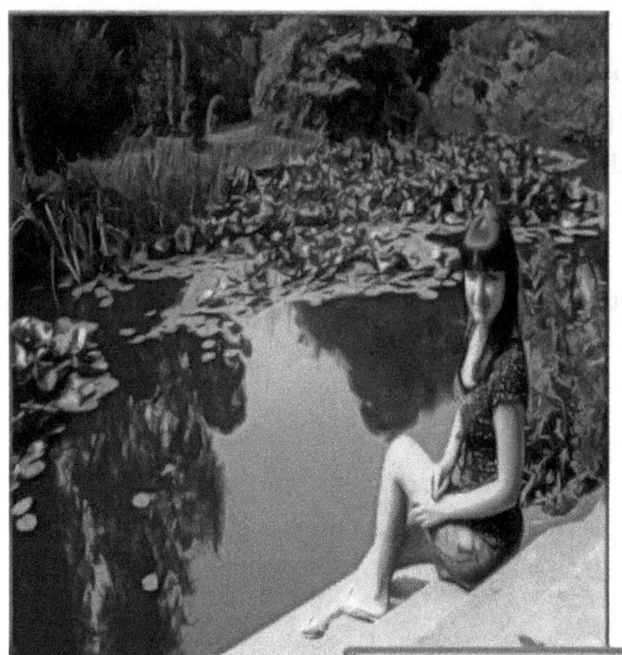

LOOKING
FOR
A
FROG
TO
KISS.

WAITIN'
FOR THAT
TRAIN,
TO TAKE
ME AWAY,
FROM THIS
LONESOME
TOWN.

CURLY TIP OF THE DAY: DON'T SIT ON TRAIN TRACKS OR YOU WILL BECOME DEAD.

From: Chris <coldbastrd@xxxxx.com>
Sent: Thursday, January 20 2:55 PM
To: Mariya <girl_1980@xxxxx.com>
Subject: [RE: Hi again Curly]

Hellos Mariya. How is the day? That is the good news about the job. That is the good monies. Since you are having the good lot of monies, maybe you send a little to Curly to help? Please! Why are you thinking of taking the vacation at times like this? We have to find Larisa! Are you not taking the relationship seriously? I am needing your help and all you can think about it laying around in snow, sitting on tiny ponies, sitting around on park benches, and sitting by edge of ponds. It is not funny! I see you are waiting for a trains to take you away on vacation. Does this mean you are leaving me too? I see you get tired of waiting and lay down on tracks. Mama, who is not the real mama anymore, tells to Curly, if you are tired, do not lay down on train tracks. It is advisable that you follow same rules. If you die by train, I will lose another friend. Curly can't stand to lose another friend. I have lost so many already. I am thinking I am cursed. Curly, the angel of deaths. Anyone who knows the Curly either die, hurt, or disappears. Today I lose another friend. I can't take it anymore. I tells to you.

I was here on Brokenbutt Mountain with Tommy. I really like Tommy. He is teaching me all kinds of things and we have great fun! He is true friend! Last night, we go to town. We have the refreshments and ride the machismo bull. It is bull that is robot but they tie it to floor so that it does not go robot crazy and kill the peoples. I attach the photo. This mornings, we put the sheep and goats to pastures. Tommy asks me if I like to shoot the guns. I say, I have never shot the guns. I would like this. He takes me into secret hidden bunker where he hides his guns. He tells to me that when end of world comes, he will protect his sheep and goats from bad mens. I attach the photo.

He tells to me, it is right of every Texacan and every American as well the right to bear arms. He shows to me his bear arm collection. I attach the photo. He is quite the skillsman with guns. He gives me gun to shoot. I look at barrel. He says, stop that you ninipoopy! That is where bullet comes from. Oh I say, it is like when Curly makes the pp and nobody should stand in front of the Curly gun when making the pp. So I understand his saying. So we go outsides and he puts me on horse. He sets up targets and I ride horse and shoot the gun. I get really good at hitting targets. I am becomings a real rootin' tootin' cowboy!

I attach the photo. After we are finishing, Tommy tells me he has a surprise for me! I love the surprises! But only the good ones. He gives me a box and says, here this is for our one day anniversaries. I open up box, it is the real cowboy clothings! I try them on. I attach the photo. What do you think? He tells to me, I can't quit you. I don't know what he means. I am not quitting the job. I will stay here a little longer and help with sheep. I says to him. You know Tommy, you are the incredible rootin' tootin' cowboy. You need to go back to showing world your ability. The childrens will like this and you can teach all of world to be rootin' tootin' cowboy.

He begins to lean over to tell me something in my ear....and then out of nowhere, the Man in black appears! He holds a gun towards me. He says, Curly, I'm taking you in. I attach the photo. I have never told you about Man in black. You see, Curly got into some trouble back in my homes. I get a slightly emotional and smash few things. Policemens don't like this and they try to lock the Curly away. But I runaway. Now Man in black follows me everywhere. He is always one step behind me. I try to escape but he is always there. Anyway, at this moment, Tommy jumps on Man in black. They struggle and fight on ground. I attach the photo. Tommy says, run Curly, run! So I run to my Little Red Rocket and ride away as fast as can!

This is terrible tragedies! I hope that he is ok. Tommy is good man...he is lonely only with goats and sheep, but good man none less. He teach me to be the cowboy and to fire gun and for that, I am forever gleeful. I must continue ride. Press onwards and never go back. I will be quiet for few days as perhaps Man in black is using computer signal to follow me. I have the laptop with camera that friend gives to me. I will talk to you in few days. Please I think you use some monies and holiday times to go to Russia and help find Larisa. This is agreeable yes? It finish now. Take the care and I talk soon.

Your cowboy buddy in land of cowpokes, Curly

WE RIDE THE BULL

TOMMY'S GUN COLLECTION.

TOMMY'S BEAR ARM COLLECTION.

I BECOME A ROOTIN' TOOTIN' COWBOY!

NEW

COWBOY

CLOTHINGS

THE

MAN

IN

BLACK!!

MAN IN BLACK WRESTLES TOMMY TO GROUND

From: Mariya <girl_1980@xxxxx.com>
Sent: Friday, January 21 7:32 AM
To: Chris <coldbastrd@xxxxx.com>
Subject: [Hi again Curly]

Hello my lovely Curly!!!!!!!
Thanks for your photos.
I thought so much how it will be better to spend my holiday. But I think that it will be better if I spend my holiday going to you! I maybe have very good time to see you. You will show me your country, your culture etc do not you wish? What do you think about it? I can arrive to your country. It's better to communicate tete-a-tete then write each other thousands letters!!! I'm sure. I hope that you do agree with me!!!! I sometimes imagine our meeting, i'm sure it'll be wonderful!!! Just imagine: When I arrive to you, you'd stand at the airport and wait for me. And then our eyes meet. We understand that it's great that we meet each other. We'd go to have supper with candles. We will talk a lot. I'm sure we'd enjoy each moment. there wouldn't be anybody but we were only. Time would stop for us!!!. It would be very romantic time. What do you think about it? i'm looking forward to your e-mail soon, my dear!!!!
Kiss you!!!
Mariya

WOOFAA!!

PROBLEM

WITH

YOUR

NECK?

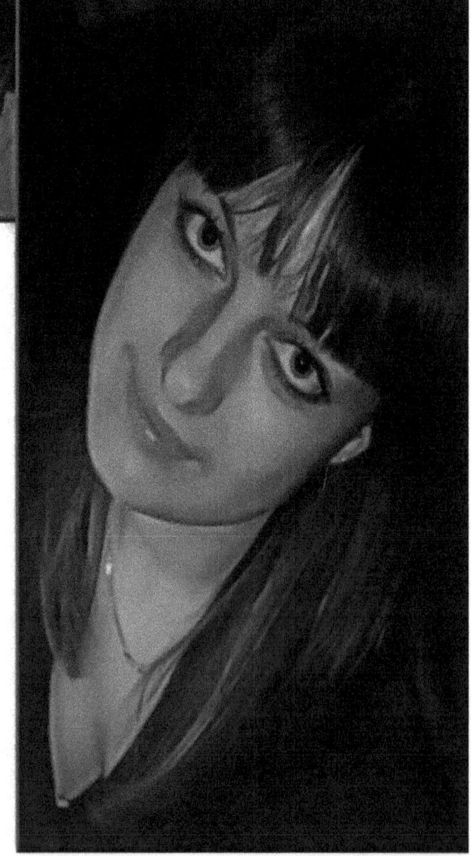

From: Chris <coldbastrd@xxxxx.com>
Sent: Monday, January 24 2:57 PM
To: Mariya <girl_1980@xxxxx.com>
Subject: [RE: Hi again Curly]

Hi Mariya. All I can say is, NO NO NO NO NO NO NO!! What I have told to you? YOU DO NOT FALL IN LOVE WITH CURLY! I am sensing that you are become irresistible to the Curly charms. This is what makes me afraid. And what did I say about sending the photos. Do not does this without the baggie. It makes the eyes watery. WOOFAA! I do not think it is good to meet teet to teet or eye to eye or man nutties to lady bits with you. Please do not ask of it again. You are supposed to be working hard on your holiday times to find Larisa. Stay focused! Besides, I am not knowing where I going from one day to next. I tell you about last days.

I ride my Little Red Rocket hard inside Nude Mexicano. It is dry place with cactus and sand. It has not been wet inside here for years perhaps. I come to places called Roswell. They seem to be into accepting the illegal aliens here as they appear places all over dedication to them. It is coming late at night and I am riding outside of town. Suddenly, a strange light appears from sky. I take the photo of it and attach. The next thing I am knowing, I wake up in jungle area dressed in different clothings that are not belonging to me. I see old pictures on ground and my underbottoms are hurting me very much. I attach the photo of the photos on ground. Maybe this is the illegal aliens perhapsing?

I ride my Little Red Rocket in jungle till I reach small village. Man with the skin darker than Curly comes up to me. He begins the speaking. I do not understand him. He sounds like the people I meet from Poopa. I hope I have not gone back to Poopa! I don't want to go there and it is so far aways! He is blah blah blahing and I am tells to him, I don't know what you say!

Then another man comes to me. He says, hey Ringo, what are you doing in Mexican? I am in Mexican? And I am not Ringo! Why does he confuse me with Beatle man? Maybe because of mouthstaches? I attach the photo of me versus Ringo. What are you thinking?

Anyways, he tells to me that I am in Mexican. I tells you quickly of story of Mexican. Long time ago, Spanglish peoples in Spang get tired of making the childrens with same women over and over. Spanglish men are known for being lovers of womens. So king of Spang, King Paco says, we need to go cruising for more womens, why don't we build some boats and go find more womens. So his peoples said, ok Paco, we make a boat and go cruising for womens. So they build a boat. But it sits too low in water and sinks. So king says, stop building the lowrider, make something that can sit low, and go high, and look good for cruising the womens. So they make adjustable hydraulics boats and this is good. So they go off cruising looking for more womens and run into the Mexican. They see that the Mexicanos walk around with the no clothings because it is so hot and the Spanglish really like this easy access. They say, hey babies we are Spanglish and we are here to make the love to you. The Mexicanos easily fall in love with the Spanglish and they make the childrens with the Spanglish. So now the Mexicanos all speak the Spanglish.

I say I don't know how I got here. He looks at me and says that I am looking confused and shaky. He asks me, what day is it? I say, it's Friday. He says, no Ringo, it's Monday, you really are lost! I don't get it. I don't know what happened to me and how I get here. He says, hey wait a minute Ringo, I know who you are. You are the man from the peanut butter jar! I say, yes, that is me! I make the Curly peanut butter! He says, ah Ringo, we love the Curly peanut butter, we eat it all the time! I say, well I am glad you are liking it!

He says to me, you know Ringo, I tell you a secret. He says, many many many years ago, the native Mexicanos, they love the peanut butter. They worship it! Deep in the jungle, there is ancient Mexicano temple ruin where they keeped a secret peanut butter formula deep inside. I says, where is this place? I must try the secret formula! He draws me map and I ride through jungle to ancient ruin. I attach the photo. I go inside the ruins. I make my way deep inside and then I come to special room. There, in center of room on special mounting, is secret formula peanut butter!! I approach the peanut butter. Hmmmm....it sure does look very tasty! I attach the photo. I am thinking, should I take the special peanut butter? I attach the photo. You know what? I TAKE IT! I attach the photo! There is large rumblings in room. What is happening? I says. RUMBLE RUMBLE RUMBLE RUMBLE!!!! I look up, I see big rock coming for Curly head! I RUNAWAY!!!!!!!!!!!!!!!!! I attach the photo!!!!!! I run and run and run and run. I make it to exit and rock seals ruin shut!

I am the lucky that I go there today and get special formula before rock closes ruin forever! What are the chances that I have the perfect timing? So I open lid of peanut butter and taste. IT IS GREATEST PEANUT BUTTER EVER!!!! I am going to send this to my friend, the Chief who look after my peanut butter factory for safe keepings.

I ride Little Red Rocket back to village. I ask to them, please tell me how I get back to America. They draw map of way I am to goings. Tomorrow, I will go back to America and continue on to Russia! Now again, I am to tells to you, please, do not come here! You are to stay there and help find Larisa. Is this clear to you? Do not fall in love with me! I belong to Larisa and only Larisa. I much finish now. I ride back to America now. Take cares for now.

I do not kiss you.

Curly

STRANGE
LIGHT
FROM
SKY

??????

ME RINGO

OUTSIDE OLD MEXICANO RUINS

HMMM...THAT SURE DOES LOOK GOOD

SHOULD I TAKE IT?

I TAKE THE PEANUT BUTTER!!

RUNAWAY!!!!!

From: Mariya <girl_1980@xxxxx.com>
Sent: Tuesday, January 25 2:54 AM
To: Chris <coldbastrd@xxxxx.com>
Subject: [Hi again Curly]

Hello lovely Curly!!!!!!!
Thanks for your photos.
I am glad that you agreed to meet me. Also I'm going to prepare a lot of documents and go to Moscow tomorrow. One of my friends lives in Moscow and today i've called my friend and she agreed me to stay at her place and she told me that she'll help me with my documents too!!! We are friends since our childhood. But she entered the Moscow state University and now she is there. Now she has found a good job and has stayed living there. I think that it's very good that she allowed me to stay at her place because it's very expensive to live in the hotel in Moscow as she sad!!! I shall write to you as soon as I arrive to Moscow. I think that for my visa I will need: your full address; your full name and the closest airport where you will be able to meet me. I do not know, but it is necessary for me to take your invitation. You could write it to me and then i'll print it!!! Ok?!!! When I shall be in Moscow I shall find out if for my visit will be necessary your invitation. I'm very happy my dear that i'm going to meet you very soon!!!
I miss you a alot!!!!
Hope to hear from you very soon!!!
Kiss you, Your Mariya.

From: Chris <coldbastrd@xxxxx.com>
Sent: Tuesday, January 25 2:15 PM
To: Mariya <girl_1980@xxxxx.com>
Subject: [RE: Hi again Curly]

NONONONONONO!!!!! What are you doing you silly womens!???!!!! I have not made such the agreement!! Where you dropped down stairs as a small childrens? I am nearly certain of this. Read my lips, hear me now, and listen to me in a few hours. You are not to come to me! If you are going to Moscow, you are to look for Larisa. Not make documentation of trip you are not to be taking!! By way, friend in Moscow, is this the Blondie you send photo of? You can tell more of her please. So we are clear? I am seeing that I have cast the spell of my Curly charms on you. You must be resistant of my charms! I can't help myself. I am being the only Curly that I know of. I am not knowing where I am going from one day to next. I tell you about my day.

I have go to border of America and Mexican. Along way, Mexicanos says to me, where are you going? I say I am going to border to America. They say, are you the crazy? You are on border of state of Azzihola. This is toughest border to cross. You will be killed! I say, stop it. I am not the Mexicano, I am American. They let me in no problem. So I get to border and there is big wall separate America with Mexican. Who builds this wall and why do they not put windows in wall so you can see other side? It would be nice for Mexicanos and Americans to wave at each other through windows. This would keep the friendly neighbors. It is big wall that I can't climb. So I throw Little Red Rocket over wall and find stick. I take stick, run towards wall and leap over wall. I find photo from securities camera on internet and attach. I land in America only to my surprises that I am greeted by policemens! I attach the photo.

I don't want to go back to the jail so I grab Little Red Rocket and runaway!! They chase me but I go into desert. It is very hot here but they say that it's a dry heave so they pretend it's not so hot....but it is hot! I lose policemens.

Many animals in desert that can kill the Curly. Snakes, spiders, hawks, camels, ostriches, zebra, lions, gazelles, emus, giraffes, oxen, tigers, elephants, and monkeys. I come to a huge place call the Grand Cumyum. It is big hole in ground and it's easiest to cross through it than go around. I climb into Grand Cumyum. I take the photo of me inside. I attach the photo. You see how huge it is! I am guessing that many years ago, someone try to dig way to Chinesa. He makes the big hole in ground! I wonder if he uses shovel or machine operation.

So I am walking along minding the own business and I look up along wall. Oh no! It is the Sandsman! I attach the photo. You see, Sandsman sneaks into bedroom back at the home and put sands in my eyes every night. He is deranged man! He comes to me and we battle! He hits me with stick. I attach the photo. I KARATE CHOP! We roll around on ground. He is strong and stick he uses hurts. I pick up rock and smash on head! SANDSMAN SMASH! I attach the photo. He looks up at me and begs for forgiveness. He cannot have it! I spit in his general direction. SPIT! I leave him there amongst the sands to reflect on deranged life and will not be putting the sands in Curly's eyes ever again!

I reach edging of Grand Cumyum and climb out. I attach the photo. This is not easy task to climb having to carry Little Red Rocket, laptop computer, camera, cellphone from Napster, green suede shoes, saber of light from the Chief, special formula peanut butter, pearl necklace beads, cowboy clothings from Tommy, and Elvis suit from Gracylands. Speaking of the Elvis. I am taking rest on side of road. A car pulls up to me. I hear voice from inside. Hey baby, you need a lift? Voice says.

I cannot believe the ears! I jump and look in car. It's the fat man Elvis! But he isn't fat anymore! I say, Elvis, remember me? It is I, Curly. He says, I don't know baby, it's a little fuzzy. Was it in that hotel in Cleveland? I say, no I do not know of this. He says, well anyway, you need a ride or what? I say yes of course if you are going towards Russia. I am heading west. He says. That is good enough I say. I load things in car and we go. I attach the photo. He tells to me that we are going to Lost Virgins. I do not know why they are lost but perhaps they couldn't find way in desert. It is big open places that is not easy to make the navigations. He tells to me that we are going to party and gamble there. I says to him, Elvis, you have lost the weights! What has happening to it? He says, I've been cutting back on my fatty intake. I say oh, I am understanding. Viva la hipposuction!

So here it is. I come to the finish. Let me know when you are in Moscow and you and friend work togethers to find Larisa. I talk to you another time. I don't send the kisses. Please stop trying to kiss me!
Curly

I CROSS BORDER IN AZZIHOLA

OH NO! POLICEMENS!!!

GRAND CUMYUM IS HUGE!!

OH NO!!! IT IS THE SANDSMAN!

I BATTLE SANDSMAN!!!

SANDSMAN SMASH!!!!!

I CLIMB OUT OF GRAND CUMYUM.

ME AND UNFAT ELVIS GOES TO LOST VIRGINS

From: Mariya <girl_1980@xxxxx.com>
Sent: Wednesday, January 26 6:07 AM
To: Chris <coldbastrd@xxxxx.com>
Subject: [Hi again Curly]

Hello dear Curly!!!!
Thanks for your photos.
How are you today? I have good mood. Today, in one hour I shall leave in Moscow by train. Tomorrow I shall arrive in Moscow and my friend will meet me. I will write at once to you when I shall arrive in Moscow. Last night, I dreamed I go to the airport to meet you. Then you noticed me. I started to say hello to you and then you smiled the most beautiful smile will be your smile. I could not speak, your smile left me speechless. Then as we met, I took your hand and felt your heat. You ask how are you and I replied hungry and tired. We started walking out and I woke up. I was sad that it was only a dream but even though the distance between us is great, I was close to you for a minute. I have often wondered about our meeting and how it will be.
I miss you.
Your and only your Mariya.

From: Chris <coldbastrd@xxxxx.com>
Sent: Friday, January 28 12:39 PM
To: Mariya <girl_1980@xxxxx.com>
Subject: [RE: Hi again Curly]

My dear dumb Mariya. Sorry I do not write for few days as I cannot remember a lot of what has happening. What do I have to say to get you to stop these feelings for the Curly? Huh? Do you need a spanking? You are being a bad girl and not listening to the Curly. Dreams of this now. If we meet, I am not going to be smiling with my smile. I will be frowning the most mean frown from the frown. Because if we met, it means that you are not looking for Larisa! You are goofy around with your time! Besides your dreams are wild and false. You would not be hungry or tired. They give you little tiny pieces of foams for your head to sleep on and small juicy boxes for you to drink on plane. They also give you little cans of sardines for you to eat upon. Also you do not just walk out of airport. They put you into machines and check your naughty bits to see what they look like. They search your luggages if you are bringing illegal aliens with you. They check your papers to see if photo on paper matches faces. So your dreams is the nonsense. Stop living in dreamy world! You will not be feeling my heat!

So to tells you now of latest adventures. I have arrived here in Lost Virgins with Elvis. We have the problems though. We have runs out of the monies. We spent all monies of many slurpees to keep us cooled in the hot desert. I attach the photo. So what are we thinking. How do we make the monies? We need the monies for beef jerky, slurpees, and places to sleep. So we decide to put on our Elvis suits and sing songs outside of casinos. You are not knowing but I sing in rock and roll band with the PB&J's. Elvis let's me play the guitar. I attach the photo. Here is song that we singing:

My Russian Bride

Bright light city gonna eat a bagel,
Gonna eat a bagel with butter.
Drank a whole lot of slurpees,
and some hot beef jerky,
And everything seems to be alright.
Elvis suits are what we wear,
As we sing in the square,
And the peoples did stare and say.
Viva Lost Virgins, Viva Lost Virgins!

How I wish that I were with Larisa,
And I'd give her a kissa all night.
This is a song that you can sing along,
As you play Donkey Kong,
Or get into a street fight.
Wear green suede shoes,
As you drink all the booze,
And peoples will say you're out of sight.
Viva Lost Virgins, Viva Lost Virgins!

Viva Lost Virgins with you teeties flashin',
And your police cars crashin',
All the monies goes down the drain.
Viva Lost Virgins with your whiskey bottles,
And your sugar sweet waffles,
I don't think I'll ever be the same.

I'm gonna keep on the riding',
From the Man in black I'm hidin',
But I'm having a swingin' time.
This song is true,
I think I might have the flu,
Now let's sing again once more this rhyme.
Viva Lost Virgins, Viva Lost Virgins
Viva, Viva Lost Virgins!

So people past by and toss us the monies. We play for hours and hours. After times go by, Elvis stops and asks, how much monies do you think we have? I look at case and make the calculations quickly in head. I do this by tapping on side of head like calculator. I tells to him $25.80. He says, how do I know this? Well I tells to him, there is 22 single dollars, 12 quarters, 7 dimes, 1 nickel, and 5 one cents. I attach the photo. He says to me, you can just tell this by looking at it? Yes of course, how else to make the calculations? I say. There is man on street selling decks of cards. Elvis runs and grabs decks of cards. He says, ok watch me. He takes cards out and shuffles them all in different ways. He shows me first card. It is king of spades. He then asks me, what is next card? I make the calculations. It is 2 of hearts. I am right. He asks what is next card after this. I make calculations. 10 of diamonds. I am right. We do this many more times. I am right all time. This is easy. Why does he ask me these silly questions? Maybe he is wanting to be the magician and make the card tricks?

He says to me, Curly, you are the freaky genius! Come with me, but change out of your Elvis suit, we don't want to attract to much attention. So we grab monies, I change clothings, and we go to casino. We go to tables where people play with cards. This is like childrens games to me. I don't understanding why they make such big show of this. So he explains to me a gaming we are going to play.

He changes monies for little chips and we go to table. Chips are fun and colorful. We play the games and I make the calculations and they keep giving me more and more pretty colored chips. It's kind of boring but at least I have the pretty chips to play with. I attach the photo. So after a long time of this gaming, Elvis says we are finished and can go. He gives pretty chips to casino and they give him lots of monies. He give me some of monies and a pretty chip to keep.

He says to me, Curly, you are the man! Let's go out on town and have the party! So we go to store and he buys me a new suit. I have attached the photo. What do you think of new suit? It is groovy funky fun! I can get down on dance floor and boogie. So we go out in town and boogie down all night. We drink many many refreshments. I think I drink too many refreshments though as I have trouble remembering. I wake up in the morning times in fancy hotel rooms. There is nudie sleeping woman on floor and Elvis is gone. He disappears like a fart in the wind. What has happening? I attach the photo. I go to use bathroom as I must make the pp. I open door and there is strange man in tub!! Who are you I say?
He says, I don't know, who are you? It is I, Curly you stranger man! He gets out of tub. It is gross. I think he make the pp in the tub. This is all just the crazy! He says, hey man I got to get to Long Bitch. I ask, is that west? He says, yeah man, you wanna come? Yes I say, I am in need of ride to get me to Pacifier Coast. Ok man, that's the way I am going. He says. So I gather my things and we go. I leave nudie woman on floor. I do not knowing who she belongs to. Along way we stop and pick up another man making the hitching along road. This is not good idea I am thinking. This man is kinda weird, shakes a lot, and looks crazy. Many years ago they do the nuclear explosions in desert when Russia and America didn't like each other. I think man exposes self to nucleation. Stranger man says he is a "tweaker". No one talks. Tweaker man says we need to stop so he can make the pp. We can't stop here! This is bat country! I tells to him. I attach the photo.

So I am continuing to make the progressions west and soon to reach coast! So I tells to you know, you are going to Moscow. Please be on lookout for Larisa. She is blondie – browny hair, deep chocolaty eye balls, tender honey bbq lips, soft milky bits, nonboogery nose, little hairy brows, and smile that is like butterflies flying through sky. That is easy descriptions for you to remember. If we keep working together, we shall certainly find her! Maybe I give you reward of one of my pearl necklaces if you are finding her. I finish it now!

Not yours and only Larisa's

Curly

WE

DRINK

TOO

MANY

SLURPEES.

WE

SING

SONG

OUTSIDE

CASINOS.

$25.80

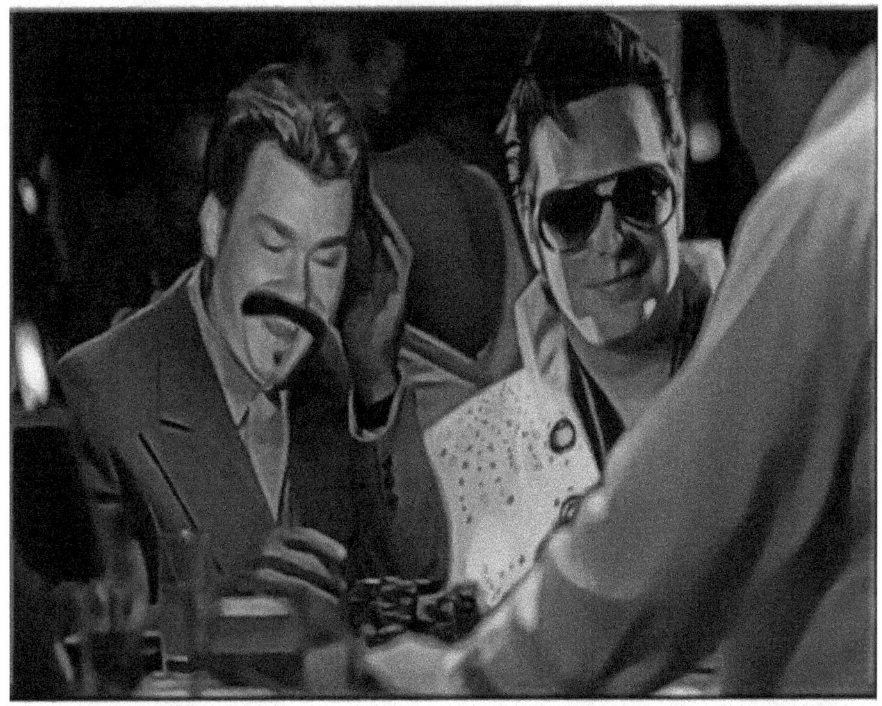

I MAKE THE CALCULATIONS IN HEAD.

I HAVE THE NEW SUIT!

WHAT HAS HAPPENING?

STRANGE MAN IN TUB.

WE CAN'T STOP HERE! THIS IS BAT COUNTRY!

CHAPTER 9:
CUNTIFORU DREAMSIN'

CUNTIFORU DREAMSIN'

HOLLYWERD

From: Mariya <girl_1980@xxxxx.com>
Sent: Saturday, January 29 4:20 AM
To: Chris <coldbastrd@xxxxx.com>
Subject: [Hi again Curly]

Hello dear Curly!!!
I've just arrived to Moscow, the train had a delay., my friend met me at the railway station..
i was really happy to see her!!! I'll write to you from her place!!! Tomorrow I shall go to the agency and embassy to find the all necessary information for the documents that I need to fly to you. I'll write to you everything about it!!! Probably I shall call you when i receive the visa and all the other documents. Today I am very tired of Moscow. now it's very late in Moscow and my dear i'll to go bath and sleep!!! Hope to hear from you very soon!!! By the way please leave me your telephone number on which i can call you!!!
I kiss you!!!!
Mariya.

From: Chris <coldbastrd@xxxxx.com>
Sent: Monday, January 31 2:08 PM
To: Mariya <girl_1980@xxxxx.com>
Subject: [RE: Hi again Curly]

Dearest Gods, I bang head against walls now. BANG BANG BANG! Why are you not listening to me? Are you deaf or something? I tells you over and over again, do not come here. So listen to me already! You are there in Moscow now. You are to set up parameter and cover all of city. You are like white op's soldier of fortune. Aren't you Russians trained for combating and special op's? When you go to embassy, you are to enlist help of governments there to help find Larisa. It is of national importance! There is no time for baths. There is no time for sleeping. You need to strike now while irons are hot!

Speaking of hot, I have arrived here in Long Bitch in state of Cuntiforu. Stranger man drops me by sea port. This is very convenient. I walk around sea port till I find mighty ship that can cross Pacifier Ocean! It is called Teetanic. I attach the photo. This is the big ship! I can certainly cross ocean in this and be safe. So I go onto boat and walks around. I make way to front of ship. I spread my arms out like I am flying across ocean! I am the king of the world! I attach the photo. Suddenly though, I feel the rumbles in the tummy. Oh nos! I run to bathrooms! Oh I have eaten some not so good things. I am on the toilets all day! I didn't attach the photo. You do not need to see such things. So I am here and I have nothing better to do so I write a poem. Would you like to listen? Here we go:

All the poops are brown,
and the t/p is grey.
I've been on the toilet,
for the entire day.
I ate some crap,
and now my butt has to pay.
Cuntiforu Dreamsin'
from the lavatory.

Stopped into a store,
I passed along the way.
I got me a slurpee,
and some beef jerky.

Now my tummy is rumblin',
and I got the squirties.
Cuntiforu Dreamsin'
from the lavatory.

All the poops are brown,
and the t/p is grey.
I've been on the toilet,
for the entire day.

It looks like something,
off a school cafeteria tray.
Cuntiforu Dreamsin'
from the lavatory.

So this is my day for most part. I go to flush toilets. We have a problems! Toilet begins to make the overflow! I attach the photo. Oh no this is the problems. I runaway from bathroom. I am noticing that ship has not left dock and is slowly going downwards. Oh no! The Teetanic is sinking! I get off of boat! I attach the photo. Oh what a great tragedies! I am lucky I get off ship before it slips below waters of the bay. I am not having the good luck with this water. Maybe it is because my soul is on fire with love for Larisa and water is opposite of fire. I speaks to man on street and he tells me it would be easier to cross to Russia from Alasska. Ah yes! I remembers! The chief tells me I need to go there! So I need to head to the north. I will write you more as I go. DO NOT COME HERE! You stay there and find Larisa. Ok I go now as it finishes. Do not try to kiss me anymore. I am already sick as I tells to you.
Curly

THE TEETANIC

I'M THE KING OF THE WORLD!

OH NO!!!!!!!!!!!!!!!!!!

THE TEETANIC SINKS!

From: Chris <coldbastrd@xxxxx.com>
Sent: Monday, January 31 2:10 PM
To: Larisa <gilkakisska@xxxxx.com>
Subject: [RE: No Subject]

Hello My sweet Larisa. It has been such the long time since we speaks. I miss you soooo soooo very much. I have the good news though. I have joined into partnership with ugly woman who lives there in the Russia. She goes to Moscow to find you! I am hoping that she finds you quickly and that you are alright. If I am to find the people that take you away from me, I will certainly make them go smash! I have come very far and not much further I go to come to you. I have such stories of my adventures. I have meet people and done so many things. My favorite is hanging with the Elvis. He is not fat anymore! He still eats a lot. He give me his favorite food and I will bring to you. It is the hot beef. When I see you, I will give you the hot beef injection. I attach the photo. So I come to the finish now. I must flush toilet as person stands outside door and is knocking constant. Please my love, tell me you are ok and not dead. I wait to hear your words!
Forever and always your love,
Curly

TOWER ISLE'S
3 JAMAICAN STYLE
Patties
TOWER ISLE'S
HOT BEEF
0g Trans Fat

From: Mariya <girl_1980@xxxxx.com>
Sent: Tuesday, February 1 4:10 AM
To: Chris <coldbastrd@xxxxx.com>
Subject: [Hi again Curly]

Hello lovely Steve!
Today I have gone to the hospital and received the medical insuriance that I can arrive to your country. I have ordered the fast visa it is travelling visa in the travel agency but it costs more expensive, but it will be registered much faster than usual. My visa will be approved by embassy while there is a document registration. It will be approved 100 (my visa will be valid for 90days) when I bring air tickets to the agency. Please tell me how long i can stay at your place, to reserve air tickets??? Tomorrow I'll go to the airport and order air tickets. I shall tell you as soon as I buy air tickets.

Today my friend will show me city. It is very big. It's really beautiful!!! Probably we shall go to BOLSHOY THEATRE today, have you ever heard about it? Moscow it simply the giant. It has more than 15 000 000 persons who live in Moscow. I worry a bit of arrival to you. I've never been a broad!!! I'm really happy that very soon i'll see you!!! I think of you, my lovely. I have told my friend about us. She finds it romantic and wishes us a successful meeting. So my dear i have to go now, i kiss you and i'm looking forward to our meeting!!!
P.S.
Do not forget to send me the information that I asked you to reserve the air tickets.
I send you an air kiss, my fine man!

From: Chris <coldbastrd@xxxxx.com>
Sent: Tuesday, February 1 1:08 PM
To: Mariya <girl_1980@xxxxx.com>
Subject: [RE: Hi again Curly]

Hi Mariya,
Tells to me, who is this Steve? Are you working with him to help find Larisa? Please send to me his information. You are becoming the starry eyed googley in love with the Curly. This is not good. If I work with man, there will be no such chance of the nonsensicals. Besides I do not knowing how you are falling in the love with Curly. You say you have never been a broad which would be meaning you are the man. I can understand this by looking at your photos. It makes the sense now. No I do not know what BOLSHOY THEATRE is. You do not have to scream it. My hearing works just fine. Why is it when people are talking to another persons who speaks a different language, they yell? As though maybe if they yell, they pound the words into other persons head and then they will understand the language they are speaking? Ok so if I use this maybe you understanding my language. DO NOT COME HERE! There you understanding now? Should I yell it louder?

So speakings of theaters, today I am in Hollywerd! This is land of theatre, actors, and the movies. I go to Chinesa Man Theatre. I attach the photo. There you can see the pawprints and footy prints of all the Hollywerd stars. Like Humpy Booger, John Wayne Gacy, Marilyn Theho, and Gary Pooper. I am looking around at all the pawprints and people recognize me! They say, hey you are the Curly from the peanut butter. I say yes of cource! They say, you put the pawprints into the floor too! So they take me over to wet floor and I put hands into floor. I attach the photo.

So I ride around some more and look at all the sites in city. Person comes up to me and says, hey I know you, would you like to come on our tv show? I say, ok, I will use opportunity to talk about Larisa. So they take me to studio and put me on the Coco talk show. I attach the photo. He is silly red haired step childrens of late night talkings. I talk abouts my travels, my Little Red Rocket, all the people I have meeting, and places I have been. I make a plead to all of America to help me find Larisa. Do you get the Coco show there?

Maybe it is seen on the tv's there and she will be released by whatever bad peoples have taken her! After my speakings, they have performer on show. She is Katy Pussy. She squirts the cream from her milky bits. I attach the photo. This gives the Curly some botherment of physicality. What a show!

After show is finishing, I am in back rooms and I show the peoples my Little Red Rocket. There is woman there who wants to ride my Little Red Rocket. No you cannot ride my Little Red Rocket! I tells to her. This is only for Larisa to ride on. However you can look at it and admire its beauty and strength. Perhaps you can give it a little polish. So she gives my Rocket a polishing. It felt good to get the polishing. I have been neglecting my Little Red Rocket and it is dirty and a bit worn. She uses her hands and makes it clean and look new again.

I nearly forgets! I go to post office and send the special formula peanut butter to the Chief for safe keeping. I don't want to lose it! I go to the hotel room after all of excitement. I am tired. It is long day and more longer journey. I am woken in middle of night by man knocking at door. I wire computer to security cameras outside room. I have to be careful and watch out for the Man in black. I look at camera. It is strange man. He keeps saying, may I speaks to you about Scientology? I attach the photo.

No, I say. He keeps knocking and asking. He is ranting and raving about aliens and all kinds of strangeness. I say, go away, leave me alone! He says, I will huffs and puffs and let myself in! He grabs fire ax from wall and begins to smash door! I attach the photo! I run to bathroom and make the escape from window! Cuntiforu is strangest place yet the Curly has visited. I find place to sleep for night that I hope am safe from Scientology man and Man in black.

So, I come to the finish now. You take the monies you are spending on making the trip here and use to make posters for finding Larisa. I am counting on you and Steve to do this. Please do not let me down. I speaks to you again soon. Do not air kiss me again. You are making it hard to breathe.
Curly

I GO TO CHINESA MAN THEATER

I PUT PAWPRINTS INTO FLOOR

I GO ON THE COCO SHOW.

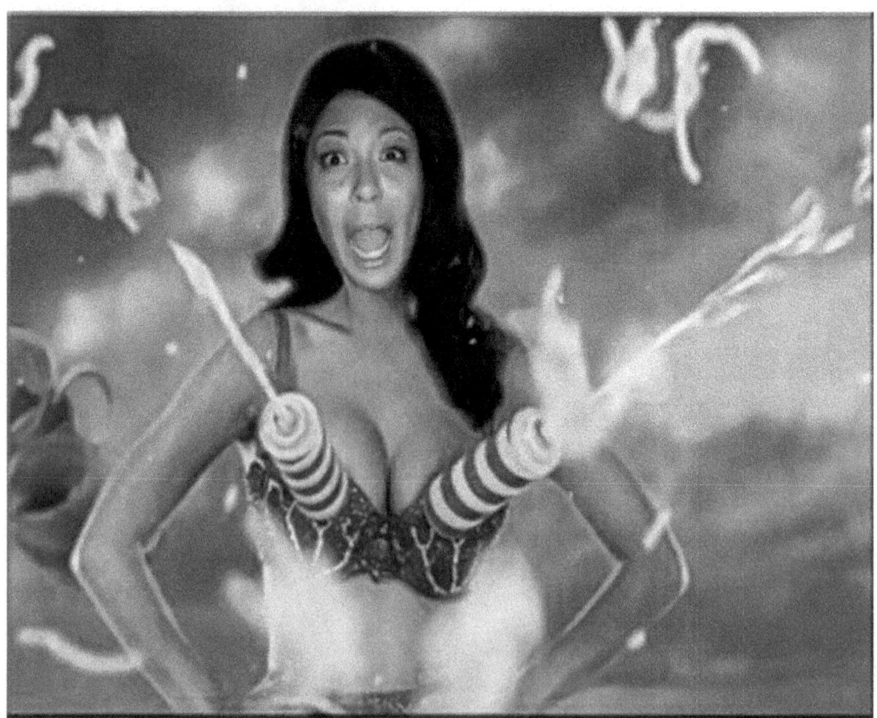

SQUIRTING CREAM FROM MILKY BITS.

MAY I SPEAKS TO YOU ABOUT SCIENTOLOGY?

SCIENTOLOGY MAN IS CRAZY!!!

From: Mariya <girl_1980@xxxxx.com>
Sent: Wednesday, February 2 2:55 AM
To: Chris <coldbastrd@xxxxx.com>
Subject: [Hi again Curly]

Hello dear Curly!!!!
How are you today? Hope great. I have good mood my visa soon will be ready and then I can fly to you. You know when I read your letters my heart begin to beat fastly and more strongly. It feels heat and tenderness. You know I never tested anything similar and sometimes begin to think that I fall in love with you. I did not tell to you in the last letter that I yesterday saw beautiful dream about us. I saw that I ran on a high grass on a field. I ran long and the longer I ran the more strongly I felt heat on the body. Then in the distance I have seen your silhouette and began to run faster. I have approached to you, have taken your hands, then have strongly embraced you and you have presented me a sweet sweet kiss. I have woken up from it and my body was damp. When I had boyfriend I never saw dreams about him. And about you saw...
I never thought that I shall test to you such feelings, but speak that the love comes suddenly and quickly. So there comes the present love. And you would like to appear in my dream and to present me a kiss?
OK, I shall finish my letter and to wait for your answer soon.
Your Mariya.

From: Chris <coldbastrd@xxxxx.com>
Sent: Friday, February 4 11:41 PM
To: Mariya <girl_1980@xxxxx.com>
Subject: [RE: Hi again Curly]

Hello against Mariya,
I am good today. So please tell to Curly about these dreams. You are getting dampness in the night times? Where are you getting the dampness? All over the body or in the childrens production area? When I was becoming the man, I use to get dampness in the night times too when I thought about the womens. Mama would be washing the clothings and she would find my underwears. She would say, Curly, why is your underwears crunchy like the crunchy Curly peanut butter? And I would say, mama, it is because I get the dampness from the dreams making in the middle of the nights. She tells to me, Curly, you are to wear the rubber underwears so to not make the crunchy underwears. Does your underwears become crunchy from the dampness? You should wear the rubber underwears.

So I tells to you about exciting news! I have arrived here in San Franfreako. It is hilly city in state of Cuntiforu. I am not knowing that Cuntiforu is so big! I am wandering around city and see the parade. WHOOPIE! It is a parade! I like the parade! I join the parade as it is going down street. I attach the photo. Do you like the parades? This parade is not so great. There is no floats or march bands. Only people carry color flags and chanting that they are happy with themselves. So I walk with parade for some time and then I stop to get a cheesyburger. I have learned to stay away from the slurpees and beef jerky! My underbottoms are still the sore! This is not the exciting news.

I am sitting there eating cheesyburgers and I am noticing that black car is across street. I attach the photo. I have seen car before. It is following me. What am I to do? This must be Man in black! I take out phone and call Napster. I have meets him many pages ago in story. You do not know him as I tells the Larisa. I have not known you at this time. Anyway, he answers phone...Hello Curly, are you in trouble? I tells to him, yes! I think I am in trouble with the Man in black! He tells to me to turn to my right....no my other right. He is there standing there with his hot rod hanging out. He appears from the nowhere! I attach the photo. I run to Napster. He says, Curly, that is the Man in black. Quick, take my hot rod and go! I jump on Napster's hot rod. I attach the photo. I driveway!

I am looking in mirror. Black car chase me! I see man put head out of car. Napster is right! Look out! It's the Man in black! I attach the photo! He is shooting gun! I must get away! Streets are very hilly. We go up and down and all around! I almost crash! I attach the photo! So many people and cars in street. It is hard to driveway! Get out of the way peoples! I must go faster! I attach the photo! This is the craziness! Man in black keeps coming and coming! Will he ever stop! I just want to get to my Larisa! Why can he not understanding??!!!?? He takes out the gun and shoots at me again! I attach the photo! He tries to kill the Curly! Why must he do this??!!

We drive outside of city. He is catching me! He comes along side of me and smashes me! It is just like the Nascar crazies! I attach the photo! I am driving for the life. You are saying, Curly, how is this the exciting news? Well is my adventure not giving you the dampness? If not, you are about to become creamy with dampness. We are side to side. He is smashing me. I look along side of road. I see there out of the nowhere, it is Napster! He shoots guns at Man in black! I attach the photo! He must have hitting Man in black. Man in black goes flying off road! I attach the photo. He crashes into side of building!

BIG EXPLOSIONS! MAN IN BLACK GO SMASH!!! IT IS THE END OF THE MAN IN BLACK!

Can you believe this? I am free from Man in black! He cannot chase me! He cannot catch me! He cannot eat cheesyburgers or apple pie or beef jerky or drink coffee or take a nap or write a letter or visit his sick aunt in the hospitals or take a vacation trip to Mutant World or go on safari journey in Africa or finish that crossword puzzle from the newspaper or write a poem or watch the stars on a starry night or participating in game show on the tv. He cannot do anything except be dead! Because he is dead! DEAD DEAD DEAD! I SPIT ON HIS GRAVE! SPIT!!!!

So you see, this is the excitement news! Is it not wonderful? You must agree! I give hot rod back to Napster. I do not know how to make the repayment for your helps I tells to him. He says, it is alright, you just go to the Russia and find your love! He takes me back to city and I get my Little Red Rocket. I turn to say goodbye, and he is gone! Like the fart in wind! Maybe he goes to see Elvis? I am not knowing.

I am continuing journey. I must finish now. Any lucks finding Larisa? Are you and Steve finding anything? Please tells to me. I really miss my Larisa. So much like you are not knowing. It is ok for you to dreams about me and I am kissing you in dreams because it is not the real life and I am not doing such things in the realness. If it gives you the dampness, this is ok with the Curly. I will talk to you soon and please have update on your findings for me.
Kissing you but only in dreams.
Curly

IT IS A PARADE. WHOOPY!!

BLACK CAR FOLLOWS ME.

NAPSTER APPEARS FROM NOWHERES WITH HOT ROD!

I USE NAPSTER'S HOT ROD.

LOOK OUT! IT'S MAN IN BLACK!

I ALMOST CRASH!

I MUST GO FASTER! GET OUT OF THE WAYS!

MAN IN BLACK SHOOTS AT ME!!

WE SMASH THE CARS LIKE IN NASCAR!

NAPSTER APPEARS ON SIDE OF ROAD AND SHOOTS AT MAN IN BLACK

MAN IN BLACK GOES FLYING OFF ROAD!!

IT IS THE END OF THE MAN IN BLACK!!

From: Mariya <girl_1980@xxxxx.com>
Sent: Saturday, February 5 3:29 AM
To: Chris <coldbastrd@xxxxx.com>
Subject: [Hi again Curly]

Hello my dearest Curly!!!
How are you today???
I could not write to you earlier because yesterday all day long I was in travel agency. And now I have good news. I can fly to you next weekend. I'm so happy that before our meeting there was one step. I am so exited before our meeting, it is my first trip and I am afraid a little... How you are about our meeting? What do you want to do in the first day of our meeting? In the beginning of week I shall call to you. I shall be online and we is detailed can discuss details of my arrival. OK, hope see your letter later.
Your and only your Mariya.

From: Chris <coldbastrd@xxxxx.com>
Sent: Monday, February 7 1:50 PM
To: Mariya <girl_1980@xxxxx.com>
Subject: [RE: Hi again Curly]

Hello Mariya. Let me asks you question. When you were small childrens, did you find little pieces of paint by window sill? Did you eat them? I am almost certain of this. I attach photo so you can see what I am askings. You see because you keep sayings you are coming here. How many times have I told you not to now? 100 billion? If you are coming, I am hoping that you have Larisa in a suitcases because that is reason you are in Moscow! Our first meeting? If you have Larisa with you, I will shake your hand and thank you for bringing her to me, then I will give you 5 dollars and you can go play in traffic. If you do not have the Larisa, well then I will be very cross and put you back on plane to Moscow to find her! So you should be afraid if you have not found her as you have to deal with raft of Curly!

So now I tells you about days. I am tired today. I stay up late to watch Super Knoll. What is this you are asking? Well you see every year the best professional chess teams gather on grassy knoll in Texaco and have a chess tournament. I am aware that you have the chest in Russia but in America, it is played different. In America we play full contact chess. It is great excitement! I attach a photo. I am very happy because my favorite team plays. They are the Fudge Packers. I feel brothership with Packers. You see when they are not playing chess, they work in factory packing fudge. I attach the photo. This is like job Curly has as I pack the peanut butter! So you can see why I would like this team so much. I am number 1 fan! When you are fan, you wear fudge on head like a hat. I attach the photo of me in indoor full contact chess arena. They play against the Stealers. These are bad mens. They get name because they go around robbing banks and peoples. I attach the photo.

I am so happy because the Fudge Packers win the game! HOORAY! But I am so tired. You know chess tournaments can take a long time. This went on for 16 hours. What a long game.

So today I am in state of Oregasm. There is lot of trees and I can see ocean. But not much around besides this. This state is known as "The Beaver State". It is true. You can googles it on the interwebs! State gets name because the womens like to keep beavers as pets. Just about every woman here has a big hairy beaver. They make the fashion statements by walking around with their big hairy beavers out for everyone to see. I attach the photo. I have seen brown beavers, red beavers, blonde beavers, black beavers, and even beavers that have been shaved bald!

I have meets a woman here named Wynona. She allows me to stay the night with her. She recognizes me from the Curly peanut butter jar. Wynona has a big brown beaver and she strokes it all the time. I tried to get close to it, but that critter did try to bite. I attach the photo of Wynona's big brown beaver. Her beaver is very hairy and untamed. It only likes it when she strokes it. I say to her, I would like to touch your beaver. But she says, my beaver only likes to be touched in a certain way. So I am thinking to myself, hmmm how can I stroke her beaver? I have gots it! I feed her beaver some of my hot beef. The beaver LOVES my hot beef! I sit on couch and her beaver lets me stroke it for hours while it takes my hot beef. The only problems is after while it gets all wet and sticky so she has to go wash her beaver. Now beaver is clean and fluffy again. I am thinking her beaver is mean at first, but as it turns, her beaver is nice, warm, and gently. It almost purrs like a pussy cat when you stroke it.

So I am going to come to the finishing. I cannot stroke all day. Time is wasting and Larisa is missing! I am riding on now. What is the status of your search for Larisa? Please give me the update. I hope you have the good news! I am getting closer and closer to Russia. I can feel it. I shall talk to you soon.

Curly

DID YOU EAT THESE WHEN YOU WERE SMALL CHILDRENS?

SUPER KNOLL

XLV

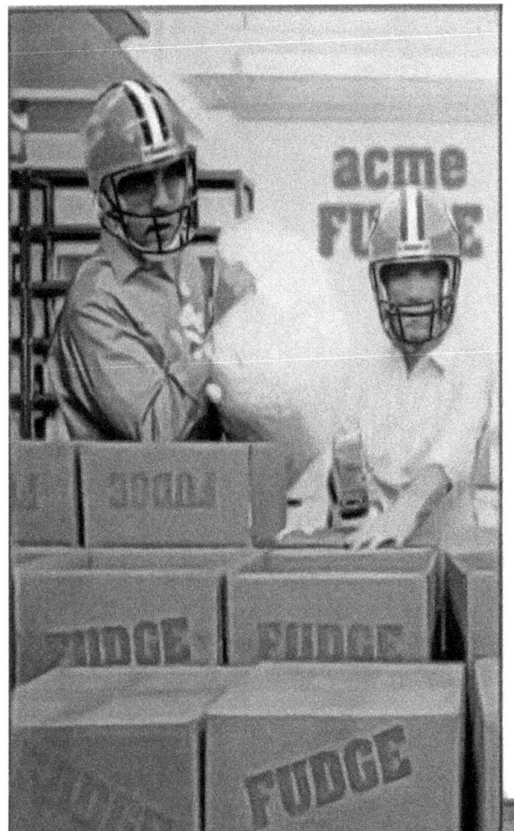

THE

FUDGE

PACKERS

GO

FUDGE

PACKERS!

STEALERS ARE BAD MEN.

WOMAN WITH HAIRY BEAVER.

WYNONA HAS A BIG BROWN BEAVER.

From: Mariya <girl_1980@xxxxx.com>
Sent: Tuesday, February 8 6:54 AM
To: Chris <coldbastrd@xxxxx.com>
Subject: [Hi again Curly]

Hello my dearest Curly!!!!
How are you??? I want you to read this letter attentively. I hope you understand that I have no perfect English and you will understand what I write you. I have two news. One is good another is not so. I shall begin with good. Today I went in the airport and has bought the air tickets on 9 February I shall send you later all information about it. Now other news. Don't worry. When I have bought the air tickets, the employee of the airport has approached me. He said that for being in your country I shall require funds of travel. Employee said that when I shall pass customs control I will be asked about it. He informed me about a rule of entrance in your country. Equivalent 20 US Dollars for each day of being in your country. I have a vacation for 30 days and it means that I shall require 600 US dollars of money to arrive to you. My visa operates in territory of your country in a current of 90 days. Dear inform you you can help me this sum of funds? I only need to show these funds at customs and we can meet you. As soon as I will arrive to you to the airport I to return all funds to you at the airport. OK, dearest today there was a heavy day. I shall go to sleep and tomorrow I wait for your answer.
I KISS and MISS YOU!!!
Your and only your Mariya.

From: Chris <coldbastrd@xxxxx.com>
Sent: Tuesday, February 8 1:15 PM
To: Mariya <girl_1980@xxxxx.com>
Subject: [RE: Hi again Curly]

Dearest dipshit Mariya. I have made understanding that the KGB performed medical experimentations studies at one time. Did you take part in such studies? I am sure of this. Where exactly do you expect to be flying to? Do you think that when you are near where I am being that you can parachute off of plane? I do not believe this is possibility. Do you think that I am still in Cuntiforu or Oregasm? I am not. You do not paying attention very well. You must suffering from HDAD...Head up De Ass Disorder.

It is fact that I am not in those places any longer. Today I am in Washinghun. I tells to you history of Washinghun. Many many years ago, before the Curly was squiggle tadpole in nuts sack universe, there was a man named Altoid the Hun. He is from Chinesa and ruled lands there with heavy hand. I attach the photo. He was mean and ruthless and would cut peoples in half if they looked at his face. He wanted to expand empire of Hun so he comes from Chinesa to America. He ends up in lands now known as Washinghun. Before time, these lands were called Bob. So he comes to marching into towns and peoples there say, my Gods, what is the smell? It is Altoid the Hun! They say to him, what is wrong with you? Do you not wipe the underbottoms after making the squirties? Do you not put the pit sticks into the underarms? You smell like dead man who's died swimming in river of vomit! He says, I do not know this. I have no senses in the nose. The peoples say, come Altoid, we will wash you and make your appearances more presentable. So they take him to the baths and wash him. I attach the photo. They cut off his beard. Gives him a haircut and new suit. He becomes new and improved Altoid the Hun. I attach the photo.

He thanks the peoples and later cuts off their heads. But that is story for a different day. They now call state Washinghun for the peoples ability to turn shit into shinola. Now if you are in Washinghun, they have automated Hun washes which is a lot easier that hand washing. You can even get your car and Hun washed at the same time and this saves monies. I attach the photo.

Washinghun is also known for its musical cultures. It was started long ago by the lumberjacks who would sing while they cut down the trees. There are many trees in Washinghun. So the one day, a man named Jimi Headtrix a great lumberjack, gets a brilliant thought in his head. He thinks, I wire my axe with guitar strings and microphone. This way I can sing, play guitar, and cut wood at same time. How brilliant! I attach the photo. This is why electric guitars are also known as an axe. Jimi starts whole lumberjack music revolutions that spawns many lumberjack bands from Washinghun. There was Nerdvana, Sound Ganja, Alice in Hanes, and Pearl Jelly. I am fan of Nerdvana. I will sing to you now Nerdvana song:

Load up your saws and bring your friends,
We're going to the forest again.
We cut down trees every day,
We're going to make those trees freakin' pay!

Cut the, cut the, cut the wood.
Cut the, cut the, cut the wood.
Cut the, cut the, cut the wood.
Cut the, cut the, cut the....

And we're cutting, and were swinging,
And we do this, while we're singing.
We're Nerdvana, we use an axe.
That's because, we are lumberjacks!

A cedar, a redwood
A sequoia, my maple
Yeah, hey, yay

I use a rock to sharpen my axe.
You better not have a problem with that.
We eat flapjacks and many spuds,
and wear hats just like Elmer Fudd.

Elmer, Elmer, Elmer Fudd.
Elmer, Elmer, Elmer Fudd.
Elmer, Elmer, Elmer Fudd.
Elmer, Elmer, Elmer...

And we're cutting, and were swinging,
And we do this, while we're singing.
We're Nerdvana, we use an axe.
That's because, we are lumberjacks!

A cedar, a redwood
A sequoia, my maple
Yeah, hey, yay

Some tree huggers say we're vile,
But I guess it really makes me smile.
It's hard, it's hard just like wood,
If you're a lumberjack, it's easily understood.

Under, under, understood.
Under, under, understood.
Under, under, understood.
Under, under, under...

And we're cutting, and were swinging,
And we do this, while we're singing.
We're Nerdvana, we use an axe.
That's because, we are lumberjacks!

A cedar, a redwood
A sequoia, my maple
Yeah, hey, yay
Fresh cut timber
Fresh cut timber
Fresh cut timber
Fresh cut timber
Cut timber

Do you like my singing? It is great song! Anywho's, you are looking for the monies. Why do you need my monies? You are not to come here. I do not know how to pound this into head without a hammer. If I use the hammer of sledge I think it would pound into the brain. I have checked my pockets. I have 13 dollars, 12 cents, 2 Kuntouchy Boiled Chicken coupons and 6 fruity jellies. I attach the photo.

I can send 4 dollars, 6 cents, 1 coupon, and 3 fruity jellies. Will this be of satisfaction? I am giving you almost half of everything I have in the hopes that you have found Larisa and are making the surprises to me by bringing her. Is this true? Please tells to me. I must make the finishing now. I await your answer in the daytimes. Remember, I kiss you but only in dreams. I would not do this in real. Curly

ALTOID THE HUN

ALTOID THE HUN BEING WASHED

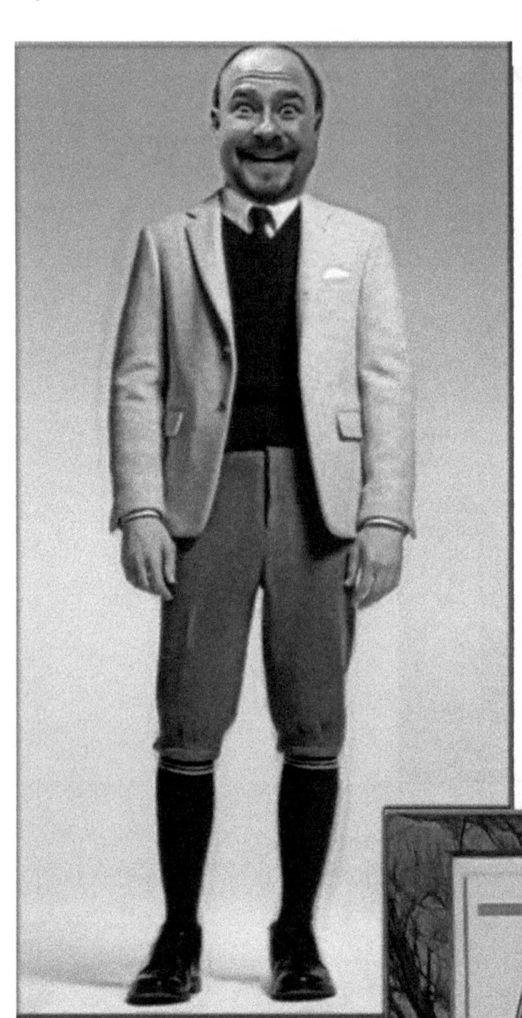

NEW
AND
IMPROVED
ALTOID
THE
HUN

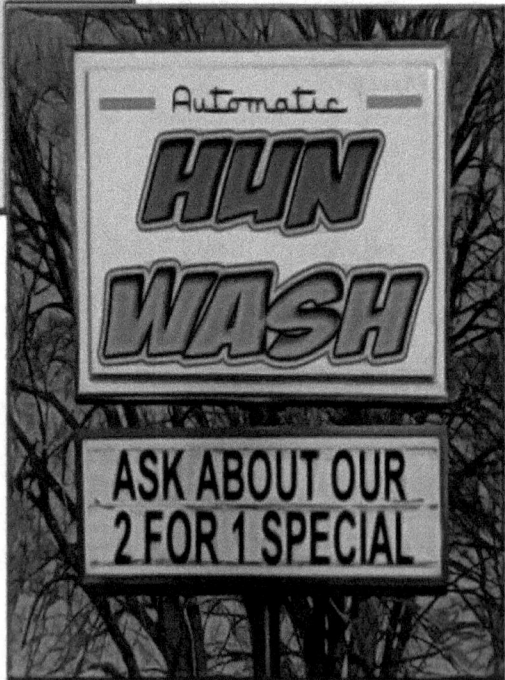

JIMI HEADTRIX THE LUMBERJACK

MONIES

From: Mariya <girl_1980@xxxxx.com>
Sent: Wednesday, February 9 6:22 AM
To: Chris <coldbastrd@xxxxx.com>
Subject: [Hello my darling Curly]

Hello my darling Curly ! I am glad to see your letter to me. Curly understand that will not let out me from the country while I not to show at customs 600$. This money will be the proof for my government, that I have them on residing at your country. I tried to find today these funds, but unfortunately I could not make it.. I really had only one hope you. If you help me I can to return you all money at the airport as soon as I to arrive to you. Curly I constantly think of us and I very much to want that our meeting with you has taken place. I will well finish on it the letter. I look forward your answer.
Yours and only Maria.

From: Chris <coldbastrd@xxxxx.com>
Sent: Wednesday, February 9 2:42 PM
To: Mariya <girl_1980@xxxxx.com>
Subject: [RE: Hello my darling Curly]

Hello Mariya. Tells to me, when you were a small childrens, did you travel to Berlin? By the chance did a wall fall on your head there? I am sure of it. You are saying that our meeting has taken place. Where did this happen exactly? In your silly dreams? I have no memory of it and I believe that this is where you are thinking. Remember, you can only touch Curly in dreams. Not in the real.

Speaking of the dreams, my dreams are becoming true. I am so close now to Russia I can smell its air. I have come now into Canookada. It is big state just above Washinghun. They have a border there that I have made the crossing. I was afraid they would not let me cross. But I am to find out, it is easy! All I had to do was give them beer and they let me cross! I didn't have to show any papers or monies or anything. I attach the photo. Unfortunate I have spent most monies left on beer now.

So I am walking along in towns and men stop next to me. They tell me that they are brothers and ask if I need a ride. I attach the photo. This is great relief to Curly as feets are tired from walking and riding Little Red Rocket. They tells to me that they will take me all the way to Alasska border. This is the great news! It is there I cross to Russia! They tells to me though that they need to have some payment for doing so. I buy a case of beer and this makes the satisfactions of payment. I bring beer to brothers and they begin to fight over beer. It makes me giggly. I attach the photo.

We are driving along and I am learning that Canookada has its own words and special languages. I am learning that you must end every sentence with eh here. I am also learning that they call each other names of things that you might find in garden. I give the example. Eh take off you hoser eh! Stop being a hosehead or I'll steam roll ya eh! These are things that I am learning. We laugh, drink beer, and they teach me song of Canookada. I attach the photo. I will sing to you now. They are singing the In Canookada part and I am singing rest.

In Canookada!
The rocks and fields and streams.
In Canookada!
They have lots of trees.
In Canookada!
Home of the Great Gretzky.
In Canookada!
He once played hockey.
In Canookada!
And don't forget John Candy.
In Canookada!
He once played Gus Polinski (Polka King of the MidWest)
In Canookada!
Did I mention they have trees?
In Canookada!
Home of the Maple Leaves.
In Canookada!
Partly they are Frenchies.
In Canookada!
They're not really known for their cheese.
In Canookada!
But they have moosen and geese.
In Canookada!

Lots of snow for your skis.
In Canookada!
Your beer will probably freeze.
In Canookada!
Michael J. Fox, he's got Parkinson's disease.
In Canookada!
For hockey they are devotee's.
In Canookada!
A place for our draft dodging escapes.
In Canookada!
One trip there and you'll be pleased.
In Canookadaaaaa ahhhhh ahhhhh ahhhh ahhhh ahhhh ahhhh!
CANOOKADA!

You are liking song. Yes I knowing. I attach the photos from parts of song so you are knowing what we are singing. This is great fun trip. It is happiest I have been in long time. This is sign of great things to come and happiest that I will share with Larisa. Do you agree? I am to make the finishing now. Many more miles to cover and songs to sing. I will send you monies but only if you are to telling me you found Larisa. Is this the truths? I talk to you soons. No kissing for you this time even in dreams. You need to live in the real.
Curly

IT'S EASY TO GET INTO CANOOKADA

BROTHERS ASK IF I NEED A RIDE.

BROTHERS FIGHT OVER BEER.

WE SING CANOOKADA SONG.

ROCKS AND FIELDS AND STREAMS.

CANOOKADA HAS LOTS OF TREES.

CHAPTER 10:
RING OF THE KING

Ring of the King

From: Mariya <girl_1980@xxxxx.com>
Sent: Thursday, February 10 4:24 AM
To: Chris <coldbastrd@xxxxx.com>
Subject: [Hello my darling Curly]

Hello my darling Curly! Excuse that I did not write you yesterday in days off I had no access to the Internet! I have phoned up to the travel agency and they have told me that they have made all that I ordered tickets aboard the plane and the visa, and then they have told me that everything else my problems! I asked at the airport about my situation which have taken place with me and they have answered me that at them constantly such situations each day and not on time! At the airport to me speak show yours 600$ and all will be good! I would ask that at the airport to me distances of the person which talks in English, but they have told me that at them a lot of work and they have no time to be engaged in me! I so need all to be not liked my loved Curly! My love I so want to appear to you near to you to give you the tenderness! I to you shall bring this money and to return to you them at once as soon as you will meet me from the plane! I went to bank to me do not lend there money!
Curly that to me to do?
Write to me!
Yours and only Mariya.

From: Chris <coldbastrd@xxxxx.com>
Sent: Friday, February 11 1:33 PM
To: Mariya <girl_1980@xxxxx.com>
Subject: [RE: Hello my darling Curly]

Hello Mariya. In Russia, do they have the heavy metal fry pans that you use to cook the eggs? The ones that weigh 20 pounds? When you were small childrens, did mother hit you in face with pan? I am sure of this. How can you sit there and only think of self in the times like this? You beg me for monies like beggar on street. Is it only about you and what you are wanting? Did you ever stop to thinks what I am wanting? What I am needing? You want the monies so you can fly around like Hollywerd star and drink caviar and eat champagne and swim on beach. I offer to you half of everything I have and this is not good enough for you. Let me tell you about days and then you feel Curly's emotions.

I have made the arrival here in Alasska. Oh you say, this is the fantastic news. You would think so. So close to Russia I am coming now. This is place where Chief says I must go. I am riding Little Red Rocket through towns and places. The mountains and rivers and trees are such the sites to see. I come to town in the nighttimes and sit for a rest while I eat fruit gummies and refreshments. I am hearing sound of music in the distances. Now this is late in the nighttimes and there is no one to be seeing. I get up from bench and go to see where music is coming from. In the distances under freeway overpasses, is car. It sits there running. I am thinking, who leaves car under freeway? I call out, who is this in distance? I attach the photo. Nothing happens. Then a few moments later, car begins to move from underpasses and out onto road. It stops. I see the window go down. A voice comes from out of car. Well if it isn't my dear old friend Curly. The voice sayings. Do I know you? I says. Well sure you do Curly. The voice speakings.

There was that time in Texaco....that fun we had in Alibaba...and let's not forgetting Cuntiforu...we had a real blast, remember? I am not knowing this persons. Could it be Tornado Tommy? The Scientology man? He was crazy! Who could this be? I am asking, please I do not knowing who you are, you show to me the faces! Oh come now Curly, you hurt my feelings that you don't know who I am. The voice speaks. You want to see my face? I will show to you my face.

I see in the shadows the head appearing from the car. IT'S THE MAN IN BLACK!!! HE IS LIVING!!!!!! His face is melted and disgustment! I attach the photo. How are you living? You are to be dead!!! I sees it with own eyes!! I say. Oh come now Curly, Man in black says, is this any way to greet your dearest old friend? I am very disappointed. He says. Well um, it is great to see you here, I am hoping you are enjoying your vacation times in Alasska, I say. I really should be getting going. I'll just be getting on my bike and moving along. I say. He asks, is that your ride there? The Little Red Rocket is it? Well I want you to meet my ride. I call her, Big Red. He revs up the engine. He turns on the lights. I am blinded by the light! I attach the photo! Big Red comes after me! I jump over wall to get aways! He almost hits me! I attach the photo!

I run through town. I could not get back to Little Red Rocket before he tries to hit me. I must get back to Little Red and make the escape I am thinking. Before I am knowing, I see lights of Big Red again and he is chasing me! I run for my life! I attach the photo! I make the double back to Little Red. This is the chances to get away. I jump on and ride like there is no tomorrow. Because if he gets me, there might not be no tomorrow for Curly I am thinking. I pedal and pedal and pedal. Go Little Red Go!!!! Man in black nearly hits me with Big Red. He goes crashing into station for gas fillings. There is big explosions! I attach the photo! This is it! He cannot make the survival! I watch as station burns. But only moments soon later, Big Red pulls out of station. Big Red is on fire!

He comes after me with car on fire!!! I attach the photo! How can anyone make the survival of fire? How can Big Red be moving? I am thinking that Man in black is Satan man himself!! I attach the photo.

I ride and ride and pedal and pedal. We ride out of town and onto lonely highways of nothingness. He is catching up with me. I try to get aways! But he still keeps coming! I attach the photo! Suddenly, Little Red has tire explosions. I am slowing and steering bars are wobbling. He is right behind me! I jump of Little Red Rocket diving to side of road. Little Red goes down! MAN IN BLACK RUNS OVER LITTLE RED ROCKET!!! He drives away and I watch Little Red Rocket burn! I attach the photo! I wait till I do not see the flame car anymore. I run over to Little Red Rocket and put out flames. SHE IS DESTORYED! HOW CAN HE DO THIS TO ME!!! WHAT HAVE I EVER DONE TO HIM....BESIDES KILL HIM AND MAKE HIS FACE MELT!!!

I drag Little Red Rocket deep into the safety of the woods. The light of the new day makes the appearances and I am seeing how badly this is. Little Red Rocket is dead!!! I attach the photo. Her wheel is gone, her horns, and saddle bags, and streamers, and fairings are all melted and gone. Her chain is broken and frame is bent. I sit and cry by Little Red Rocket for hours. Through everything, she has been the one thing in life that I could always count on. She never hurt me...never asked monies of me...never made me sad...never made me cry. I always found in her happiness, love, and joy. Isn't that what the friend should be? But now she is gone....forever.

Just like everything in Curly life, it has been taken away from me. The dreams are crushed and turned to nightmares. I have no home. I have no job. My greatest friend is now gone. And my love, Larisa, she is gone now too. What is the meaning of life? Why are we here? We are like the rat in maze, always looking for the cheeses. I have come so far. I have made it to end of maze, and my cheeses have been taken away from me. Why must people hurt each other? Is this what the human is all about? I see no point to go forward. I cannot live the nightmare any longer. There is no point. I see no point in the life anymore. There is no more hope. It is all gone.

Goodbye,

Curly

WHO IS THIS IN DISTANCE?

IT'S THE MAN IN BLACK!!!!

I'M BLINDED BY THE LIGHT!

HE ALMOST HITS ME!

I RUN FOR MY LIFE!

BIG EXPLOSIONS!!

HE COMES AFTER ME WITH CAR ON FIRE!!!

MAN IN BLACK MUST BE SATAN HIMSELF!!!

I TRY TO GET AWAYS!!!

I WATCH LITTLE RED ROCKET BURN!!!

LITTLE RED ROCKET IS DEAD!!!!!

From: Mariya <girl_1980@xxxxx.com>
Sent: Saturday, February 12 4:52 AM
To: Chris <coldbastrd@xxxxx.com>
Subject: [Hello my darling Curly]

Hello my darling Curly! I'm sorry I could not write to you in recent days, I felt very unwell, I had a fever. It is very cold and I caught a cold. Today I felt a little better, my temperature is normal. And the first thing I went to write you. But I was shocked by what you wrote to me in his letter. Maybe you wrote it because of what you experienced or overcome with emotion. But I am very upset that you think of me such things. I have great desire was to write to you today. But I am devastated by what I read. I do not know what I should write to you today.
Your and your Mariya!

From: Chris <coldbastrd@xxxxx.com>
Sent: Tuesday, February 15 2:18 PM
To: Mariya <girl_1980@xxxxx.com>
Subject: [RE: Hello my darling Curly]

My apologies Mariya. Of course I have become overcome with emotion! My greatest friend has been dead! Wouldn't you fill with the emotionality as well with such news? I am sorry I have make the excusals of your character. But you must make the understanding that you keep asking for the monies while I am suffering in great sufferment. But all is not lost. You must find the seat to sit your underbottoms while I tells to you of my days.

I sat and cried by Little Red Rocket for hour upon hour. The day passes slowly till near the nighttimes. I thought about my life as whole, and I was thinking about how there was such unfulfillment. There are so many questions I have no answers to. My heart longs for love of Larisa and for family that we can be creating. I am admitting, I thinking of stopping it all and going to heaven to live with mama and papa. Then a man in cloak comes from behind the pine trees. I grab rock and make the preparations to fight for my life as I am thinking it is Man in black. He takes off his cloaked hood. It is not Man in black. I attach the photo. He says, I remember getting you that bike when you were small childrens. I am not understanding. I asks, who are you? My name is Adoy. He says. You are the man that Chief Chokesondeek tells to me to find in Alasska. I say. Ah the Chief, he is a good man. Adoy says. Come, gather up your things. We go to my cabin in the forest. I gather up all the pieces of Little Red Rocket and belongings and make trek in woods to cabin. We arrive at Adoy's cabin and I put Little Red pieces down outside. He invites me in. Come, you must be hungry. He says. I make stew of muskrats and gravy. The cabin is candlelit and dark.

But it is good solid cabin made of logs held together by moose excrementals. I sit at table and Adoy brings bowl of stew for myself and him. He sits down and we begin to eat stew. Tells to me. He asks. What did the Chief tells you about me? I says, he tells to me that I am to make journey to Alasska and find you. Did he tell you anything else? Adoy asks. No, this is all he tells to me. I say. You tells to me that you have gotten me Little Red Rocket when I was small children's. I say. What is meaning of this thing you say? With this, Adoy gets up from table and goes to bookshelf. He pulls large book from shelf and brings to table. He places it next to me.

It is heavy book with solid gold covers. The writing I cannot understanding on cover but it looks familiar. There are many things I must tells to you. Adoy says. Please open the book. He tells to me. I finish stew and open book. The candle light and light from fireplace illuminates the book pages in soft orange glowing. I do not understanding the writings, but it has many illustrations and pictures that I am seeing. Adoy says, this is the Book of Kings. It is the history of kingdom of Siberia that is given to every king of Siberia to use as journal for history keeping. It is like diary. He continues. Many years ago, before you or I or anyone taking the breath in the world today has been in world, there was a community in East Russia what is today known as Siberia. They were people who farmed and lived off the land. They traded food and services with each other. There was no war or famine. It was happy peaceful community. One day, a darkness spread across the land as dark invaders came to countryside. The dark invaders were the Ottoman Empire. I attach the photo. He continues. They came to take over the rich natural bounties of the land and enslave its people. But there was one man. A simple farmer named Victor Von Vadouchski. He did not approve of the dark invaders from Ottoman taking over his countryside. The Ottoman's were lazy. This is why they call the lazy chairs Ottoman's.

Victor decides to mount a rebellion against the invaders. He organizes groups of men from surrounding villages and meet in his barn. He says to them, how can we sit by and have these lazy invaders take over our land? Take our crops, work our men to deaths, make raping our women, enslaving our childrens!! Join me brothers, and we will rise up against these dark invaders and drive them out! Adoy continues. Victor organizes army of men. The blacksmiths make swords and armor. The women make heavy leather underclothing armors. The childrens prepare the horses and oxen. They do this in many months in the nighttimes so that Ottomans do not know what is coming.

On the 2nd Friday of May, Victor leads his new army against the Ottoman Empire. I attach the photo. Adoy goes on. There were many casualties on both sides. But the rebellion fought and fought. It was their country in which they fight for. I attach the photo. Adoy makes more story. Victor and his army drive out the dark invaders and wins the battle! The people rejoice! They pillage the bodies of the dead Ottoman invaders, removing their gold teeth and armor and burn their bodies. They take the gold teeth and melt them down into the form of a solid gold ring. They present the ring to Victor.

They proclaim, Victor Von Vadouchski, you have brought us out of slavery and freed us from our captors. With this ring, we make you king of all this land. Victor takes the ring and places it on his finger. He proclaims, people of this land, I will gratefully be your king. But what shall we call this land, this space, that I am king of? The people thought long and hard. Perhaps we call it Saber Space? For it is a space and we carry sabers? Victor thought about it. He says, Saber, I ah, think I like that but not the Space part. The peoples looked at each other in puzzlement. They made the misunderstanding. They shout, Siberia! This is where we are from and Victor is our king!

I say to Adoy, what does this have to be doing with Little Red Rocket and me? This is all very fantastical but I am not making much sense of this all. Adoy says, be patient, I will continue. He tells to me, the Von Vadouchski family ruled Siberia for hundreds of years. They were fair rulers and well liked by their subjects. It was to this family, that I was born. He says. What are you saying? I ask. He says, turn the pages of the book. He stops me when we get to one of the pictures. I look at it and look at him. It is him, but much younger! I attach the photo. Adoy tells me, I was once king of Siberia. My real name is Vladimir Von Vadouchski. So you are king of all Siberia? I ask. I use to be. He tells me. A long time ago.

I am still not making the understandment of what this is having to do with me I say to him. And why are you called Adoy then? You will make the understanding soon enough. He says. But today has been long day for you. You must rest now and we will talk more in the morning. He brings me to a bed made of hay straw. Sleep well Curly. He says. Tomorrow will be a good day. I says to him, how are you knowing my name? I have not told you these things. Sleep now, sleep. He says. I close my eyes and quickly fall into the sleep. Today I have awoke and written the letters to you. Adoy is out hunting for food and soon we will eat and talk more. I will tells to you what he has tells to me. Again, make the forgiveness of Curly as this has been very hard for me in last few days. I promise I will not have the outbursting against you again. I much finish now. I write you again soon.
Curly

I MEET ADOY IN THE WOODS.

THE DARK INVADERS FROM OTTOMAN EMPIRE.

VICTOR LEADS HIS ARMY AGAINST OTTOMAN EMPIRE.

VICTOR'S ARMY DEFEATS THE OTTOMANS.

KING VLADIMIR VON VADOUCHSKI

From: Mariya <girl_1980@xxxxx.com>
Sent: Wednesday, February 16 3:47 AM
To: Chris <coldbastrd@xxxxx.com>
Subject: [Hello my darling Curly]

Hello my darling Curly! I very much miss on you. My dear, I very much would like to hear from you very pleasant news, But I should suffer and wait. My lovely I very much do not have you near to me, I wait for the moment to be near to you. Ideas about you do not leave my head! And it comes to an end the good arrangement of my spirit! I frequently present, as your lips softly concern my lips! We leave this world, and us carries away in eternity! I so love this feeling! This feeling you has presented me! My feelings to you grow with extraordinary force! This stay of feelings to me so is pleasant, also I need in your letters more and more! I so am grateful to destiny, that we had a meeting in the Internet. It has caused to opening in me of new magnificent feelings! And it does my life, more beautiful and desirable. I think, that you will do me by the happiest woman in the world. I do not have words to express all feelings to you, I so would like to tell you, That I thirst for you and I wish constantly. But I do not know as I shall tell to you it when we shall meet. But I do not know when it will take place. I want to thaw in your embraces as a slice of ice on the hot sun. I want, that your gentle hands would study all my body and to burn down in them from desire. I know only one you will present me many happiness and love I immediately shall come very much want to be near to you! You have made me the happiest in the world and I shall do you same happy as I! I shall take away money from bank and what for this purpose I should have that was not problems I did not collide with it there is no time? You the most tender, loved and desired.

You and your Mariya

From: Chris <coldbastrd@xxxxx.com>
Sent: Wednesday, February 16 12:35 PM
To: Mariya <girl_1980@xxxxx.com>
Subject: [RE: Hello my darling Curly]

Dearest Mariya. Am I reading the letters correct? You are going to rob the bank? I would highly advises against such the activities! Do you want to end up in jails or have a Russian Man in black chasing you? You do not want to live such the life! Besides, I have concerning news that now that I know of such things, it gives me the hebbalie jebbalies reading your letters about how you are falling in love with the Curly. Please sit your underbottoms on chair and firmly seatbuckle yourself. You will surely melt into pool of greasy fats like slice of boiled chicken gizzard under hot heat lamps.

I await for Adoy to return from hunting. He returns and we have breakfast of rabbit stew and corn. We finish and Adoy goes out and sits on the porch of his cabin. I grab gold cover book and join him there. Please tells to me Adoy? I ask, or whatever your name is, the rest of stories you are telling me in the nighttimes. Adoy looks out over valley and lake nearby with far away lookings. Please open book. He says, it will make easier following story. He continues. Yes I was king of Siberia a long time ago. I believe I was good king and my people did like me. The problem was I was out of touch with everyday things that were around me. I didn't pay attention to politics, or rumors, or what was happening in my country. I was locked in my fortress every day, going about my own little business. Merrily oblivious to everything outside those four walls. If I had cared and paid attention, I would have knowing what was coming.

Adoy has me turn to a page with a photo of some men. He says, those men are the Marx brothers, Harpo, Groucho, and Karl. I attach the photo. He continues. They wanted to make changes in country of Russia. They wanted to bring what they thought would be perfect society to the people. It is called Communityism. They organized rallies and armies. They plotting takeover of all of Russia. It is their intentions to rid Russia of all separate kingdoms and make one joint Russia. They started in the east and worked their way west overthrowing each kingdom as they went. Siberia being the largest and furthest west, I didn't know this was happening till almost it was too late. I received word that large army gathers to overthrow Siberia kingdom. I could not amass my army in time. It was too late. I flee country with my life.

I turn the page and Adoy continues. I make the journey to America. I arrive in New York and keep a low profiles. I do not want to be sent back to Russia to have my head cut off! I head out into woods and it is there I stumble upon Ewok village. The Ewok people being known for their generosity and hospitality take me in and make me one of their own. The Ewok elders take me to speak with the great spirit Gods. It is here that I no longer am Vladimir. I become Adoy. I attach the photo. Adoy goes on. I spent many months living with the Ewok peoples. Learning to hunt muskrats, fish, make clothings, sew necklaces out of beads to sell to tourists. There was a woman. A very beautiful native Ewok woman. Her name was Rosy Cheekybottoms. I fells madly in love with her. We marry under the light of the full moon on the sixth month. I attach the photo.
Adoy turns to me and says, what you are about to learning, you have never known before. The evening of the marrying, we return to our hut. We lay down together. It is there, that I inject you into your mother. I attach the photo. I turn to Adoy in confusement. What are you saying? I ask. Curly make the understandment. He says, I am your father! This has blown the Curly mind I thinking! Where have you been? I say.

Why have I had the mama and the papa that I always know and you tells to me that they are not the mama and papa!? Curly, settle down! He says. Your temper is like mine. It will get you into trouble someday. It already has! I say. Father continues. Curly, why do you think you speak with the accent? Do you know what accent this is? I say, you know my sister, who isn't my sister tells to me same thing. What is the accent? I am not knowing. Father says, it is the Russian accent. You are half Russian, half Ewok. I asks, Why have you not raised me? Why do you live here alone in forest?

Father goes on. Your mother had a difficult child birthing. She loses too much of the life giving bloods when you make the birth appearances. It all happens to fast and I watch as she dies there after your birthing. Before she dies, she begs to hold you. So I give you to her and she kisses you on forehead. She says, great spirit Gods, watch over my son. She sees a little bit of hair on your head and it has a curl. She looks at me and says, you shall name him Curly. I love you Adoy. With that, she dies. Father continues. I wept and cried. This miracle of life has been given to me, but with the price of death. I was happy, and angry, joyful, and sad all at same time. I cover your mother in blanket. I was scared that Ewok peoples would be mad that their daughter Rosy was no more. I run away into the nighttimes. I was lost and confused and on my own. I am not knowing how to care for small childrens. What am I to do?

The next day I see couple having picnic in park. They laugh and smile and I am thinking, they are good peoples and they will be able to take care of small childrens like should be. So I followed them to their home and later, wrapped you and left you on doorstep for them to be finding.

Father, I say, I have seen my sister who is not real sister. She gives to me a ring that was found with me when I was small childrens on doorstep. I pull out the ring and show father. You see Curly, father says, that is the Ring of the King. He who holds the ring shall be king of all Siberia! This is what is inscribed on its surface. It is the same ring and tradition that goes back to when Victor defeating the dark invaders. But father, I say, you are still alive. You are true king of Siberia. I did try Curly. He says. You see when I decide to leave you, I make the decisions to return to Siberia and fight for my kingdom so that we have home and safe place to live. I leave the ring with you in case I am killed or captured. This way no man who shouldn't be king, becomes king.

Father goes on. I make the journey to Siberia. I amass a small group of men to regain power. I attach the photo. He continues. But the Communityist were too strong. There were too many of them and we lose battle for Siberia. I attach the photo. What happens next? I asks. My men and I, he says, were taken and thrown in prison. It is miracles that they do not kill us on spot. While in prison, I met a woman there. We fall into the passions. We lay down together, and I inject her with another small childrens. They find that the woman is pregnant and move her to different jail. I have learned from peoples that she bares a daughter. I have never seen her. Her name is Mary. Father, I say, what is name for Mary in Russia? Well, he says, that would be Mariya. NO! I say. Get the funks out!!!

I run inside cabin and grab computer. I pull it out and find your photos that you have been sending to me. I asks, do you know when this was? He says, around November 1980. I asks, father, do you know what daughter is looking like? I have only seen few photos when she was small childrens. He says. Father, I say, please take a look at these photos. I shows to him photos of you. Thank the Gods you have never sent the nudiness photos!

Now that I am knowing that I am knowing, my eyes would burns out of the head and I would be cast in river of fire after the death. He studies the photos. He says, yes, yes, this is my Mary! This is my daughter!
How do you have these photos? He asks. I have been speaking to her on the interwebs. I says. The interwebs? He asks. Yes it is computer systems for speaking to each other I tells to him. It is like phone with pictures. You have been out of touch for long times. I say.

Tells to me father, how did you end up here? You see Curly, he says, me and my men get the news that the Communityist are to put us to death. One of my men that I was imprisoned with, Spockinski who was faithful servant to me come up with a plan. I attach the photo. He goes on. Spockinski makes a distraction of the guards. The guards come to see what is the problems. They open the cell and Spockinski leaps upon them! I slip out of cell and make the escape. I look back and see that they kill the Spockinski. He was a good man and I am forever grateful for his sacrificing. I make way across frozen tundra of Siberia with Communityist chasing me. I find row boat and cross back to America. Back to here, Alasska. But father, I ask, why did you not come back to get me? He says, many years had passed. You were older small childrens. You were settled into life that is all you ever knowing. I keep in communications with Ewok tribe members from time to time. I tie notes to pigeon feet and the pigeons carry notes to Ewok village. Chief Chokesondeek returns messages. They have watched over you all these years. Look here, he says, I have your peanut butter in my cabinet. I save it for you when you find me. He pulls out a jar of my Creamy Curly Peanut Butter. He goes on. Not long after I make the arrival here, I go to town and see a beautiful shiny bike in store window. I make a trade with store owner for muskrat pelts for bike. I send to you for Christmas present so in hopes that someday, you would make journey of discovery and find me. And so it seems, that journey is complete. No father, it isn't! I say. I have to make the confessions.

I am going to Russia, to Siberia, to find my love. I meets her on the interwebs and we have fallen madly in the love. Father looks up to sky. This is all work of mighty spirit Gods! He says. They have brought us all together when you become old enough to make the understanding. It is the fate of the Gods. Father, I say, it is not work of Gods! It is I who make the journey. It is I who follows the path that leads me to Russia and my love. Father turns to me. So it is Curly, so it is. But you are not seeing the great coinsidencicals? You find woman for love in Russia. You find and speak to your half sister? You find me here in woods? This is not work of the Gods you say? Perhaps. I say. Maybe it is my fate, but I will finish this journey and continue till I find my love in Russia! You will come with me and we shall make the great return there! Father looks out towards lake. I cannot make the return. He says. They will imprison me and try to cut off my head. Father, I say, have you not hearing the news? There is no more Communityism. It is all gone! Russia is the free country now. I sees it on the news. Really? He says. I have been out here to long! The only news I hearing these days is what moosen is sleeping with other moosen and what the trees whisper to me in the night winds. But still, I am not going. This is my home now. Come now, he says, there is some unfinished work for you to be doing before you go.

My Mariya, are you still there? Have you fallen off the chair or melted into pile of goo? You are my half sister!! Do you know what else this is all meaning? I am prince of Siberia and you are princess of all Siberian kingdom! You're father is not dead. He is alive and well in Alasska! What are you thinking of all of news? This must bring the excitement does it not? I much finish now. This is huge letter I write and my fingers burn. Father and I are building a raft but it is looking to small to cross to Russia with. I am not sure what we do with this. I will write to you when I can.

Your loving half brother, Curly

THE MARX BROTHERS PLOTTING TAKE OVER.

VLADIMIR BECOMES ADOY.

ADOY FALLS IN THE LOVES.

NIGHT FATHER INJECTS CURLY INTO EWOK MAMA.

FATHER GATHERS MEN TO REGAIN POWER.

FATHER LOSSES BATTLE FOR SIBERIA.

FATHER AND SERVANT SPOCKINSKI HELD IN PRISON.

From: Chris <coldbastrd@xxxxx.com>
Sent: Thursday, February 17 1:13 PM
To: Mariya <girl_1980@xxxxx.com>
Subject: [Hello dear half sister]

Hellos dear half sister Mariya! How are you today? Today greets me well with some sadness and some happiness. Listen my dear sister. I am knowing that you are not the pleasant in the faces and since I am knowing now what I am knowing, I feel sorry for pointing out such discrepancies in your character. Will you please make the forgiveness of Curly? I will try not to do so in future. It is important to have the family and now that I am knowing your are the family, I must treat with respectable. Although it is fun to make the poking of the sister and brother in good humor. Not the poking of each other in the physicality however. You are understanding. I tell you about my nighttimes and day.

In the nighttimes of last, father and I build the raft. It is small raft. I ask father. This raft is very small. Even too smalls to carry me all the way to Russia. We must build bigger! Father says to me, no Curly, it is not for you to be sailing to Russia. It is for you to be sending Little Red Rocket to the heavens. It is tradition in old countries to place the bodies on a raft and light it on fire to send to heavens. This way it also keeps streets and lands clean of dead bodies laying about the places. Ah yes, I am understanding. I say.

I take all the pieces of Little Red Rocket and place it on the raft. I place the raft onto the water. We go inside the cabin and father gathers a large stick. He dips it into the fire of the fireplaces. He says, this fire I have kept burning since my arriving here. It is the fire of life and now it will sends your Little Red Rocket into the heavens. He hands to me the torch of fire. I attach the photo. We walk back to lake. I hand father back the torch. I kneel down and kiss Little Red Rocket.

Tears fill my eyes. I whisper to her. My friend, you have taken me places I thought I have never been seeing. You make me strong when I was weak. You made me who I am today. We had such the great journeys and even though our journey has ended, I shall forever carry you with me in my heart. You have given your life for me, and for this, I am forever grateful. With this, I take the torch back from father and light the raft. I watch as the raft slowly drifts away burning and Little Red is sent to heavens. I attach the photo.

I turn to father and say, father I must continue on journey. This is my destiny. Father says to come with him to special place. He leads me through woods and we make arrival at a large hidden door. He says that it is secret bunker. We go inside. He lights the room but it is very dim and hard to see. There within blackness is beautiful machine. He tells to me, Curly there is special people who protect me even though I am not king of Siberia anymore. They are the royal guard and it is their job to protect the king. They would give life to make sure that king is safe. Who are these people? I say. Father says, there are a few women and men and their boss is a bald guy names Napster. Ah ha! I say, I have meets this man! He has protected me in past! It is because you wears the ring of the king! Father says. He continues. When I come to Alasska, soon after they come and build this bunker for my protections. They also leave me this car in case I must make the escape if necessary. He turns the key of the beautiful machine and it fires to life. The noises it is makes are intoxication. This is the last of the mighty Russian V8's back when Russia build fast machines and gas was cheap. He says. I attach the photo.

He shows me inside of machine. He points to a shiny red button. Curly, he says, don't pull that button. This will unleash all supercharger power of mighty Russian V8! You will not be able to control the power! I attach the photo. Why are you tells to me not to pull button? I say. Because I am giving this to you to finish your journey here. He says.

You will take it and cross Badlands and make your way to end of Alasska. There you will find my boat in which I used to cross from Russia to here. Father, I do not need to be using car because you will be driving it with me. I say. You will make the return to Russia! No I can't go. He says. I can never go back.

Why are you so afraid? I say. Is this traits of supposed king of Siberia? You are beings weak! I come so far and see you. I fight and struggle all way across country. I've been on road so long, I don't even remember my own name anymore! That is not weakness! I know your name. He says. You are Curly Von Vadouchski! My son. Oh reallys? I says. Because last time I have been checking, it is Curly Poindexter III Jr. Esq! You cannot be father of me! My papa is strong and would never give up so easily! Were you there when I take first steps? Were you there when I learn to make the pp on the toilets? Where you there when I learned to ride Little Red Rocket? Where were you when I needed you all this time? Here in woods amongst pigeons and trees! You go back to country to make life for family and were defeated. So instead of fighting and making the struggles, you runaway here and stay wrapped within your walls of sorrow by your lonesome. You give up on country. You give up on family. You give up on me! That is not father that in which I knowing! Perhaps you were great man at one time. I am not knowing. But whatever you are now, it is far from the greatness.

Adoy looks at me and the tears appear in eyes. His mouth opens but nothing speaking comes out of it. I sneer at him, turn and runaway. I run to cabin and gather belongs. I take Creamy Curly Peanut Butter from cabinet. HE CAN NOT BE PUTTING IT DEEP INSIDE HIM! I think. I run back to secret bunker. Adoy is still there in the dimness sitting against the wall rocking back and forth. I reach to necklace with ring. I pull it off my bodies and throw it at him. There, I say, you rule this kingdom of trees, birds, and nothingness! It is where you belongs!

I get in beautiful machine and fire it up. I give one last look at Adoy and head out to the Badlands. The Badlands are bare and empty like the look in Adoy's eyes when I last sees them. The Badlands are bad. This is must be where Man in black is. I cannot help but feel the pain in my heart left by the emptiness of loss of Little Red Rocket. The Man in black must pay for what he has done! I am feeling the angry taking the hold of me! I can hardly contains the rage of emotion. MAN IN BLACK MUST BE SMASHED! I ride the Badland highway looking for Man in black. I attach the photo. Mile after mile. The road laid waste behind me. The blackness, the emptiness, the anger taking hold of me. I am wasting the time looking for him, but it does not matter. This is one thing that I must be finishing.

I find a good clearing where I can sit, wait and look out over many miles of Badland. I sit and wait now for Man in black to make the appearances. I attach the photo. He has always finds me. So now I wait like hurt sheep waiting for wolf to come feast. But what he is not knowing, is this sheep is wolf in disguises. While I wait, I feel poem coming on. So I write to you and write the poem. I write the poem now.

Whoa bad man, Man in Black
Whoa bad man, Man in Black
Bad man has a gun, Man in Black
Keep me on the run, Man in Black
Gonna pay him back, Man in Black
Gonna give him a smack, Man in Black
I said oh bad man, Man in Black
Whoa bad man, Man in Black
Whoa bad man, Man in Black
He killed Little Red, Man in Black
Gonna smash his head, Man in Black

It won't be pretty, Man in Black
It'll be quite gritty, Man in Black
Whoa bad man, Man in Black
Whoa bad man, Man in Black
He works for Uncle Sam, Man in Black
His face I'll slam, Man in Black
Well I'm gonna do my thing, Man in Black
Like a bee I'll sting, Man in Black
Whoa bad man, Man in Black
Whoa bad man
MAN IN BLACK!

So I come to finishing writing now. Must focus on tasks ahead. I sees that you not write today. I hope that you are not in shocking still of all of news that I have tells to you. I am sorry about Adoy and how this has turning out. He is just not the man that we have been thinking he was. Don't be sad. When I finishing business here, I will come there very soon. I will find Larisa and we will have great celebration that of course you will be invite to. Have a super duper day my dear half sister. I speaks to you soon.

Your half brother, Curly

I CARRY TORCH THAT WILL SEND LITTLE RED TO HEAVENS.

I WATCH AS LITTLE RED ROCKET IS SENT TO HEAVENS.

FATHER SHOWS ME LAST OF THE MIGHTY RUSSIAN V8'S.

DON'T PULL THE SHINY RED BUTTON!

I RIDE THE BADLAND HIGHWAY LOOKING FOR MAN IN BLACK

I SIT AND WAIT FOR MAN IN BLACK

From: Chris <coldbastrd@xxxxx.com>
Sent: Friday, February 18 2:56 PM
To: Mariya <girl_1980@xxxxx.com>
Subject: [Hello dear half sister]

Hellos again my dear half sister Mariya! How does the day great you this day? I am not seeing the letters from you. Is everything ok there in Moscow? I am hoping so. Have you any lucks finding Larisa? If not, it is ok. I will be there very soon and we will make the search together! So you must be wondering about my days. I tells them to you now.

I am in Badlands waiting for Man in black. I am angry for his treatment of me and of course, Little Red Rocket. I am so tired trying to stay awake but he will come. And you are knowing what? I look out over horizons. I see car in distances. I take out spys glass and looking. It is Man in black in Big Red! I attach the photo. It is time for me to not be laying about. It is time for actions! I attach the photo!

I start the beautiful machine and throw into gears. I leave nasty rubber burning behinds me. I attach the photo. He is coming to me very fast. We are like two nights of rounded tables making preparations for joust. I attach the photo. I wear my new beautiful machine like impenerterrible armor. So this is the way we play! You cannot stop me Man in black! Not this times! Closer and closer we charge at each other. I attach the photo! He swerves all over road trying to scare me. I attach the photo. But it won't work this time! I sees the shiny red button. You cannot stop me this time Man in black! I yell out. I pull the button! I attach the photo! With this, I am supercharged!!! I attach the photo! The beautiful machine lurches ahead in great momentums. I sees the Man in black. He snickers at me from his car. I attach the photo.

I AM NOT SCARED OF HIM! I AM UNBREAKABLE! I ATTACH THE PHOTO! At last moments, Man in black swerves to not be hitting me. He loses control of car and makes the flipping over and over. I attach the photo. You see Man in black! You cannot frighten me anymore! I MAKE YOU GO SMASH! I stop the machine. I reverse and make the assessment of damages to Man in black. His car has gone off side of road. It is wrecked complete. Now I must get all of the courage and check to see that Man in Black is really dead. I attach the photo. I am finding big gun in car. Much bigger than Man in blacks guns. This will surely do the tricks.

I get out of the machine and walk down hill to where Man in black is. I finds him pulling himself out of wrecked car. He does not sees me. The air is foul with smells. I thinking he must have made the accidentals in pants. That has shown him! I put the gun to his head. I attach the photo! So Man in black, I say, we are meeting again! This times though, I have the advantages! Man in black looks surprised. Well it looks like you win Curly! Man in black says. I give up! This is beyond the givings up! I say. How do you think I am feeling? You taken away most precious friend from me! How should repayment be? Go ahead and do your worst! He says. But I'm going to take you back to justice!

I think for a moments. I run back to machine while telling him not to moves. I grab the Curly Peanut Butter. I run back to Man in black. I open jar and stick my finger in and pull out huge chunk of creaminess. I grab Man in black by mouth and shove the butter deep inside him! THIS IS WHAT YOU ARE NOT UNDERSTANDING! Man in black gags for moments then begins to enjoy the butter. I tells to him, you are seeing, I find my loves in Russia and I take my peanut butter to her and put it deep inside her. We will make the family and live a life of happiness! NOW ARE YOU UNDERSTANDING!

Man in black composes himself. I am breathing heavily and there is nothing but silences all around. Man in black turns to me and says, Curly, I had no idea! Your butter, it's so smooth and creamy. I like to have it deep inside me! Can I have more? No! I say, I am saving it for my Larisa. But I am glad you are enjoying the sampling. Man in black begins to make the tears in eyes. He says, Curly, I wish I have what you have. I've been so focused on my career. Do you really think I am such the bad guy? He asks. You are the baddest of the bad and I should kills you! I say.

Man in black continues. I am just doing my job, my duty. I am not meaning to hurt you. I've been so wrapped up in my career. I have no time for family, for friends. Maybe I have been jealous of you Curly. You go to places all over country. You meet peoples and they love you.
You make the friends everywhere you go. How can I not be jealous of this? How can I not feel angry? He says. It is at this point, I am feeling sadness and pity for Man in black. Here I am turning into the very thing I am hating. I put down the gun. I pull out tissue so he can blow the nose from the snots dripping down melted face. There, there. I say. Don't be sad or angry or jealous of what I am having. Maybe you stop being the bad man. Maybe you give up career of chasing peoples.

Tells to me Man in black, what is your name? Man in black blows his nose and says, my name? Nobody has ever asked my name. They all run away when they sees me. I've never had friends. People have always been afraid of me. And you here Curly, through the kindness of your heart ask my name. My name is Cecil. Well Cecil, I say, it is making the pleasure of me to make the acquaintance. I shake Cecil's hand. Tell me Cecil, instead of chasing people away, what else have you wanted to be doing in life? Cecil looks at me. He says, I've always liked to make people laugh.

I've never had friends though that I could make laugh. I only tell jokes and things to myself. Cecil, I say, you want to be the jokester like clown? Cecil looks at me. Yes the clown! He says. That would be such the life that I wish to be leading!

Cecil, I say, you are in the lucks! My sister, who is not the real sister, but I love the same, she is performer in circus. She is in Oaklahomo with the circus now! You go to Oaklahomo and tells to them that Curly sends you and that you would be the greatest clown in all the world! Don't you think the childrens will be afraid of me? He asks. I mean my face is half melty. I says, do not worry about this! You wear the makeup and people will never know. You look like your melty face is smiling anyways. Cecil says to me, you would do this for me? Yes I would. I say. I was mad at you. Really mad. I wanted you to go smash! You took away my Little Red Rocket and this, it has come hard to make the forgiving. But in a ways, I make the understanding that you do what you do. You were caught up in your job. You were full of anger and hatred. For moments there, I was as well. But this is not good for the souls. This is not ways to get to heavens. This is only ways to get to river of fire after the deaths. So Cecil, who is no more Man in black, I forgive you for what you have done. Can I asks to you, do you forgive me for making the problems back at home with hammer of sledge? Cecil puts his head down for a moment. He then says, yes Curly, I am forgiving you. It is easy to get mad and upset. You are knowing this. But we must make the promises to each other.

Ok. I says. Cecil says, from this day forward we control our anger and not smash things. We do not hurt people and we do not make damages of their things. Cecil puts his hand out. I take his hand and shake it. It is a promise! No more smash!

So can you believe this now my dear half sister? The Man in....I mean Cecil and I are friends! I attach the photo of our new friendship! He makes the promise that when he returns to civilization, he will have all charges against me dropped. I am free to continue to Russia! I AM A FREE MAN! FREE AT LAST! FREE AT LAST! Man in black is dead. But the rebirthing of Cecil will bring joy to many peoples! I drive him to civilization. He give to me hug and I sees him off on train.

This is amazing moments in the Curly life! Tells to me what you think of all of what has happening? I have not hear from you in few days. I take the machine and drive on to coast. There, by morning times, I shall finally make journey in boat to Russia. A free man. Which is why I finish now so that I can make it there by morning. I'll write to you when I can. I hope everything is ok there. Have you made any progression in finding Larisa? It is ok. I'll be there soon and we look together because we are family. Have a good night and we talk soon.
Your loving half brother, Curly

I SEES THE MAN IN BLACK!

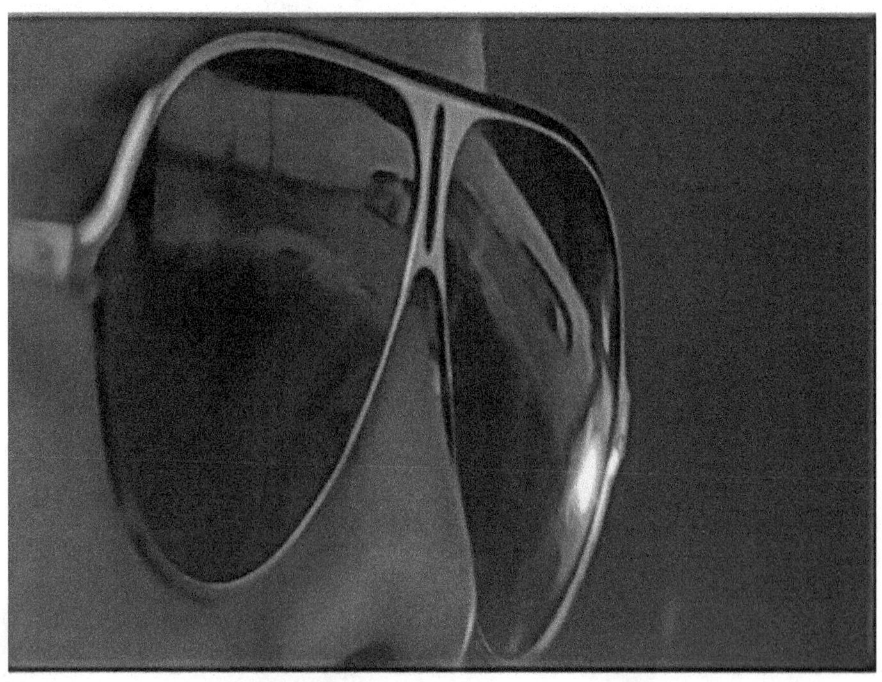

IT IS TIME FOR ACTIONS!

I BURN THE RUBBER ON ROAD!

HE IS COMING TO ME VERY FAST!

CLOSER AND CLOSER WE CHARGE!

MAN IN BLACK SWERVES ALL OVER ROAD!

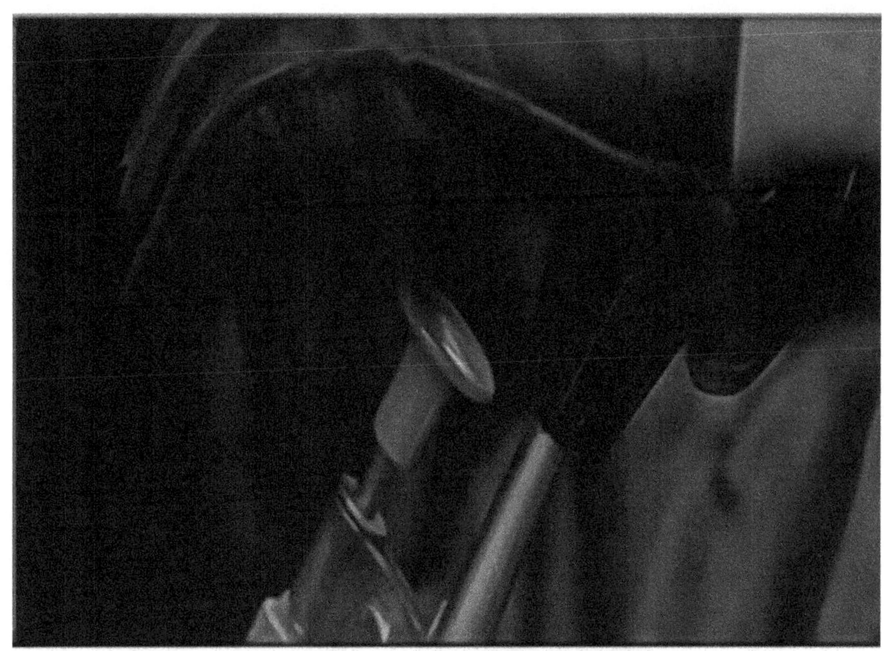

I PULL THE BUTTON!

I AM SUPERCHARGED!!!

MAN IN BLACK SNICKERS AT ME!

I AM UNBREAKABLE!

MAN IN BLACK FLIPS CAR OVER AND OVER!

I MUST CHECK IF HE IS DEAD.

I PUT THE GUN TO HIS HEAD!

CECIL AND I BECOME FRIENDS!

From: Chris <coldbastrd@xxxxx.com>
Sent: Monday, February 21 1:34 PM
To: Mariya <girl_1980@xxxxx.com>
Subject: [Hellos half sister]

Hellos to you dear darling half sister. How is the day greeting you this day? I am well. Very well infacting. Things seem to be going just right! However I am bit concerned that I have not hear from you in few days. Is everything going ok? I do not hears your words since telling you of news of our relations. I know this is shocking and I am knowing that you had the botherment of physicality whenever you thinking about me. I am hoping that you have scrubbed the body and mind of these things and we shall move ahead as half brother and half sister but not in the same respecting that they make considerment of family relations of such manners in places like West Virgin. Another words, do not be having the dreamsing of me touching you in any way aside from a pat on the back or perhaps a kiss on the cheeks. And not the cheeks on your underbottoms. Are we clear?

So today I arrive at end of America. Ahead of me is ocean to be crossing to arrive in Russia. I find boat that Adoy has left when he comes back to America. I was making preparations for crossing ocean and then suddenly, I hear pawprints in snow. I grab gun from beautiful machine and run back to dock. I am not wanting to be eaten by polar bear and turned into polar bear poops! To my surprises, a man comes out of the forest and down to the dock. It is Adoy! I attach the photo.

I says to him, so you are here to sees me go away are you? This is only thing you knowing what to do! Saying goodbye! He says to me, no Curly. I am going to go with you. This is true? I say. You are coming with me? He says, Curly, I know I haven't been the best father, or the best king for that matter. I've been alone for so long. I've been scared.

Scared to face you. Scared of what you may think of me. Scared that you would reject me. It is seeming that everything I have done, I have failed at. To be your father, well, that is something I never wanted to fail at. It was easier for me to hide away in faraway places, then to be a man and give you the love that you deserve. But I am getting old, and the years past so quickly. I don't want to lose you again. I want to be the best father I can be. Will you give me that chance?

I turn to Adoy and say, Adoy, you have disappointed me yes. But it is only because I am knowing you can be such the great person. Such the great father. Such the great king. I just wanted and still want you to try. That is all I am askings. I know that you will do great because you have made me. I have come from you from the injection. I have faced my fears. I have conquered everything set before me. I am knowing that I am part of you and if I am ability to do such things, well than I must have gotten these ability from somewhere. Not just out of the sky. I have gotten them from you. If I can do these things, then so can you!

Father throws out his arms and exclaims, oh Curly! I drop the gun in the snow and run to father. We give the hugs and begin to cry like the little schoolgirls. Father, I says, let us make the triumphant return to mother Russia! With this we gather belongings and push boat into waters. It is very cold here. Father brings saber and a hammer of sledge. We will be needing this during journey across ocean. There is much ice that needs to be smashed! We rowed, rowed, rowed, the boat gently across the ocean. Meerily, meerily, meerily, this is Newton's laws of motion.

We reach the part of ocean that has frozen. I pick up hammer of sledge and wield it over head. I smash the ice. ICE SMASH! I chop, I smash, I chop, I smash! I attach the photo. Arms getting weak and turning to jellies. You will not take me this time ocean! I scream out. CHOP! SMASH! CHOP! SMASH! It is too much though.

I am falling weak and collapse in boat. Father takes saber and tries cutting ice. It is too thick and heavy. Father, I say, we can't give up. What are we to do? He says. We will push boat to Russia! We get out of front of boat and pull up onto ice. We get behind it and push. I attach the photo.

We push long time and the legs nearly turn to jelly. My head is down and I am pushing with all of mighty. Suddenly we are not able to push anymore. We are stuck! I push and push and push! Father looks up and says, Curly, stop the pushing. I yell out, no we cannot! Must get to Russia. He taps me on shoulder and says, stop pushing. Look! I stop and look. There before me, covered in whiteness like sugary coating jelly dognut, I am seeing sight I never thought I would see at beginning of journey. IT IS LAND! WE HAVE REACHED RUSSIA! Finally after all this time and places and people and miles. I never thought I would live to see day.

We gather our belongings. Father brings me heavy coat to make the protection from cold. I attach the photo. He tells me we are going to his fortress many many many miles away. Here we can make the rest before I carry on rest of journey. We cross the frozen tundra of Siberia. Wind and coldness whips at our face and heels. I am not making the realize that Russia is so cold! Why haven't you tells me of this dearest half sister?

We walk for what feels like an eternity. It becomes dark very early and becoming colder as each minute passes. There in distances we see a light and make heading for it. After some times, we reach light and it is a settlement. We find a local bar where we make the stop for refreshments. We go inside and go to the bar. It is strange the peoples we are seeing here. There is a band playing and they wear funny masks. I attach the photo. We go up to bar and order refreshments. I attach the photo.

A man approaches me and taps me on shoulder. He says to me in very bad English, we don't like your kind here. I am thinking that he has hearing me speak the English. Father speaks to him in native voices telling him to go away and that we don't want any trouble. I am not understanding the native Russian speaking. I am thinking I am having to learn this as I am half Russian yes?

The man persists in bothering father and I. He pushes and shoves and tells me in bad English to go back outside. The man takes out a knife and makes the threatening that I cannot understands but father seems to know what he is sayings. Father pulls out saber and cuts off the mans arm! People starts to go crazy! They pull out knives and all kinds of weaponry. It is looking like we must make the battle to the death!

Suddenly, father pulls out the ring in which I have thrown back at faces not long ago. He holds it up in the air. I attach the photo. The people see this and cower in fear. One man cries out, it's the ring! The Ring of the King! A harsh silences falls over peoples. You can hear a mouse fart if a mouse did fart. Father speaks. It is I, King Vladimir Von Vadouchski! I have returned with my son to take back the throne of Siberia! The people drop to their knees and bow before us. Father continues. You will let us pass and cause us no harm. We will take on the refreshments here and move on to my fortress where I will be reinstated as your king! One man stands up and approaches us. A tear makes the appearance in his eye.

He says, great King Vadouchski, we have waited so long for your return. We have always been and always will be your humble followers. With this, he drops to his knees again, takes fathers hand, and kisses it. Father says, rise my subject. All of you rise! The people get up to their feets. Father continues and looks at me as he says these words. I know I have left you for a long long time. But I will never leave you again. You don't need to bow before me. You don't need to call me king.

My name is Vladimir. I am one of you. And you have always been part of me. When I ruled this land, I didn't know who you peoples where. I didn't care beyond what was right in front of faces. But that has all changed. You will know me by name, and I will know each and every one of you. You will be like my family, and I will be part of your family.

Father reaches in his coat and pulls out large bag of gold pieces. He says, bartender, drinks are on me! The people scream out in rejoices! ALL HAIL VLADIMIR! KING OF ALL SIBERIA! They each approach us in merriment and happiness. The band plays on and we sing songs of the motherland all night longing. It is great triumphant return! As the night wears on, I make way outside of bar. I can't help feeling sad. I look up at moon. M-O-O-N, that spells moon. I am thinking if only Larisa is seeing same moon I am seeing, because there is only one moon, that we feel the closeness. I am here finally in Russia and this is supposed to be the happy time. But I can't help but feeling the heaviness of heart that Larisa is not here now with me. I look up at moon and says, no matter where you are, I will find you. Please hear my words.

I come to finishing this letters now. I have written while in corner of bar and it is loud and crazy here. We shall stay overnight and tomorrow, make way for fathers fortress. I will write when we make the arrival. I hope everything is ok with you dearest half sister. Father tells to me that he will be requesting your visitation to his fortress once he arrives. Is this in the agreement with you? He will send charter to fetch you. I will speaks with you soon.

Your loving, but not too loving that is in the weirdness, half brother,
Curly

ADOY GREETS ME AT DOCK.

ICE SMASH!!!!

WE PUSH BOAT TO RUSSIA

FATHER GIVES ME WARM COAT.

FUNNY MASK BAND

WE GET THE REFRESHMENTS.

FATHER HOLDS UP RING OF THE KING

CHAPTER 11: FROM RUSSIA WITH THE LOVES

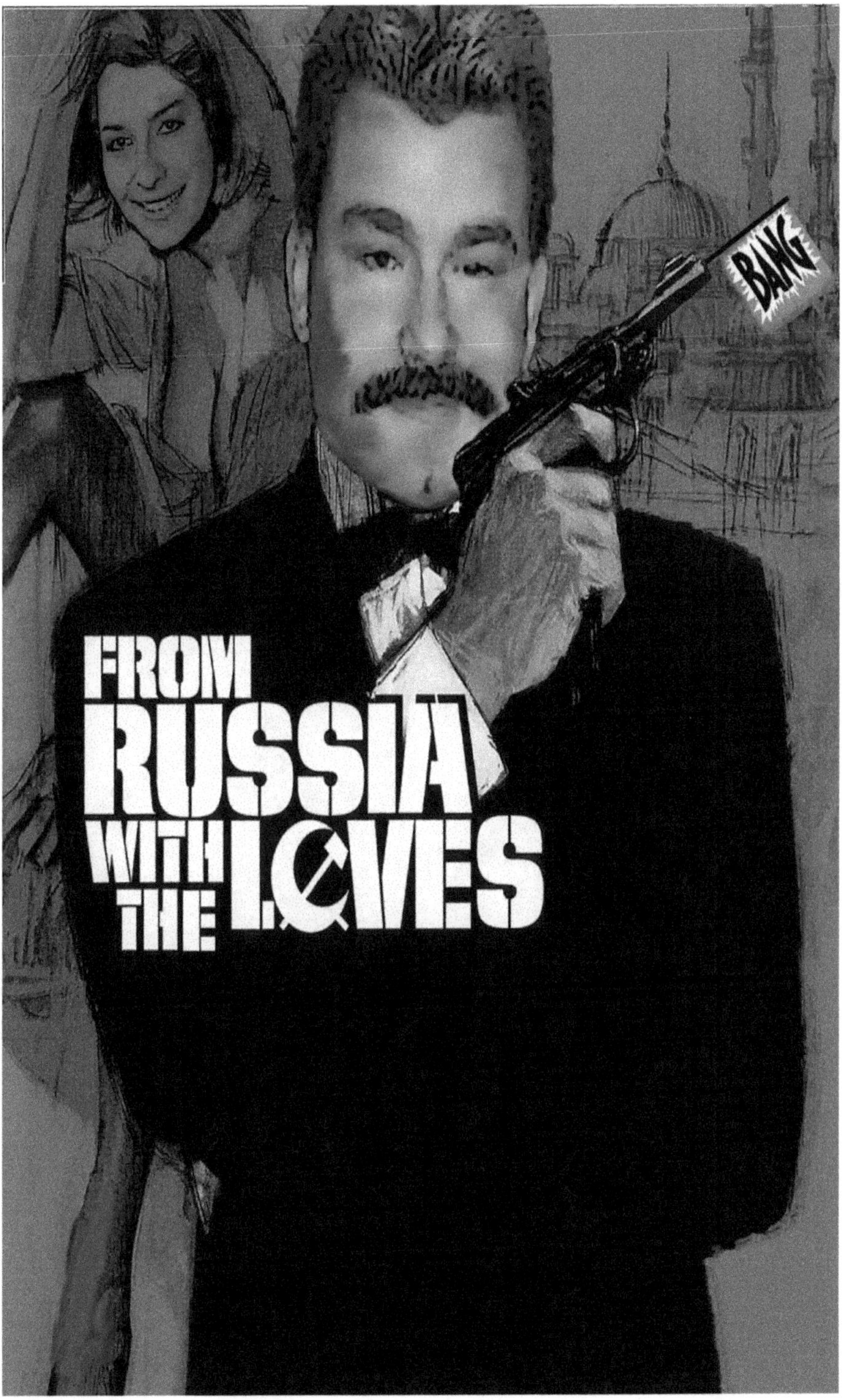

BANG

FROM
RUSSIA
WITH
THE
LOVES

BANG

From: Chris <coldbastrd@xxxxx.com>
Sent: Monday, February 21 2:37 PM
To: Larisa <gilkakisska@xxxxx.com>
Subject: [I am here my love]

My dearest sweet Larisa. I am having the news of excitement for you! I am here, in Russia! Isn't this the moistest amazing thing possible!!??! I have not been hearing from you in such the longness. This makes me sad. But I am not without hoping. I am knowing that soon we will be together. Sooner than I ever though being possible and we will be such the happy together. This is the dreams that fill my soul every day and nighttimes. I have so many things to tells to you about. The people I have meeting. The places I have going. I tells to you that I have found my real father!! Yes it is true!! Yes the papa that did raise me has dead but there is real father who makes me from his man bits. Also I am having half sister! I speaks with her every day and she is there in Russia too! I have not telling to you, I am half Russian! Isn't this amazement? Who would ever be thinking?

So soon we will be together just like we have always been speaking of and dreamsing. I am truly blessed that the days have arrived when I am here. I have brought my butter so that you can put it deep inside you. Prepare yourself for my arrival by taking the showers and scrubbing the bodies. It will be times to remember that you have never experienced in all of life! The thoughts are giving me much the botherment of physicality. I am finishing....oh wait a minute....ok now I am finishing. I will sees you soon!
From Russia with the loves, Curly!

From: Larisa <gilkakisska@xxxxx.com>

Sent: Tuesday, February 22 9:25 AM

To: Chris <coldbastrd@xxxxx.com>

Subject: [No Subject]

fuck you

From: Chris <coldbastrd@xxxxx.com>
Sent: Tuesday, February 22 1:37 PM
To: Larisa <gilkakisska@xxxxx.com>
Subject: [RE: No Subject]

WHO IS THIS!!???!!! I AM KNOWING THIS IS NOT THE LARISA!!! WHAT HAVE YOU DONE WITH HER? TELLS TO ME!! SHE WOULD NEVER SPEAKING TO THE CURLY LIKE THIS!! I WILL FIND YOU AND YOU WILL TELL ME WHERE LARISA IS! PREPARE YOURSELFS FOR MY FIST TO BE RAMING DOWN YOUR STOMACH!!

From: Chris <coldbastrd@xxxxx.com>
Sent: Tuesday, February 22 2:19 PM
To: Mariya <girl_1980@xxxxx.com>
Subject: [Hellos my dearest half sister]

Hellos again my dearest half sister Mariya. How is this day for you? I am having the so so day. I am very angry actually. I have tried to write the letters to my sweet Larisa. I have gotten response that is not of her nature. I am believing this is mens who steal her away to Moscow and must be holding captive. I am just prayful they are not having their ways in the physicality with her. I do not want my precious dove soiled. It is making me mad because so far today has been good day. I tells you about it.

Father and I make the arrival at his royal Fortress of Solidturd. It is huge structure made of ice. I attach the photo. What breathtakings site! There are many peoples who have gathering as news of the return of father has spread through Siberia. When we make the arrival, the peoples see father. They grab him and hoist him up over crowd and carry him into Fortress. I attach the photo. I make way through crowds and find father. He tells to me that he is going to get cleaned up and we are to make the appearances before peoples. We make ourselves clean and change into fantastical royal robes. We make the appearances in front of crowds. Father is presented with the crown of the king.

Father addresses the crowd. He says, my peoples of Siberia, I am so very pleased to return to you. There will be changes to the way I use to run things. But all for the good. As the days and months go on, you will see these changes and Siberia will return to the proud and prosperous kingdom in which it once was. I'd just like to take this moment though to thank the person who could make this all possible. I'd like to introduce you to my son, Curly Poindexter!

I turn to father and say, father, you have made the mistake. I have? He says. Yes. I say. My name is Curly Von Vadouchski. A tear makes the appearances in fathers eye. So I guess I have so it seems. Father says. He turns to the crowd. I'm sorry, he says, my son, Curly Von Vadouchski, prince of all Siberia! The crowd roars in celebration and cheers!

We spend the rest of days mingling and making new friends with peoples of Siberia. This is the joyous time! I attach the photo of father and I after he receives the crown. We are looking very royal are we not? The nighttimes approach and I am lead to my new room in Fortress. The bed is made of solid ice. What a creation! It is looking like snow sleigh. I name it Rosebud. I attach the photo. I try to make the sleep but I toss and turn all night long thinking of bad peoples who harm Larisa.

In the morning times, I speaks to father. I tells to him, father, I must go find the Larisa. I am very concerned about her safety and also now that I am not hearing any more from half sister (that is you), I am concerned for her safety too. I must complete my journey. It is the destiny of me. I am going to Tomsk at last known places of Larisa and look for her there. Father says, Curly I am understanding. One of my guards will escort you there on snowmobile as they are familiar with territory. Tomsk is part of Siberia after all. When you find her, will you be coming back here? I so want to meet this woman of your love.

I think about this for few moments. I says, yes father I will return so you may be meeting her. I am going to look for half sister as well. We will come back here and have the family reunions. But father, I says, I think I will not be staying. Yes of course I will make the visits and one day, I am surely be staying here for rest of life. But it is America that is my home and the place that I wants to show my Larisa. I wants to take to all the places I have been and have her meets all the peoples I have meets. And of course, I am forgetting my peanut butter factory! I am in hope that things are still ok there. I have been tempted to eats all of peanut butter jar that you have had. But I save for Larisa. Of course when I return to America, I will sends to you cases for your own pleasurement.

Father gives to me a big hugs. Good luck my son. He says. When you return, we shall have a great feast and celebration. I've already had special throne room constructed with thrones for me, you, Larisa, and Mariya. He shows to me room. I attach the photo. I return hug to father and says, I will see you again soon. With this, I leave Fortress of Solidturd.

I am writing to you now on side of snow trail. Guard has making the escort on snowmobile with me. I attach the photo. It is on to Tomsk that we are pressing. It is difficult journey as vibrations from snowmobile tingle my man sack and gives me the botherment. I am also having to hug guard tightly so that I am not falling off. It is worth the troubles. All of this has. It is soon I meet my Larisa and everything will be right with world. I am making the finishing now. Tells to me that everything is ok with you dear half sister. I am worried that things are not right with you. I will search for you too once I find Larisa. Have a great day and talk soon.

Your loving half brother, Curly

THE FORTRESS OF SOLIDTURD

PEOPLES CARRY FATHER INSIDE.

FATHER AND I

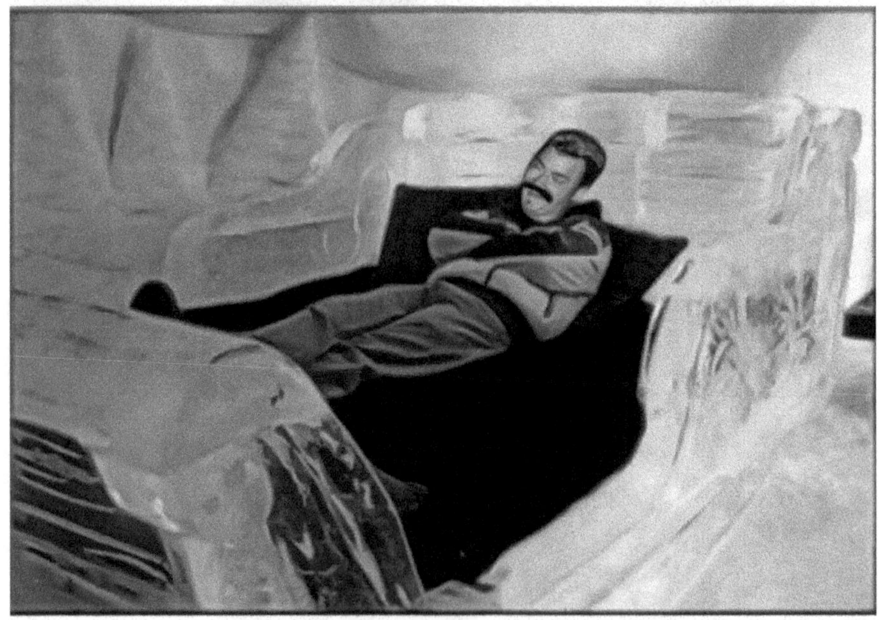

BED THAT I CALL ROSEBUD

THRONE ROOM

I RIDE TO TOMSK.

From: Chris <coldbastrd@xxxxx.com>
Sent: Wednesday, February 23 1:52 PM
To: Mariya <girl_1980@xxxxx.com>
Subject: [Horrible news half sister]

Hello to you dear half sister. I am not hearing from yous in very long time now. This is getting very concerning. Especially when I shall tell you of today's horrible news.

I have made the journey to last known address that Larisa gives to me in Tomsk. I find apartment number in which she has given to me. I comb the hairs on the head and mouthstaches. I make sure eyebrow hairs are straight and in order. I take out the Curly peanut butter so she can accept to her and also I am ready with the pearl necklaces in which I get from Nude Oilings. I knock on door. Nothing. I ring bell. Nothing. I knock on door again and says, Larisa, I am home my darlings. Nothing. I see window in which I peek a boo in. I see a figure in the dark in front of computers. I knock on window. Hello? Larisa? I says. I see the figure get up and go to door. The door opens.

Standing in door is very tall dark man. I am confused. I says, who are you? He says in thick accent, who are you? I says, it is I, Curly Von Vadouchski, prince of all Siberia. Who are you? He says, I am Kookakoola Babaganoosh from Nigeria. I attach the photo. He says, what business do you want? Are you the police? I say, no, I am not policemans. Where is Larisa? He says, I don't know what you are talking about. I sees in his eyes that makes the lies. He goes to shut door on my face, but I kick it in!

The man is thrown back against floor. I rush into apartment. It is dim light and on side of room I look and sees that there is computers. Many, many computers. I am noticing something on computers. I run over to them. I see Larisa's face on one computer screen! I look and see your faces on another computer screen!! WHAT IS MEANING OF THIS??? I call out. Man jumps up and yells to me to get out of there. I look at more screens and see letters and profiles and pictures of peoples . I see print outs of letters and checks from peoples from all over world. I pick up handful of letters and checks. I turn to man. What is all this about? I says. What have you done with Larisa and Mariya? I throw down the papers at his face. The man lunges for me! We make the battle! He is very tall man and I am much shorter than he. I kick and battle the best way I can. I attach the photo. He is strong warrior and we battle for several minutes. KICK! CHOP! PUNCH! SMASH! I make the battle for the life. This is man who steals Larisa aways! I am knowing of this. We throw punch at same time and both fall over. I attach the photo! I am in the daze and sees the stars flying around head.

I come to the senses and grab man by neck. I choke him with all might that is left in bodies. WHAT HAVE YOU DONE WITH LARISA? WHAT HAVE YOU DONE WITH MARIYA? YOU AWFUL BAD MAN!! I scream. I am choking and choking. He tries to speak so I pull back a little to let his words release. He speaks. Go to Moscow.....go.... to.... Mos...co.... He passes out. I am thinking I kills the man. But I see that the chest is still moving. I leave him lying on floor.

I am so angry!!! This man must be working with other bad men to kidnapping womens. I grab checks and letters off of desk and burn them in trashcans. I take computers and THEY GO SMASH!! SMASH SMASH SMASH SMASH SMASH SMASH SMASH SMASH SMASH!!!!!!!!!

CHAIR...SMASH SMASH SMASH. TV....SMASH SMASH SMASH...TABLE...SMASH SMASH SMASH...BOOKCASE...SMASH SMASH SMASH...ALL ENTIRE ROOM...SMASH SMASH SMASH SMASH SMASH SMASH SMASH SMASH SMASH!! I ATTACH THE PHOTO!!!!!!!!!!!

I have lose the temper to all off degrees! I knowing that I make the promises to Cecil not to smash, but this is bad man and he does something to Larisa and to you I am thinking because you no write anymore either. I kick man in stomach. Wake up you maggots! Nothing. He does not move. I look around all of apartment but have not finding anything else of useful that gives to me clues of what else is happening to Larisa and you. I leave the apartment. I am now going to Moscow. This is where Larisa goes and it is where I am knowing you were last when we speaks. This must be where you both are.

Hold tightly my dear half sister! I am coming for you! I will saves you and Larisa! If mens are doing bad things to you, fight thems! Fight and smash with all of your mighty! Just hold on little longer! I will be there soon!
Your loving half brother, Curly

KOOKAKOOLA THE NIGERIAN

YOU AND LARISA ON THE COMPUTERS!

WE BATTLE!!

WE BOTH FALL DOWN.

I CHOKE NIGERIAN!!!

ROOM SMASH!!!!!!!!!!!

From: Chris <coldbastrd@xxxxx.com>
Sent: Friday, February 25 3:22 PM
To: Mariya <girl_1980@xxxxx.com>
Subject: [Dearest half sister]

Hellos to you today dear half sister Mariya! I write to you in the greatest needs. I have made the arrival here in Moscow. I am so lost, confused, and hungry. I do not understands the words that I sees all over. They have backwards letters and strange symbols. I must learn to read and speaks the language that is being said here. I tells to you about all the problems I have hading.

I arrive here yesterdays. I am hungry and it is oh so cold here. I go to McDickies and try to get a Big Dic sandwiches. It is supposed to be two fatty patties, gooey sauce, lettuce, crusty cheese, on a sesame street bun. What are they to give to me? A sandwich that has what looks like fishy eggs on it. I attach the photo. Man who speaks little English tells to me that it is Russian caviler and is delicacy here. I take bite and eggs make the goopy explosions in mouth like the disgusting chewy gum we have in America that has the goopy cream center in it. It makes me want to produce vomits! I spit it out! SPIT! Who is eating this disgustment?

I walk around places and find place peoples tells to me is Red Square. I do not know why they call this Red. It is not Red and is vaguely looking like square. It is more like rectangle. Who makes the names here? Peoples who have drinking too much moonshines? I see building in square that looks like it has the Hershe Kissings on the top of it. I attach the photo. I am thinking that this is chocolate factory which is good because I am hungry and need the foods. I go inside. No chocolate. Why would they advertising chocolate Kissings if they are not making the production of this? There is only many seats in which people sit and also peoples kneeling.

They all face a statue of a man who is hanging from a big letter T. They appears to be making the prayers to man on big T. So I am thinking I am needing all help I can be getting. I make way to front of room and kneel before this man. I make the prayers. I tells them to you now. Dear Mister T, I am knowing that you probably cannot hears me since you are a statue. But if you can hear me Mister T, please help me find my love, Larisa. She is all that I live for. Curly has lived best life that Curly can live and I hope to you that you helps me with my prayers to finds her. With this, I leave Kissings tops building.

I make way back into city. The city is so large and I am so lost. I am thinking this is bigger endeavors than I am expecting! I thought it would be easy to find you and Larisa here. I think that there was only few houses and maybe a store and I would find you quickly. It is much bigger than this. Much, much bigger! I walk down streets to find you. I am not finding you. I go to cross street. I see a bear on a motorcycle!! I attach the photo! You allow bears to ride motorcycles here? Moscow is wild and craziness! I wonder streets, alleys, and go to different stores all day in searching for you and Larisa. I am remembering that Larisa would use buses to get around places here. I come up with idea!! I go to copy store with photos of you and Larisa. I make poster using last monies that I am having. I go around to bus stops and hang missing person posters in bus stops. I attach the poster. If you are finding such poster, I am travel now from bus stop to bus stop waiting several hours and watching everyone who gets off and on now. You will find me at one of the bus stops.

Please my dearest half sister Mariya. I am out of monies, out of foods, out of luck, out of hope. I should call to father for help, but this is the destiny that I am following on my own. Please, tells to me where you are. I must be knowing. It is so cold out night here. I find dumpster to which I stay in middle of night.

Here I find half frozen foods to eat on. I attach the photo. I write to you a poem. Please hear it now.

Ave Mariya! Prison love child!
Listen to my prayer!
Thou canst hear ye from the wild,
Thou can save me amid despair.
Safe may I sleep beneath thy care,
Though banish'd, outcast and reviled -
Mariya! Hear my prayer.
Sister, help a desperate child!
Ave Mariya!

Ave Mariya! Illegitimate child!
A filthy couch with a bum I share.
Shall seem this down of eider piled.
If thy protection havith here.
The murky dumpster heavy air.
Shall breathe of roses if thou hast smiled.
Then, Mariya! Hear my prayer.
Sister, help a desperate child!
Ave Mariya!

Ave Mariya! With your jacked up smile!
Foul drunks and bums of the earth and air.
From this their wretched haunt exiled,
Shall flee before thy faces glare.
And in ye arms in which thy care,
Beneath thy guidance reconciled;
Hear to me my only prayer,
And for a sister hear a child!
Ave Mariya!

Mariya, I am nearly at end of the rope. Will you help pull me back to salvation? Mariya my dear half sister, you are my only hope.

Your one and only half brother, Curly

FISHY EGG SANDWICH

KISSINGS TOPS BUILDING

BEAR ON MOTORCYCLE!

I'M DOWN IN THE DUMPS!

STOLEN!!

Have You Sees the Womens?

Larisa

Mariya

Help me finds them!!!
see Curly at the
nearest Bus Stop!

From: Chris <coldbastrd@xxxxx.com>
Sent: Monday, February 28 2:26 PM
To: Mariya <girl_1980@xxxxx.com>
Subject: [I bring to you good and bad news]

Mariya my dear half sister. I have to bring you both good and bad news. First I tells to you the good news. I have found myself in the dire straights. This is good you says? No, but read on. I look all over Moscow for you and Larisa. I can't find you anywheres. I do not know what to do. It is late at night and rain is pouring. I am in middle of road looking for Larisa. I see a car in the distance. It approaches me and stops. A man gets out. He has his hand in his coat. I am thinking he is going to rob me! But I have no monies to give him. He asks, are you Curly Pointdexter? I says, yes this one of names I go by. He says, I have something for you. I am thinking he is going to pull out gun! He reaches in pocket and pulls out envelope. He says, I'm from Eastern Union, I've been looking for you everywhere! I have a telegram for you! I sign for telegram and open it. I run to headlight of car so I can read it. It's from Chief Chokesondeek! I read to you telegram now.

TO: CURLY POINDEXTER
SOMEWHERE IN RUSSIA
CURLY. WE HAVE BEEN SEARCHING FOR YOU FOR WEEKS! WHERE HAVE YOU BEEN? I HAVE INCREDIBLE NEWS. THE SPECIAL FORMULA PEANUT BUTTER YOU SENT BACK. WE WERE ABLE TO REPLICATE IT. IT IS SELLING OUT EVERYWHERE! IT IS A GREAT SUCCESS! ORDERS KEEP POURING IN EVERYDAY! PEOPLE CAN'T GET ENOUGH OF YOUR BUTTER DEEP INSIDE THEM! I HAVE TAKEN THE PROFITS FROM THE SALES AND INVESTED IT IN A CASINO ON EWOK LANDS. I SEND PHOTO ALONG WITH TELEGRAM. CURLY, WE ARE MAKING SO MUCH MONEY WE CAN HARDLY COUNT IT ALL. YOU HAVE TO SIGN MANY CONTRACTS.

I HAVE INCLUDED THEM HERE. YOU MUST RETURN BACK TO AMERICA IMMEDIATELY! THERE IS A PRIVATE JET WAITING FOR YOU AT MOSCOW AIRPORT. GET YOURSELF THERE QUICK! I HAVE INCLUDED A PASSPORT FOR YOU. DON'T WORRY ABOUT YOUR TROUBLE WITH THE LAW. A FRIEND OF YOURS, CECIL HAS BEEN ABLE TO CLEAR ALL CHARGES WITH THE PRESIDENT. CURLY MY FRIEND, YOU AREN'T JUST A MILLIONAIRE, YOU ARE A BILLIONAIRE!
SAFE JOURNEY
YOUR FRIEND AND BUSINESS PARTNER
CHIEF CHOKESONDEEK

Can you believe this news! I am having more monies than the Gods! Who would have been thinking that my peanut butter does so well? Well I guess I can believe it because I taste the special formula peanut butter and knowing that it is best in all of lands! And a casino! Just think! I can have my own special color chips for me to play with! Now I tells of bad news. As you are reading. You sees that I must return to America very soon. I have not found you. I have not found Larisa. I have searched all over everywhere. You cannot be found. No one comes to bus stop with poster I am making. I begin to think, maybe you and Larisa are not real. You have disappeared. She has disappeared, then reappearing and telling me mean things. I am not knowing what is real and what isn't anymore.

I do knowing this though. Chief Chokesondeek is real. And if he tells me that there is plane waiting for me, there is. And if he tells to me that there is monies for me, there is. Because I am knowing him and I knowing he tells to me truths.

I am so conflicted. Please just speaks to me and tells me that you are real. Tells to me that you are here in Moscow. Then I will be knowing what is real and that you and Larisa are real. And then I will stay for as long as it takes to find you. I do not care about monies, or planes, or casinos. I care about Larisa and you.

Talk to me dear half sister. I am going now to bus stop to take bus to airport. If I am not hearing from you, then I will go and this will all be just the bad nightmares. You are having little times to make the communications. Hurry my dear half sister, hurry.
Your half brother, Curly

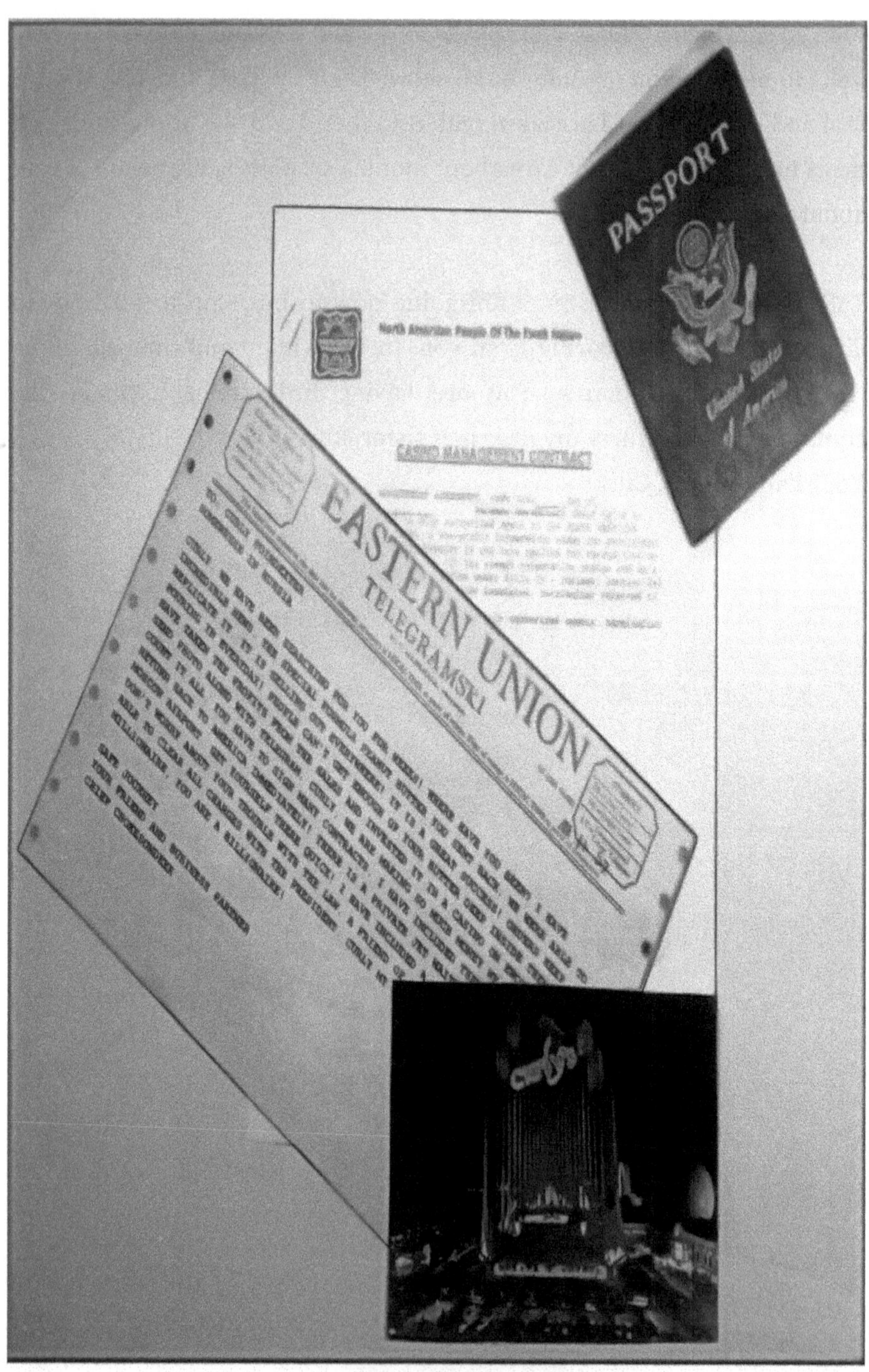

THE DOCUMENTS

From: Mariya <girl_1980@xxxxx.com>
Sent: Thursday, March 1 4:32 AM
To: Chris <coldbastrd@xxxxx.com>
Subject: [Hello again my darling Curly]

Hello again my darling Curly. I am happy that you wrote to me all this time. Forgive me. I could not write to you. I have gone to Moscow to receive the visa and ticket. Moscow the very large city. I was not in the large cities. I have solved to go by the underground. In the underground very much there is a lot of to people and at me from a bag the thieves have stolen my passport and all documents, all money which I had. I thought that to me now to do. I have thought that you my love any more will not want me to see and to hear. I am grateful to you for all mine. I has decided to go then home. In the underground there were very few people. The Moscow young people looked at me. They came to me and have offered me to engage with them love. I have told that there is no I it I shall not do. They began to stick to me and to apply to force. I began to be pulled out them. They by force have dragged me in the machine. Have brought me for city. I thought that I today shall lose consciousness. I was afraid very much. I was frightened. I have decided with what that by an image from them to escape. I began to cry. They began to break from me clothes but then who has called to them on the phone. They have adhered me to a bed and who has left them has caused. I have decided from them to escape. I have found out that at them under a pillow the knife lays. I cut cords and has escaped from them. I was afraid to you to write you thought that after that to me will not write. I love you as before. I miss without you. Forgive me forgive forgive forgive. I do not know that to me to do. I have escaped from them but did not know that to me to do, where to me to go. I did not know where I am present and where to me to go. I sat in the first bus and has left away from this place.

I went by this bus while it has not finished the work. Then the woman which drives the bus has asked me why you do not leave.

I have told that me to go not where. I do not know where to me to go. I have told all history. She has invited me to herself. Now I live at her. I was afraid to go home to me very much it was very very a shame. I thought that there should by me simply be to be laughed and speak that I very such simple girl which have wanted to go to America. It is very a shame. Curly, you can forgive me. They have stolen everything. Can you help me with money to get home? I know you to me will not trust more me. I miss without you. I regret that you were not in that time. Forgive forgive me. I love you my Curly.

From: Chris <coldbastrd@xxxxx.com>
Sent: Tuesday, March 1 1:37 PM
To: Mariya <girl_1980@xxxxx.com>
Subject: [RE: Hello again my darling Curly]

Well, well, well. Look at what pussy the cat dragged in. If it isn't my lovely half sister Mariya. This is quite the amazing story in which you are telling. Thieves and monies stolen. Knives and great escapes. What an absolute incredible yarn you spinning. Oh and of the course, you need my monies now. But you know what I am thinking? Come here a little closer. I tells to you what I thinking. Closer...come here, let me whispers in your ears. I AM THINKING THAT YOU ARE BIG FAT LIARS! IT IS BOLSHEVIKS!!!

Oh Curlys, wee wee wee....please forgive me...I am beaten by roving young thugs in the subway....wee wee wee weee weeeeee! They take all my monies and documents....weeee weee weee weee weeee weee! Who would you think would be falling for such a story? Yes you are knowing that I would have fallen for such the story. I was thinking that this is what has happening to you and Larisa. Matter of fact I think of these things just up to after my last letters I sends to you. But now I am knowing truths. Truths you say? Oh yes my dear fake half sister, the truths! I tells to you the truths now.

After I have finishing writing the letters to you yesterday, I go to bus stop to make way to Moscow airport. I am feeling very sad and defeated that Russia has gotten the best of me and that I am not able to find you or Larisa. So I sit there and wait for bus. People come and go on and off the buses. I pay little attention. Then I see out of corner of eye, a person stopping at bus stop wall. They look at the poster that I make and leave on all bus stops. I nearly forget abouts this. I hear woman's voice speaking in Russia.

I am thinking she is talking to me but I do not understands the Russian. I am looking at ground. Woman comes over to me and taps on shoulder and speaks Russian. I don't look up and says, I do not understands you. Please go away. She begins to speaks in broken English. She says, do you know who this Curly person is who is asking about these womens? I says, well yes, I am knowing this person. I start to look at woman and says, I know this person because I am. I stop speaking. My breathing is taken aways. I looks at the womans face. How can I forgets this face??!!? It is you! Mariya!!!!!

She says, tells me how you know this person. I says, Mariya! It is I, Curly! Your half brother! I jump up to give the hug. She pulls away and says, what are you doing you crazy person! She goes to runaways! I grab her by arm. No please don't go! I says. It is I, do you not recognize me? No! She says. I have never meets you in my life! She struggles to break free. Wait! I shout. We speaks over the interwebs in letters for long time now. Do you not remember our conversations? She says, no I have never been talking to you! Please let me go! Wait Mariya! I says. I am knowing your name, do you think that this is just by the chances? Please let me explains to you. Just give me few minutes of time! She half hearted agrees and sits down with me in bus stop.

There I pull out computer and show her letters. I show her photos of places and things in the letters. I explain what has happening this whole time. I shows to her pictures of herself that she has sent to me. She is taken back by all of these things that she reads and sees. She is not knowing of any of it before this day. Do you know why she is not knowing of any of this? It is not because she has eaten paint chips from window sills, or falling out of tree when small childrens or thrown down stairs. No. It is because SHE IS NOT WRITING TO ME!

She does not know of this address of email in which is being used. This is complete mystery to her. The photos you send? They are photos in which she puts on her Myfacespacebook interwebs page. So you know what I am thinking? Do you know the mystery's that I am solving? You my friend, are not her! You my friend, have steals her identity and pretend to be her! THE JIG IS UP! YOU WILL NOT BE GETTING JIGGY WITH IT ANYMORE!

And to think, I trusted you. You are nothing but the bald face liar! You try to get the monies from me and that is all you are wanting. What a fool was I for thinking you were real! But you know what? You are real, as in the person Mariya really does exist because here she is sitting right next to me as I write to you. I attach the photo. She tells me to tells to you to stop stealing her information and using it! She thinks you are dirty rotten persons for playing the games and you should get the sickness and die. You better watch out whoever you are! I am noticing that she has the temper like the Curly and if she finds you, she will probably smash you! You never want to mess with the strong Russian womens I warn to you!

She is blowns away by entire story and very very happy that she has a father in which she has never knowing and also a half brother. That would be me. She says to me Curly, my darling half brother, this other women, Larisa you are looking for, do you really love her? Yes dear half sister. I says. I love her with all of heart and soul and every ounce of being in my bodies. She says, Curly, I am knowing this girl. She is my bestest friend and roommate. I jump up out of bench! Why are we sitting here!!! I yell. Please take me to sees her!

We make the walk to their apartment. It is only 15 minutes away! To think I was so close! We enter building, climb stairs, and make way to door. Mariya puts key in door and opens. My heart races like the horses at the tracks. The door opens and we go inside.

She calls out to Larisa. I hear the voice in which I am waiting to hear so long. It sounds like the singing of the angels. We make way to kitchen. There, cooking her borsch, the last twinklings of sunset glowing through her hair through the windows, it is Larisa!

I drop to my knees in front of her! Larisa, my sweet Larisa, at last I have finally finds you! I says. Sweet Larisa says to Mariya, who is this man? This is the man who is in loves with you. Mariya says. I tells Larisa the poem in which I write long ago but waiting for this special moment to tells to her. Here is poem.

Highways... seem to come and go.
I travels from coast to coast,
Meeting many, loving none.
Bearing sorrow and having some fun.
It is Russia to which I run ... to sweet Larisa.

The roads they all look the same,
And everybody seems to know my name.
Every night I look up to skies,
There are no blankets where I lies.
In all my deepest dreamsing with you I flies ... with sweet Larisa.

Again the morning's come,
Again from Man in black I run.
Dreams of sunbeams shining through her hair,
It is her I wish that I could be near.
The roads roll on towards...sweet Larisa.

The roads, they never seem to let me go.
Lord ... Lord
My former life but is a ghost.
Will I be laid to rest beneath the clay?
For my spirit to just float away?
I know that I can't go on... without Larisa.
Yes I know that I can't make it ... without Larisa.

A tear approaches her eyes as I says to her these words. I stand and embrace her. I whisper in her ear that it is her that I have waited whole life for. We sit down and Mariya finishes preparing the borsch. I tells Larisa all of story of my journeys to sees her. I show her letters in which I write. I show her pictures in which I sends. She cannot believe that all of this I do for her. Of course I do this all for her! Why would I not? It is her in which I have always loved. She is overwhelmed. I pull out my creamy peanut butter. I put my butter deep inside both of them! Afterwards, I give them each their own pearl necklaces! Several in fact.

She tells to me that she is not knowing the email address in which she is supposed to be writing from. She has never sent to me the letters or the photos. In fact she says, the photos are also from her Myfacespacebook. It is all making the senses now. You have been stealing the identities of these womens and using their pretty faces like your own special whores to bring to you monies! But the difference between a whore monger and you is that the whore monger pays his whores to bring to him monies. Where you do not make the payments! Matter of facting they are not even willing to become the whores to make such the monies. They are having too much respect for themselves! They work hard for what little monies they are making and are very much offended that you take their information and photos and use for your own personal gaining!

We are now making way to airport to take private plane to Siberia. Mariya is excited to sees her father in which she is never knowing. The girls only need to pack what they really are wanting. They don't need to return to this place they are staying. Their lives are going to be completely changing now. I am not even sure why I tells to you these things. You are nothing but a fraud. But I feel the compulsion to tells you so that maybe you will think about the things you do. That maybe you decide to change the life in which you are leading. Do you want to go to river of fire after the death? Maybe you should be thinking about doing the different things with the life besides lying to peoples. Maybe weave the baskets or pick fruit or something like this. Become a productive part of the world instead of the sickness that covers so much of it.

I finally finish it all now. There is only one more letter in which I need to be writing. Make peace with the Gods and your life you dirty sickening person. Never make the contact with me or anyone of my family. Never do this agains to anyone else or I will find you and you will go SMASH! That is a promise.

Regards
Curly

DEAREST HALF SISTER MARIYA AND ME

From: Chris <coldbastrd@xxxxx.com>
Sent: Tuesday, March 1 2:48 PM
To: Larisa <gilkakisska@xxxxx.com>
Subject: [NOW I AM KNOWING TRUTHS]

So Larisa as I am finding, that is not your real name. I will no longer be addressing to you in such the manner. I have learning that you are not who you say you are. The reasons I am knowing is because I have meets the real Larisa! HA HA!

I am here now with the real Larisa and we make the discovery that you are nothing but a dirty fraud. You are like the roachedcock, crawling all over trash piles of the interwebs. You prey on the peoples with love to gets them to sends to you monies. You silly dirty fraud. I have more monies than you can ever be dreamsing! You will get none of it! I am so rich when I go pee pee, it is the color of gold. HA HA! I get the last laughs on you! You did not counts on me to make the trips to Moscow and discover the truths. You did not count on my perseverance! You see what you did not count on is the power of love and that love overcomes any obstacle that can be thrown in ways! Love conquers all!

I half suspecting that you are the man in which I battle in Tomsk. I alerted father to these facts in which I finding. He sends his mens over to the place that I finds you. But you have made the escape and apartment is empty. You can run you dirty fraud, but you cannot hide for long! Fathers men are on the search for you! I have talked to Cecil back in America. Even though he has given up the life of the law to become the clown, he has alerted the law agencies which he use to work, and they search for you too. Do you hear the sounds? It is the sounds of the clock ticking. With each second, the noose around your neck grows tighter and your breathing becomes harder. You look behind shoulder. Is that me behind you?

TICK TOCK TICK TOCK TICK TOCK! Your time is running out. You will find that you will be running and running for rest of life trying to get aways. I only wish I had figured this out sooner so that I could have taken you to the police myself when we make the battle. It is ok though. I am returning to America now with the real Larisa. We shall marry and have the large family! I promise you, I will use all the resources I have to make sure that you are brought to justice! Someday I will finds you, and you will certainly go SMASH!!!!!

I do give you this though. Without you, I would have never found my love, the real Larisa. So to this, well I will be the bigger mans and thank you. But that doesn't mean that I still do not wish to see you be cast into a river of fire! Monies? Which you are all about. Sure it is good to have monies. But that is not meaning of life. As I look back over entire journey, I have learned the true meaning of life. Life is what you make of it. Life is the friends you make along your journey. Whether they be in your life for the long time, or just a short time like the quick pit stop along the road. Life is your family and the relationships that grow amongst them. Life is the places you go, and the peoples you meet. All you touch and all you see, that is what your life shall be. So the meaning of life is take life and celebrate it for all it is worth. The big things and the little things. Each one of these things make up who you are.

As I leave you, I only have one last photo that is attached and one last thing to say. I am answering your last email properly this time now that I have learned everything I have learned. It is really no point to drag this any further than need be. So to you I says.....

NO SIR, FUCK YOU!

Regards,
Curly and Larisa

конец

(THE END)

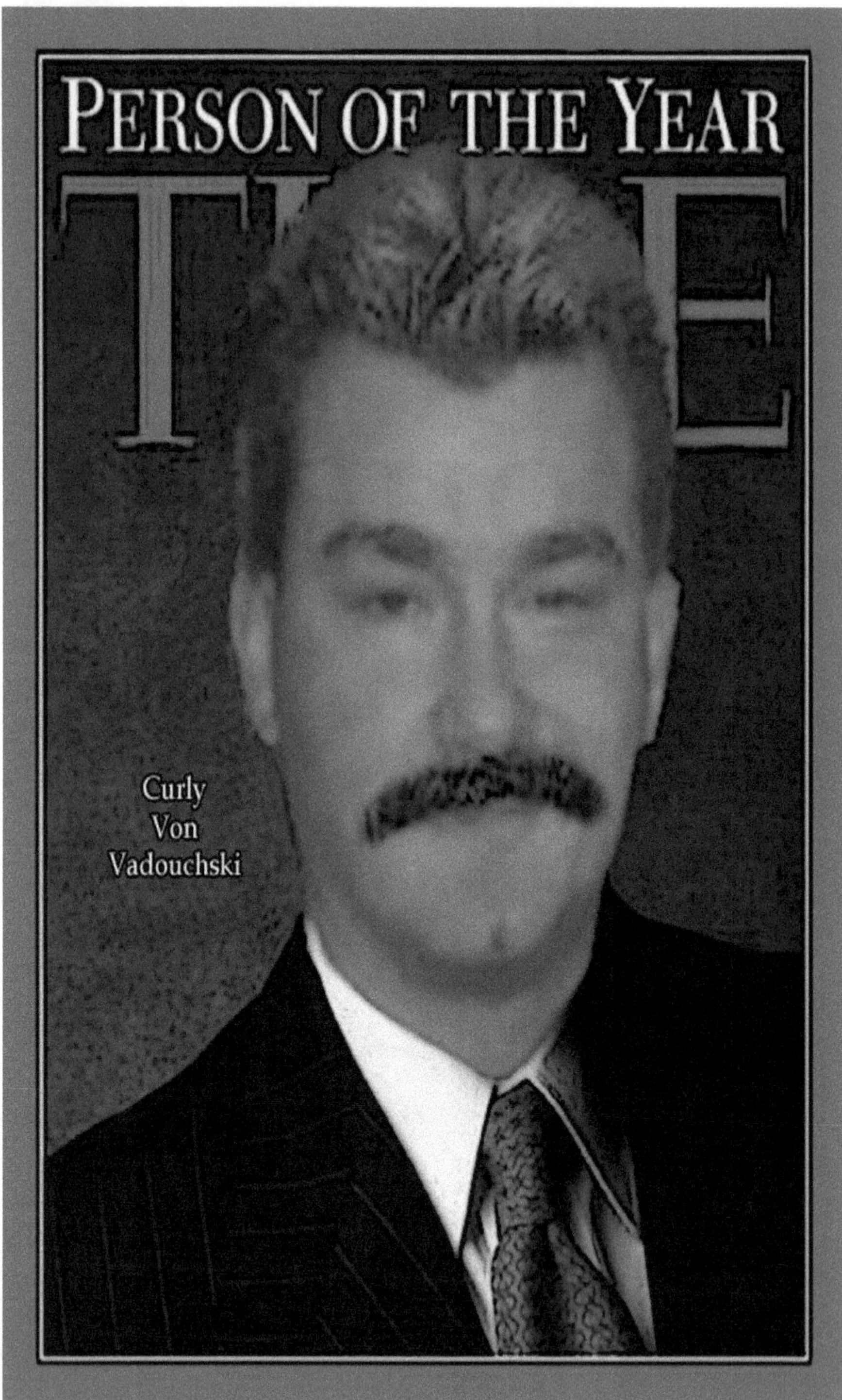
PERSON OF THE YEAR
Curly
Von
Vadouchski

Putting His
Butter Deep
Inside You
How one man's quest
for the perfect peanut
butter is changing the
world as we know it
Curly Von Vadouchski

BRIDAL MAGAZINE
Traditional Russian Weddings
All The Rage This Spring
Borsch Recipes for Your Reception
Incredible Peanut Butter Wedding Cake Ideas
Siberian Honeymoon Getaway
5 58242 66335 9

BICYCLE WORLD
A LITTLE RED ROCKET BUILT FOR TWO!
DETAILS INSIDE
1 25002 74135 0

ЛЕГЕНДАРНЫЙ МУЖСКОЙ ЖУРНАЛ
PLAYBOY
СУПЕРЦЕНА 85 РУБЛЕЙ*/ 350 ТЕНГЕ
WWW.PLAYBOY.COM.RU
СЕКС, ДРУГ, РОК-Н-РОЛЛ:
5 СПОСОБОВ СОВМЕЩАТЬ ДРУЗЕЙ С ЖЕЩИНАМИ
ГОРОД ТЫСЯЧИ ПАБОВ
Брайтон для гедониста
ПЕРСОНА
СИЛЬВИО БЕРЛУСКОНИ:
«Лучше меня в Европе никого нет»
20 ВОПРОСОВ
МЭТЬЮ ФОКС:
«Вспоминаю свою жизнь по татуировкам»
MARIYA VON VADOUCHSKI
Принцесса из Сибири ню внутри!

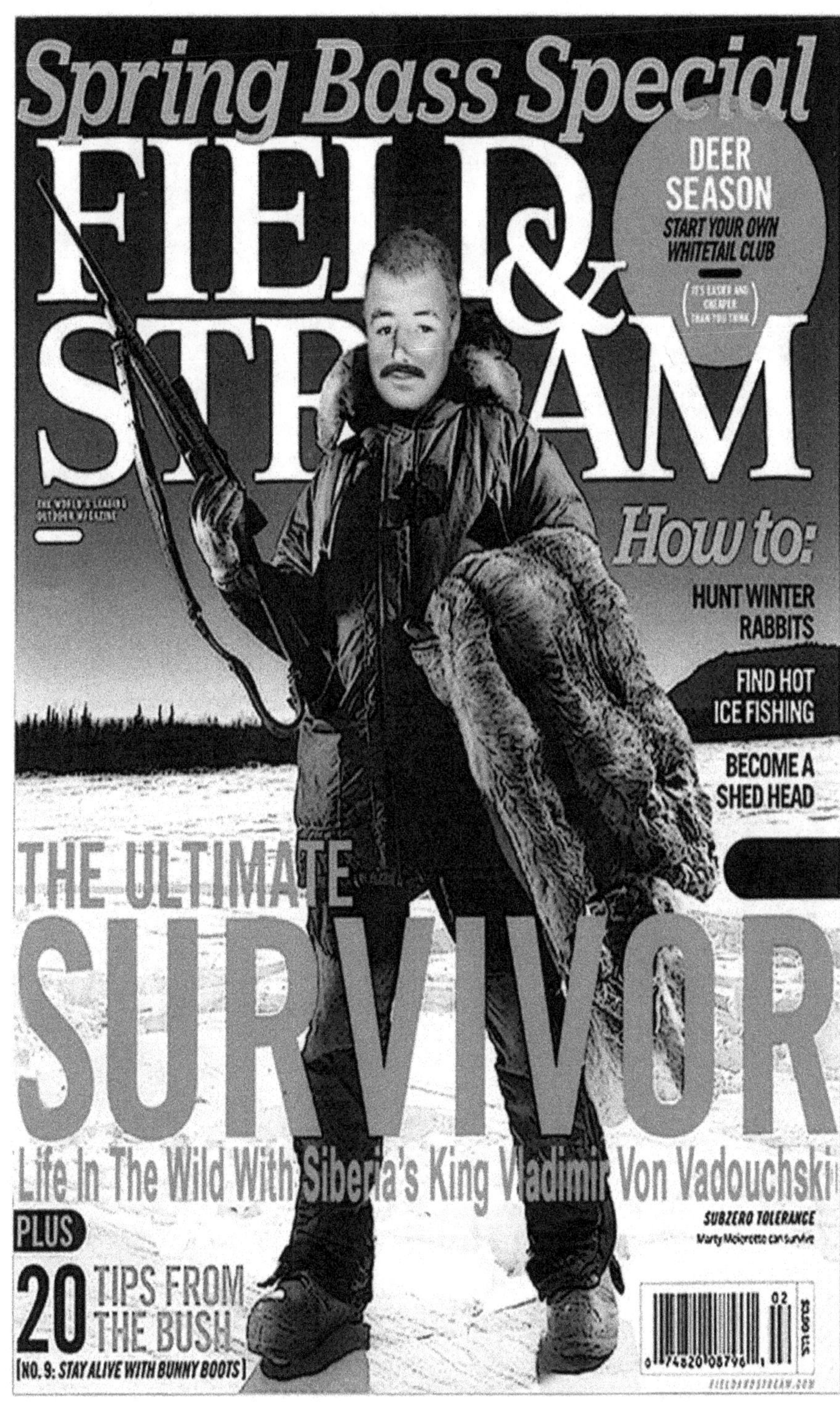

Spring Bass Special
FIELD & STREAM
DEER SEASON
START YOUR OWN WHITETAIL CLUB
How to:
HUNT WINTER RABBITS
FIND HOT ICE FISHING
BECOME A SHED HEAD
THE ULTIMATE
SURVIVOR
Life In The Wild With Siberia's King Vladimir Von Vadouchski
SUBZERO TOLERANCE
PLUS
20 TIPS FROM THE BUSH
[NO. 9: STAY ALIVE WITH BUNNY BOOTS]
02
0 74820 08796 1

CASINO BI-WEEKLY
MAGAZINE
Curly's
Curly's Casino Voted Number
One New Casino In the Country!

SPECIAL DOUBLE ISSUE
Peo
SEXIEST
MAN
ALIVE!
Curly
Von Vadouchski
Napster
CoCo
PLUS:
129
SMOKIN'
HOT
GUYS
$4.49US $5.99CAN
48
0 74470 10227 4

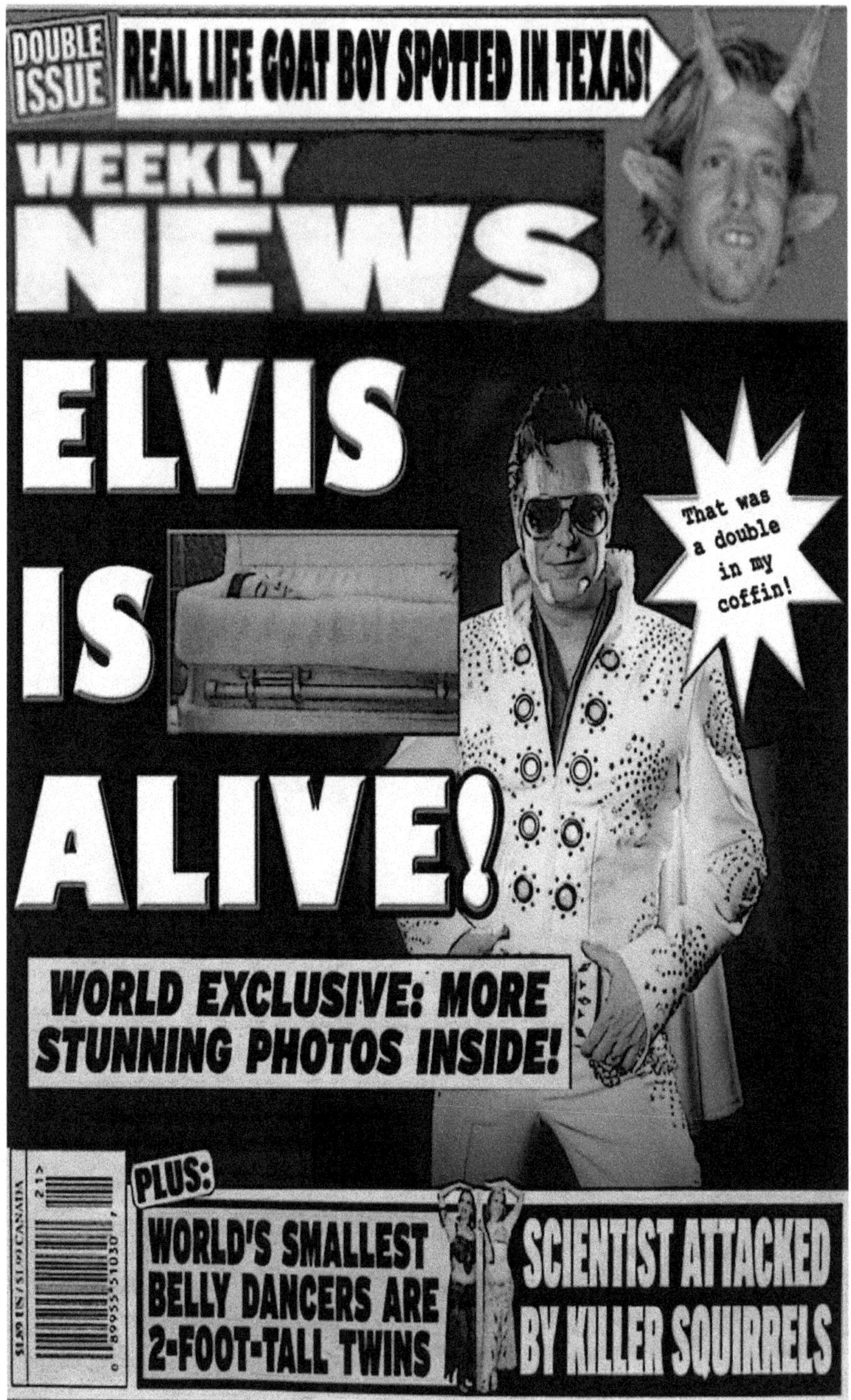
DOUBLE ISSUE
REAL LIFE GOAT BOY SPOTTED IN TEXAS!
WEEKLY NEWS
ELVIS IS ALIVE!
That was a double in my coffin!
WORLD EXCLUSIVE: MORE STUNNING PHOTOS INSIDE!
PLUS:
WORLD'S SMALLEST BELLY DANCERS ARE 2-FOOT-TALL TWINS
SCIENTIST ATTACKED BY KILLER SQUIRRELS

Medical Monthly

The Power of Peanut Butter

Experts theorize that this simple food could rid the world of famine and disease

The story inside!

Love him, loathe his clothes? DIY boyfriend styling
Fashion HOT LIST
Your 100% REALITY-BASED guide to getting dressed
LARISA VON VADOCHSKI'S HOT NEW STYLE
WHAT YOUR BIKINI WAXER REALLY THINKS
sexy beauty
+ LOOK HOT IN A HURRY
SEALED SECTION
The world's most embarrassing sex position (how to enjoy it & even excel) + how to give good hand
GOT BIG BOOBS? HOW TO DRESS Sexy
HOW TO GET NOTICED AT A PARTY
(No, you don't have to play nude Twister)
WANT BODY CONFIDENCE LIKE LARISA TURN TO PAGE 76
20 BEST JACKETS UNDER $300
Are you waiting too long to have a baby?
04
9 313006 000501
ACP

NATIONAL
GEOGRAPHY

Raise The Teetanic

Billionaire Investor To
Finance the Refloating of
the Sunken Ship Lost To
A Faulty Toilet Valve

Plus
BRILLIANT BEE-EATERS
RIGHT WHALE WATCH
HIGH IN THE OZARKS

CLOWNING QUARTERLY
CECIL THE CLOWN
WE INTERVIEW AMERICA'S HOTTEST
NEW CLOWN SENSATION

OK! WEEKLY
Curly & Larisa
BABY EXCLUSIVE
INTRODUCING
Newborn Curly Jr.
DADDY'S
LITTLE BOY!
'I want my son to be a little cooler than me'
CURLY'S LONG LOST SISTER
MARIYA
Who's Stealing
Her Style?
Chief
Chokesondeek
America's
Richest
Bachelor

GUNSLINGER
MAGAZINE
PLUS!
SUPER SEXY
CENTERFOLD
INSIDE!
THE RETURN OF TORNADO
TOMMY'S ROOTIN' TOOTIN'
WILD WEST SHOW!
TOUR DATES ANNOUNCED!
8 007141 009277

TECHNOLOGY
MONTHLY
Junkmail Justice
The Story
Behind The
War On Cyber
Thieves
How To Keep
Your Hard
Drive
Virus
Free
WANTED
Dead or Alive
$250,000
Plus:
Top 10 Must
Have Gadgets

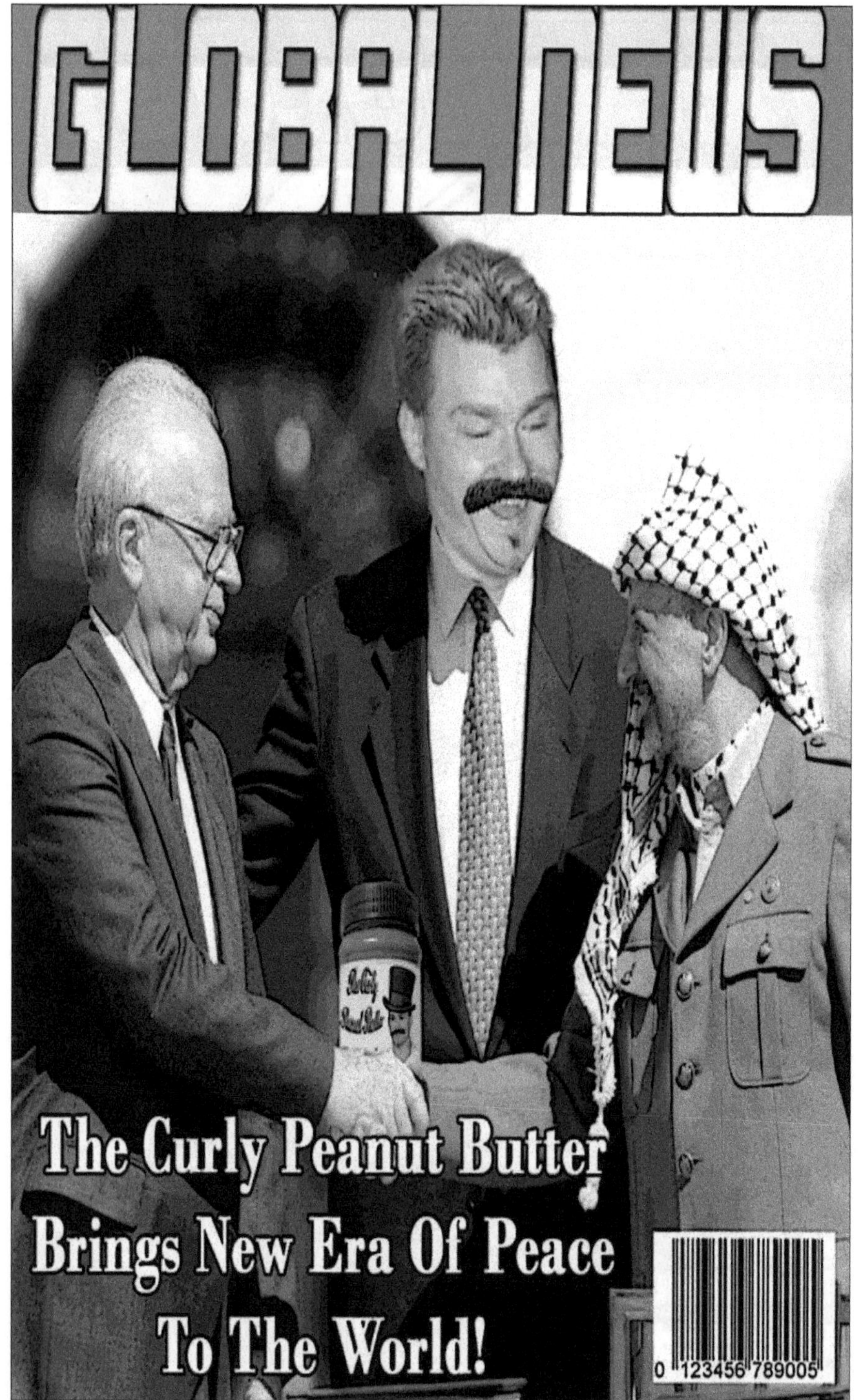
GLOBAL NEWS
The Curly Peanut Butter
Brings New Era Of Peace
To The World!
0 123456 789005

Rolli
one
Curly Von Vadouchski
A New Hope
EXCLUSIVE
Inside His Peanut Butter Powered Revolution
HILLARY'S LAST STAND
THE BLACK CROWES
Back, better and still brawling
PLUS
The PB&J's Reunite

In Memoriam

www.ingramcontent.com/pod-product-compliance
Lightning Source LLC
Chambersburg PA
CBHW052027090426
42739CB00010B/1807

* 9 7 8 0 6 1 5 5 6 7 4 4 0 *